THE ACCIDENTAL AMERICAN

THE
ACCIDENTAL
AMERICAN

Immigration and Citizenship
in the Age of Globalization

RINKU SEN
with
FEKKAK MAMDOUH

BK

Berrett–Koehler Publishers, Inc.
San Francisco
a BK Currents book

Berrett-Koehler Publishers, Inc.
235 Montgomery Street, Suite 650
San Francisco, CA 94104-2916
Tel: (415) 288-0260   Fax: (415) 362-2512
www.bkconnection.com

Ordering Information

Quantity sales. Special discounts are available on quantity purchases by corporations, associations, and others. For details, contact the "Special Sales Department" at the Berrett-Koehler address above.
Individual sales. Berrett-Koehler publications are available through most bookstores. They can also be ordered directly from Berrett-Koehler: Tel: (800) 929-2929; Fax: (802) 864-7626; www.bkconnection.com.
Orders for college textbook/course adoption use. Please contact Berrett-Koehler: Tel: (800) 929-2929; Fax: (802) 864-7626.
Orders by U.S. trade bookstores and wholesalers. Please contact Ingram Publisher Services, Tel: (800) 509-4887; Fax: (800) 838-1149; E-mail: customer.service@ingrampublisherservices.com; or visit www.ingrampublisherservices.com/Ordering for details about electronic ordering.

Berrett-Koehler and the BK logo are registered trademarks of Berrett-Koehler Publishers, Inc.

Printed in the United States of America

Berrett-Koehler books are printed on long-lasting acid-free paper. When it is available, we choose paper that has been manufactured by environmentally responsible processes. These may include using trees grown in sustainable forests, incorporating recycled paper, minimizing chlorine in bleaching, or recycling the energy produced at the paper mill.

Library of Congress Cataloging-in-Publication Data

Sen, Rinku.
The accidental American: immigration and citizenship in the age of globalization / by Rinku Sen, with Fekkak Mamdouh.
      p.   cm.
Includes index.
   ISBN 978-1-57675-438-2 (hardcover : alk. paper)
   1. United States—Emigration and immigration.¯2. Mamdouh, Fekkak, 1961–¯3. Immigrants—New York (State)—New York—Biography.¯4. September 11 Terrorist Attacks 2001–¯I. Mamdouh, Fekkak, 1961– .¯II. Title.

   JV6465.S44 2008
   304.8'73--dc22
   2008022231

First Edition
12 11 10 09 08   10 9 8 7 6 5 4 3 2¯1   28

Project management, design, and composition by Steven Hiatt / Hiatt & Dragon, San Francisco
Copyediting: Steven Hiatt   Proofreading: Tom Hassett

Dedicated to the memories of
Bouchaib Mamdouh and Arun Kumar Sen,
and to migrant workers everywhere

CONTENTS

COMING TO CITIZENSHIP
IN A NEAR-GLOBAL AGE

At 8 a.m. on September 11, forty-year-old Fekkak Mamdouh was asleep, having worked the previous night's late shift from 4 p.m. to 12 a.m. His wife, Fatima, lay beside him; she had dropped off their daughter at kindergarten four blocks away and then climbed back into bed. For six years, Mamdouh, whom everyone knew by his surname, had been a waiter at Windows on the World, the luxury restaurant on the 107th floor of the World Trade Center's North Tower. He had started working there in 1996 when Windows reopened after the 1993 terrorist bombing in the building's basement. Mamdouh's wide brown eyes and the round apples of his cheeks gave him a disarming look of innocence. These mellow features hid the scrappiness that had made him a beloved, though sometimes controversial, union leader.

The first call came from Mamdouh's sister Saida, who lived in Italy. She told him to turn on the TV. The second call was from his brother Hassan, who lived down the street. "Listen, brother, there was a plane that just crashed through the Twin Towers," Hassan said. "Guess what? You're not going to have a job for a couple of months while they fix the place."

Mamdouh and Fatima turned on the TV thinking of terrible accidents when the third call came—their neighbor telling Fatima to get their girl out of school. Fatima hurried to retrieve her daughter Iman. When she got back, Mamdouh was still transfixed by what was flashing across the television screen. He said, "You watch. They're going to say it's Muslims."

Fatima asked him why he thought so.

"Because they did it in ninety-three," he said, referring to the earlier attack.

Without eating, Mamdouh left their house in Astoria, Queens. He went to 8th Avenue and 44th Street, the offices of his union, Local 100 of the Hotel Employees and Restaurant Employees (HERE). He and other union members made two lists: one of all the workers who would have been catering breakfast for Risk Management employees that morning, and another of all the places they might be found. Then teams of shop stewards and union organizers set off to search for the workers and track their families. Mamdouh paired up with a colleague, an Egyptian immigrant and now former captain at Windows. The two started out at hospitals, asking who had been brought in. They met many families of people who had worked at the World Trade Center, but they found no actual casualties of the attacks. They made their way down Manhattan's West Side, where all its hospitals are located. After the fourth one, Mamdouh's companion, who had been crying steadily, said he couldn't take any more. He went home, while Mamdouh headed to the morgue on First Avenue and 30th Street, staying there until 3 a.m.

The following night, Mamdouh gave an interview to a cable news channel. One of his friends, another Moroccan, saw the interview and called him the next day to ask why he hadn't said that Muslims—meaning regular, real Muslims like them—hadn't done this thing. Mamdouh told him that people already knew.

For the next five days Mamdouh ate and slept very little. He spent hour after hour circling the morgue's lobby carrying a sign: "If you know anyone who worked at Windows or if you worked at Windows, please call the union." Mamdouh was able to cross barback Mario Peña's name off the missing list on September 12, and he found cashier Faheema Nasar a full week later, but in the end, seventy-three of his co-workers weren't coming back.

A couple of days after the attack, Mamdouh and Fatima went to their neighborhood Pathmark store. She had covered her head in *hijab*, as she had since her mother died three years before. It was evening and the store was not at all crowded. They were the only people wanting to buy fish, and Mamdouh stood at the counter with her while she tried for several minutes to get the fishmonger's attention. Eventually, Mamdouh's patience gave out.

"Hey, she's trying to talk to you," he said to the clerk, who continued to ignore them. "She's trying to ask you a question."

"Don't you know what you guys did?" was the response.

"What?"

"The World Trade Center." It was a mumble, but Mamdouh heard it clearly enough.

He snapped. His eyes widened, his smallish frame puffed up.

"What are you talking about, what we did? I lost seventy-three of my friends there. Maybe you didn't lose anybody, and you don't know what you're talking about." The clerk backed up from the counter while Mamdouh yelled, "I want to see the manager!" He yelled some more at the manager, who apologized. Neither Mamdouh nor Fatima would ever return to that store.

Something shifted in Mamdouh that day. The clerk's accusation had wounded him. Two days after the tragedy, he was ever aware that he himself could easily have died. He suffered for the loss of his colleagues, and the idea that someone would associate him with their deaths because he was Muslim was shocking. Until then, he had been living the life of a lucky immigrant, getting great jobs in high-end restaurants because he spoke fluent French. He had come to the United States to make money and to be near his younger brother, and although he missed Morocco, he had felt American enough to marry here and have two children who were born U.S. citizens. Despite his prediction to Fatima that Muslims would be blamed for 9/11, he had actually managed to get by for twelve years without noticing American discrimination in a daily way, not toward black people or Asians, and certainly not toward himself. Now he rewound his history, noticing things that he hadn't clearly seen before. He couldn't yet know, however, that these new insights would reshape his life as an immigrant worker in America.

Wall vs. Amnesty: Old Debates and New Perspectives

This book tells the story of modern immigration through the life of Fekkak Mamdouh, an ordinary, if somewhat fortunate, immigrant who found himself at the center of historic events. Situations like his have given rise to a contentious debate across the United States about immigration and the purpose of contemporary policy. Politicians, media pundits, populist organizations, and policy advocates have focused either on stopping unauthorized immigration or on legalizing undocumented immigrants. The current discussion prompts seemingly discrete questions. How big should the fence along the southern border be? Should undocumented immigrants be allowed to correct their status, and if so, how easily? The debate is intensely polarized, yet too narrow to lead us to real solutions.

The wall-versus-amnesty framework hides the far more fundamental question: Should the United States continue to welcome immigrants in large numbers? To answer that question in a humane manner that promises the best possible outcomes for both immigrants and current residents, for both the United States and for the countries that send immigrants, we need a holistic new framework within which to plan future action.

Substantial numbers of people are making new homes in this country. Each year, about 1.5 million come here to live and work. The largest single group, comprising about 40 percent, come from Mexico; the rest arrive from other countries of the Global South or former Eastern Bloc European countries, including India, China, the Philippines, Cuba, Vietnam, the Dominican Republic, Korea, Colombia, and Ukraine. Worldwide, immigrants have been a major source of economic support to their home countries; 190 million people sent $300 billion to their countries of origin in 2006.[1] Immigrants also make enormous economic contributions to their new countries.

Demographers and sociologists estimate that two-thirds of these 1.5 million immigrants arrive with official sanction; the rest either cross the border without documents or overstay tourist visas. It is impossible to know exactly how many immigrants are undocumented, since the Census Bureau doesn't ask about immigration status. The most commonly quoted source of projected numbers, the Pew Hispanic Center, calculates a national figure by subtracting citizens and legal residents from the total population reported by the Census Bureau. Using admittedly limited projection techniques, demographers generally believe that between 7 million and 13 million undocumented people now live in the United States, and that the number grows by 500,000 or more each year. The Pew Hispanic Center estimated 11.1 million in 2005 and as many as 12 million in 2006.[2]

Participants in the mainstream debate on immigration typically take one of two sides: a secure-the-borders/punish-the-"illegals" side, and a side that argues that we should legalize undocumented workers and improve the immigration system. On the punitive side, immigration restrictionists make three arguments. First, they assert that the country cannot bear the growing material burden of illegal immigrants; second, that illegal immigrants threaten the American public's psycho/social sense of identity; third, that lax immigration policy has enabled terrorists to enter the country. While restrictionists who advance these arguments largely focus on unauthorized immigration, they have also opened the door to proposals to limit legal immigration.

In making their fiscal and economic argument, restrictionists express concern about the ability of our public school systems to absorb so many non-English speakers, and about our public hospitals' having to provide emergency care to the undocumented. Employers pay lower wages to immigrants, they point out, thereby dragging down the average wage rates of the lowest-paid American workers. In this story, the immigrant is a parasite.

A second set of opponents focuses on cultural identity issues: immigrants' alleged refusal to learn English; their large extended families, all piled into overcrowded homes and apartments; their practice of separating themselves out in neighborhoods and business districts that then become unwelcoming to "real" Americans. All this multilingualism, restrictionists assert, is changing the character of the United States, and it will end with a complete takeover of this nation-state by Mexicans or the Chinese. In the harshest expressions of this narrative, immigrants behave so differently from Americans that their very humanity is questioned.

Finally, restrictionists advance the law-and-order argument. It begins by making the single misdemeanor act of crossing the U.S. border a person's sole defining characteristic (illegal) and ends by equating immigration policy with national security. In this narrative, the immigrant is a criminal and a terrorist.

On the other side of the current mainstream debate, the business community and some immigrant rights advocates have argued that immigrants, on the whole and over the long term, generate more resources than they consume. These advocates cite studies showing that about 75 percent of undocumented workers actually do pay taxes through fake Social Security cards, and that immigrants in general use far fewer public health resources than do native-born Americans. Today's immigrants assimilate at exactly the same pace as yesterday's immigrants. They commit crimes at far lower levels than native-born Americans. The characterization of immigrants as a socio-cultural threat, this side argues, is overblown and racist. While this attitude is obviously more sympathetic to immigrants than that of the restrictionists, it frequently reduces the immigrant to a hard-working but one-dimensional economic actor. The immigrant might have a family, but he or she has only a little bit of culture (usually culinary), virtually no politics to speak of, and contributes nothing to the United States other than labor to ensure long-term economic growth.

Conducting the debate within these boundaries—punishing undocumented immigration or legalizing the undocumented people who are here now—has not and will not deliver an effective, humane solution that can produce the greatest benefits for the largest number of people. Captive to the rhetorical status quo, both sides have decided, for various tactical reasons, to ignore three important realities. First, globalization is incomplete, creating a situation in which corporations are free to move jobs, operations, and capital anywhere they wish, while workers' mobility is limited by borders and immigration laws. Second, a permanent, unchanging American identity is neither possible nor desirable; the culture of the United States has changed many times over the course of its history, and further transformations are always already in motion. Finally, the current debate posits immigrants and U.S. residents as foes, when in fact our destinies are closely tied together. Without focusing attention on these three blind spots, we cannot gather enough information to make rational, innovative choices.

What we currently call "globalization"—or "neoliberal economics"—was promoted by Margaret Thatcher and Ronald Reagan in the 1980s to propel most of the world into an expanded system of unchecked capitalism designed to give corporations more flexibility than either workers or governments. Clarifying its mechanisms and effects is the key to understanding why so many people are moving around the world, scrambling to make even a basic living. "Globalization" has three major characteristics: smaller governments that levy lower taxes and provide fewer public services; deregulation of business so that corporations have fewer labor, environmental, and pricing limitations; and opening new markets for consumer goods by removing tariffs and other trade barriers, which are essentially taxes on international commerce. Since the 1980s, when the Reagan and Thatcher administrations controlled the international financial system, any country that hopes to borrow money from global financial institutions like the International Monetary Fund (IMF) or the World Bank has been forced to make "structural adjustments" to bring its economy into line with these principles.

As a result, corporations have assumed ownership of many of the major resources—resources previously managed by government—on which the poor rely, including utilities, water, land, health care, and a host of others. These resources have become increasingly expensive for consumers, not just in the countries of the Global South, but everywhere. Deregulation was touted as a way to help poor countries attract foreign investment—corporations are far more likely to locate their operations where the costs of doing business are minimal, whether because the legal minimum wage is low, or unions are weak, or health protections are not required. In addition to structural adjustment programs required by the World Bank and IMF, free trade agreements like the North American Free Trade Agreement (NAFTA) generally build upon these principles without questioning their value or applicability. With corporations pressing for lower labor costs, and governments caving in to that demand, workers are squeezed between two gigantic forces—with no countervailing force to protect their interests.

Neoliberal globalization creates the conditions that drive people to migrate. Without that understanding it is difficult to see why all our laws designed to keep out undocumented migrants are self-defeating. Large numbers cross borders illegally in the first place because it is their best choice to achieve a dignified life—if not for themselves, then for their children—in a neoliberal world. They come, and they stay, even at the risk of losing any legal standing in their adopted country. The response of receiving countries has been to treat these migrants as purely economic beings, allowing a limited number to fill "temporary" labor shortages that corporations might claim they have. The migrants are then supposed to go home.

If we continue to ignore the true reasons people come to the U.S., characterizing their actions as a matter of decontextualized individual behavior ("They chose to break the law"), they will continue to come, no matter how many fences are erected or how dangerous it is. Militarizing the U.S.–Mexican border by deploying ever increasing numbers of Border Patrol officers (tripling the force from 1980 to 2000) and building fences has not discouraged migrants from crossing. These measures have, however, driven them into the most remote reaches of the desert. During 2005, at least 473 people died under such circumstances, a historical record.[3] Such a death, some people say, hurts far less than slow starvation.

Thanks to our second blind spot, we assume that cultures and national identities do not change. This assumption prevents us from acknowledging the full humanity of immigrants, which in turn leads us to reject their potential cultural and political contributions. Immigration restrictionists seem to imagine that Americans have thought and behaved in pretty much the same way since 1776. Americans and immigrants alike, they imply, encounter each other in economic situations and are otherwise untouched. The mainstream national response to the collective trauma of September 11 has been to draw and freeze a particular definition of the true American: white, Christian, English-only-speaking, and hungry for nothing but hamburgers. Foreigners are cast not only as strange, but also dangerous. We apply our fears and biases selectively, however: Arabs, South Asians, and Muslims are all seen as potential terrorists, while Mexicans are seen as criminals. The Irish, not so much.

In this view the good immigrant does nothing but work, and the bad immigrant does nothing but undermine the rule of law. Pro-immigration advocates who try to deflect the culture war argument by stressing that immigrants just want to work hard and raise their families imply that if immigrants are allowed to do that, they will keep their cultural and political ideas to themselves.

Stasis, however, is a fiction. Cultures do not stand still, nor should we want them to. The English language, for example, is full of words that originated far from England. The word *jungle* is related to the Bengali word *jangal*, the word *shmuck* is actually Yiddish, and the word *gumbo* comes from the Bantu *ngombo*, meaning okra. Hamburgers and hot dogs began as hearty German fare, slapped onto buns by intrepid immigrants to meet the needs of New York street life in the late nineteenth century. American jazz has its roots in ancient African musical traditions.

As immigrants change America, so too does America change immigrants. The clashes between generations of immigrant families, so deeply written into American literature, testify to the inevitability of identity shifts. The language of immigrants shifts, as do their culinary, educational, political, and romantic habits. All these modifications can be both positive and negative. It is not acceptable, or even possible, to prevent any change at all. Instead, it's up to us to drive the changes that are occurring in a positive direction.

The debate over cultural change reflects a deep racial anxiety in our country. Although whites are still a significant majority, their proportion of the population is definitely shrinking. California, New Mexico, Texas, and the District of Columbia are already majority-minority jurisdictions; New York, Maryland, Mississippi, Georgia, and Arizona are next in line. But these populations already exist—shutting down immigration today, or restricting it to only white countries, will not reverse the trend. Continuing to define the American as a white person can only lead us to institutionalizing racism, a system in which only whites are considered entitled to the privileges and rights conferred by citizenship.

The third assumption embedded in the current debate is that immigrants and U.S. residents have opposing interests stemming from competition for limited resources. In fact, our interests and our fates are closely linked. The Reagan/Thatcher program of corporate globalization has hurt us all. While a punitive, limited immigration policy might make current residents feel better, it won't magically refill the public coffers or bring back thousands of formerly high-paying jobs. For example, the North American Free Trade Agreement, which was presented as the key to stimulating both the U.S. and the Mexican economies, had so few labor and environmental protections that it was virtually ensured to harm workers in both countries, although corporations have certainly done well from it. Sadly, all the data shows that NAFTA has been a dismal failure for almost all involved, driving millions of Mexican workers to migrate within their own country and farther north to survive, while simultaneously enabling the loss of over 750,000 jobs in the United States.[4]

Our punitive approach to illegal immigration harms Americans in equal measure. First, making immigration difficult while doing nothing to change conditions in sending countries creates the whole category of illegal immigration in the first place. If people could immigrate legally, or if they had other options for making a living in their home countries, few would take the option of entering illegally. Second, when undocumented people cannot protect their rights, employers are able to abuse them, which makes them the labor force of choice and drives down working conditions for everyone else. Third, immigrants who are driven underground out of fear become vulnerable to all kinds of crime, from fraud to mugging, undermining the rule of law rather than strengthening it. By refusing to join forces with immigrants, we damage labor rights, forgo substantial tax revenue that could be used for the public good, and, most of all, sacrifice the social and economic benefits of a free and open society.

Living in a New Immigration Framework

Grappling honestly with these three realities—that globalization is incomplete, that cultures are always changing, and that immigrants and U.S. residents have more to gain from embracing each other than they do from an adversarial stance—is the key to driving the immigration debate in a positive direction. Organizing workers in New York City's enormous restaurant industry after September 11, Fekkak Mamdouh saw the effects of the national debate on the average immigrant—a person of color, stuck in a low-wage job, about one-third of the time without documents and therefore without a legal identity. These immigrants suffer greatly to keep New Yorkers in great meals at low prices. They often live in severely overcrowded apartments. They earn little, and are frequently cheated of their wages by their employers. They send back much of what little they do earn to support families in their home countries. They perform the industry's most dangerous jobs, documented in burn scars and missing fingers.

Mamdouh's work to transform the restaurant business, one of the largest sources of local economic growth in the country, echoes the efforts of other immigrants upon whose backs this country's prosperity was built, and who transformed the Industrial Age with strikes, protests, and political action. The industry also holds lessons for other parts of the economy. It is both a gateway—an entry point through which low-wage immigrant workers can make their way in a new country—and an archetype, offering important models for building local economies that are less vulnerable to the negative aspects of neoliberal globalization.

Ironically, Mamdouh's association with such immigrants brought him closer to, rather than alienated him from, native-born Americans. Through a series of unpredictable events, he learned that the key to making things better for everybody lies in focusing on the most reviled, the people at the very bottom of the hierarchy. He learned that everybody really meant *everybody*, from kitchen workers to New Yorkers who ate in restaurants on a weekly basis to employers who were trying to live by the rules. To learn these lessons, he would struggle with his own mythic ideas about what it meant to be an American. He would also struggle with the role of September 11, an event that both inspired and limited his work.

While Mamdouh was organizing in New York City, Cecilia Muñoz, an immigrant rights advocate in Washington, D.C., was laboring to change policy from the top down. Muñoz was on Capitol Hill with a direct view of September 11's effect on the immigration debate. Through her, we track the federal debate from the day before the attacks to the death of comprehensive immigration reform in the 2007 session of Congress.

Together, these two stories reveal an ironic truth: even as Mamdouh's work on the streets of New York continually broadened his community, the discussion of appropriate federal policy went the opposite way. The scope of congressional proposals to create a legalization program shrank while enforcement measures grew, the whole process giving the impression that the United States is an increasingly narrow community, disconnected from the rest of the world. The contradiction suggests that our public officials are deeply, even tragically disconnected from the actual communities in which we live. When allowed to, those communities work things out with broad analysis and promising solutions, solutions that Congress appears to be missing.

We need a new framework for addressing immigration, a global framework that both takes a clear-eyed view of Americans' struggles and enables the birth and fruition of forward-looking, humane, and effective policies. The immigration "problem" cannot be solved through immigration policy alone, nor even in the United States alone. We can go a long way with a system that eases rather than restricts people's movement, that respects immigrants as more than cheap labor. Such a policy would decriminalize immigrants by increasing legal immigration (rather than temporary worker programs), while protecting their labor and civil rights.

An open immigration policy, however, won't resolve the deep inequities that exist among countries. For that project, we need to bring countries closer together—not by ratcheting down workers' wages and rights in the receiving countries, but by raising wages and rights in the sending ones. Such a project may sound politically impossible, but we already have a global political and economic system that is remaking the world in the name of neoliberalism, based on trade, war, and diplomacy. The task before us is to complete the process of globalization in such a way that it benefits the largest number of people, rather than only the economic and political elites who gain so much from the current system. We can imagine and build regional transnational taxation, governance, public service, and labor systems that allow us to end the cycle in which corporations race to the bottom, forcing workers to race, fruitlessly, to what they perceive as the top.

Without intending to, Mamdouh uncovered the seeds of a new immigration and economic framework. He came upon them by accident—as a child, he never imagined traveling even 200 miles from his home in Casablanca. But larger forces presented challenges and opportunities, as they always do. He figured out how to speak back to those forces and, in that speaking, how to act in the best traditions of the United States, when its instinct for ingenuity was turned toward the project of inclusion. Mamdouh is neither hero nor criminal, but just an ordinary immigrant. If he can find a way, so can we all.

Chapter 1

LEAVING HOME

Mamdouh's own migration history was typical for his generation in many ways, from the conditions in which he grew up to the family relations that propelled his moves. Even before he left Morocco, Mamdouh's life took shape in a global context, politically, economically, and culturally. He was born poor in a country that had achieved independence just before his birth. Those were heady times for Moroccans, but a good portion of their optimism turned out to be misplaced. Although independence freed them from French colonial control, it didn't transform Morocco's monarchy and political system, nor did it improve life for most Moroccans.

Mamdouh's circumstances and decisions were closely tied to those of his family. He was actually part of a second generation of migrants; both parents had made the universal trek from the countryside to the city within Morocco. He himself followed his brother, who was the first to leave the country altogether. In each generation, the decision to move was motivated primarily by the need to survive, but also reflected a healthy anticipation of adventure and change, of breaking out from old patterns and expectations.

Desperate as they are, once emigrants decide to leave, they try to choose not only the most geographically accessible place, but also one that seems welcoming or exciting. Like most migrants, Mamdouh came to the United States after an earlier stint in Saudi Arabia—trying life in multiple countries is extremely common. As he traveled, working for very wealthy people, Mamdouh was allowed to see, and sometimes to participate in, luxurious lifestyles based on rampant consumption. Living in proximity to riches he couldn't have imagined as a child didn't make him greedy, but it did show him the vast distance between the poverty in which he'd grown up and the wealth that was possible. It made him more determined to gather at least some of the good things in life for his own family, and made it impossible for him to return voluntarily to his old life in Morocco.

Over the course of his journey, Mamdouh experienced life in all the possible immigrant statuses—as a guest worker, as an undocumented person, as a legal permanent resident, and as a naturalized citizen of his new home. As it does for many, restaurants provided him a gateway to a new country. And like most immigrants of color, he started in the lowest wage jobs the industry had to offer. Unlike most, however, he quickly rose to a position at the front of the house, which put him on the path to what can only be called the top of the profession— waiter in one of the world's most famous restaurants. The timing made a difference. He was fortunate to arrive in the United States in the late 1980s, when the attitude toward undocumented immigrants was far more accepting than it would be fifteen or twenty years later. He was also lucky to work with restaurant managers who recognized his skill, including his multilingualism, and who therefore gave him opportunities to rise.

Mamdouh's family history of migration began with his father, Bouchaib, who left the countryside for the city in 1938. Bouchaib grew up in a poor village 60 kilometers south of Casablanca. By the time he was fourteen, Bochaib had suffered the deaths through illness of two brothers and his father. Most of his neighbors were farmers, but Bouchaib learned commerce by traveling with his uncles to local markets where they sold tea and sugar.

As a young man, Bouchaib joined the independence movement, protesting the "voluntary" arrangement between French presidents and Moroccan kings that made his country a French protectorate. When King Mohammed V refused to renew the agreement in 1931, France brought in its Senegalese colonial troops to force his hand. Bouchaib found himself in the midst of a mass protest that turned to panic as a pro-independence crowd ran from French cannon fire. Bouchaib survived that night by lying down among the dead and pretending to be one of the victims.

As he approached manhood Bouchaib watched his friends leave the countryside to make money in the city. He told his mother that he too wanted to go to Casablanca, where he could do something with his life. He took the bus, arriving with nowhere to stay and no work. But he made do. He always found someone who took him to a friendly café where he could spend the night, or pointed him toward day work in the mornings. Eventually, he got a small job in Mohammedia cutting the grass on a Frenchman's farm; he soon became the farm's foreman and was given a small house on the grounds. He returned to the village a year later at the insistence of his mother, but within four months he returned to Casablanca. There he met Americans for the first time—GIs who had arrived to fight the war in Europe.

Bouchaib finally opened his own little grocery in 1942, a small shop next to the little shack he called home. In 1953 a friend introduced him to Aicha, a young woman who had also come from the countryside. The two married just as the French sent Mohammed V into exile for once again refusing their "protection." Together Aicha and Bouchaib had seven children who grew to adulthood. Within the next fifty years, four of them would continue their parents' migration trajectory, leaving Morocco altogether.

Bouchaib raised his family through the postwar and postcolonial period in a country ruled by monarchs who maintained close ties with the West even after Morocco gained independence in 1956. The family's history illustrates the consequences of postcolonial economic schemes that consisted too much of privatizing state functions to enrich elites and foreigners, and too little of encouraging democracy and real development. As a result of the monarchy's policies, Mamdouh's childhood was marked by both poverty and repression, which together pushed him to search for something better. He wanted the material means to live a dignified life, certainly, but also the freedom to stop looking over his shoulder. Rumors of grand opportunities to find such things outside of Morocco would eventually pull him halfway around the world.

Mamdouh was Bouchaib and Aicha's fourth child, born in June 1961, just months after Morocco celebrated the crowning of a new young king. Hassan II's thirty-eight-year reign would eventually be known as the "period of fire and steel," but at that point the country was still somewhat placidly enjoying the aftermath of a relatively bloodless independence struggle. By then the family was well established in Ben M'sik, a neighborhood of tin shanties and unpaved streets; most of the streets around them were too narrow for even a single car to drive through. They had three shanties—one to live in and two for the grocery store. Bouchaib sold coffee, sugar, tea, flour, and other dry goods, and by Mamdouh's tenth birthday the business had prospered for thirty years. The family shop was located between other neighborhoods and a hugely popular open-air bazaar, so the constant flow of foot traffic guaranteed steady customers. Mamdouh and his brothers got up early every morning to help Bouchaib lift the shop's heavy metal door. His parents had opposite personalities, his father gruff and loud, his mother shy and housebound. The couple regularly fed friends and strangers along with family, sometimes more than a dozen people in a night.

Still, they were poor. Nine people created four bedrooms out of a roughly 10-x-10-meter space. The house froze in the winter and steamed in the summer, and the lack of running water or indoor plumbing meant that the children took shifts getting water and washing up at one of the mosaic-tiled public fountains that dotted Morocco in the tens of thousands, or bathed occasionally at the local *hammam*.

From an early age, Mamdouh admired his father's independence and entrepreneurial spirit. The family saw Mamdouh as an honest, straightforward child whose siblings didn't torment him excessively. He was especially close to his eldest brother, Mohammed, who taught him how to swim and later how to drive. Mamdouh's early childhood didn't feel deeply deprived, but he was accustomed to making his own toys like soccer balls out of any material that could be made to roll.

Despite the family's poverty, Mamdouh had plenty of typical childhood fun. During the summers, his father sent him to the countryside to stay with his uncle in Ben Hamed, about 70 kilometers south of Casablanca, and Mamdouh traveled to the surrounding towns with his uncle, who had continued the family tradition of selling goods at the market. One of Mamdouh's favorite treats was watching Hindi movies from Bombay, which united Asia and the Middle East culturally, providing a major source of entertainment for a relatively low price. On Sunday mornings, when it was cheapest, he would indulge his obsession with Bollywood actors like Rajesh Khanna, Rishi Kapoor, and Amitabh Bachchan.

Mamdouh learned to make money early on. By the age of fourteen, he was picking through the European and American castoffs at thrift shops, finding items he thought he could resell, taking them home to wash or mend, and then marking them up slightly for sale on the street. His friends knew him as smart, ambitious, and generous, a sharp dresser yet perfectly willing to sell the shirt or jacket off his own back. People regularly asked him about his clothes, "Are you ready to sell that?" and he often was. Once he sold the sneakers he was wearing and walked home in his socks. By the time he was seventeen, Mamdouh had opened the family's first bank account. He talked constantly about his plans to change his life, lecturing his friends about how they needed to make money, go to school, give their parents what they deserved, and never lose hope.

But Mamdouh could not escape the political and social context of his own society. King Hassan II did try to introduce some reforms, expanding the public school system, providing food subsidies, and raising the wages for government workers, but global conditions made hampered these efforts. The French had conducted a friendlier form of colonization in Morocco than they had elsewhere in their empire, but they had still retained economic control of the country. Hassan II wanted both to modernize the nation and keep government control, and these two ambitions marked his tenure. The result of Morocco's large-scale development projects on Mamdouh's family was to aggravate their economic need rather than to bring prosperity. Without democratic rights, however, there was little they could do. The combination of poverty and political repression drove many young Moroccans of Mamdouh's generation to leave the country as soon as they could. The best they could hope for in Morocco was a government job—but the number of those was shrinking and they were in many cases part of a system of corruption.

The Moroccan royal family traced its lineage to the Prophet Mohammed. Although they had created an administrative structure that was formally separate from the monarchy, after independence that structure and the monarchy effectively merged. Suspecting an assassination attempt, Hassan II suspended parliamentary elections in 1971. He also established a secret police force that searched out seditious behavior.

Morocco's economy wasn't strong enough to support Hassan II's ambitions, and Morocco's relationship to the West remained suppliant even after independence. In the end, France had released the protectorate relatively easily, choosing instead to focus on its bitter war against rebels in Algeria, but Europe limited Moroccan imports after independence and kept the country at arm's length economically. In exchange for an International Monetary Fund loan granted while the country's population was growing, Hassan II agreed to reduce public spending on basics like food and education. Throughout the droughts of the 1970s, peasants abandoned the countryside for cities. Food prices shot up in the 1970s: sugar by 37 percent, butter and milk by 45 percent, and flour by an astonishing 76 percent. The cuts prompted food riots, which in turn set the state's repression apparatus in motion.[1]

These events affected Mamdouh's family. In 1971 the family got word that the government planned to build a new airport at the outer edge of Casablanca, then a four-lane highway from Rabat to Casablanca. The neighborhood would eventually be razed, the Mamdouhs were told, but they vowed to stay as long as possible in their home of thirty years. As a white wall went up all the way around their community and highway construction started, the foot traffic that had kept the store so lively over the years slackened, the store's profits shrank by half, and the family entered hard times for real. Their own poverty grew apace with everyone else's—the country's resources were largely going into fighting to control Western Sahara or paying for large infrastructure projects that could attract foreign investment. The police and army kept the populace in line with violence. Seeing state authoritarianism at such close proximity made Mamdouh consider political action courageous—for other people.

Despite government repression, by the 1970s their neighborhood had become the site of radicalization for trade unionists and political activism. The early 1970s were marked by enormous demonstrations and strikes, some lasting a full year. The conditions encouraged protest. The *Washington Post* reported of Mamdouh's neighborhood that "the problems are easily visible. Only a 10-minute drive from Casablanca's beachfront resort and chic night clubs lie the crowded tenements of Boush N'touf, where street boys were seen playing soccer with a dead rat instead of a ball, or the makeshift huts of Ben M'sik, where thousands of families live without electricity or sewers in what resembles a Palestinian refugee camp in Lebanon."[2] Mamdouh joined the occasional window-breaking demonstration with his friends, more out of youthful exuberance than moral commitment. He never got caught, though, and his father continued to think of his sons as good boys who worked hard and stayed out of politics.

Soon after Mamdouh graduated from high school, an acquaintance told Bouchaib that he would make a good recruit to the secret police, since he was known to be smart and capable.

"What are you planning to do now?" Bouchaib asked Mamdouh.

"I want to keep studying," he said. "School is good and I'm doing well in it. I want to keep going."

"But you will need to start working sometime." Bouchaib told him about the secret police idea, eliciting an uncomfortable chuckle from his son, who knew the police to be wildly corrupt. "Why are you laughing? Because you think I'm crazy?"

"You know, Baba, you've done a lot and been through so many hard times. You've raised us all well and we are all doing good. But if I go to the police, I will be feeding my family bribes."

In June 1981, two weeks after Mamdouh's twentieth birthday, Morocco's trade unions called for a general strike in Casablanca to demand reinstatement of food subsidies. The strikers called in particular for a gas boycott—no one was to buy gas or move their cars all day—and effectively shut down the city's economy, including airports, train stations, factories, and shops. When the government started running buses along the highway to get around the boycott, Mamdouh watched from the wall as people threw stones. The general strike itself was controlled, but the unions couldn't predict or manage the level of frustration among the city's people, and full-scale riots broke out two days later. The army brought in its tanks, helicopters, and armored cars and ordered a curfew, essentially imposing martial law on the city's poorest neighborhoods. People stood on their balconies and threw rocks at the police.

Mamdouh rarely ventured out during these three days. On the first day of rioting he watched from the family home as people took over the highway, burning cars and trucks. On the second day, the day of the most intense repression, he, his brother Hassan, and several friends stood at the edge of a soccer field when tanks started rolling down the street perpendicular to them. He watched as two people were shot down, then saw a mass of people running across the field, trying to get to the shanties on the opposite side. The tanks continued shooting, and the field was soon littered with bodies. The rioting and repression went on all night and into the next morning, and the police continued to hunt for rioters for days afterward.

The family learned that the police had walked into the house next door and taken Aziz Khetab, Mamdouh's childhood best friend. Khetab had woken up from an afternoon nap to find soldiers standing in his bedroom; they dragged him off to jail, releasing him the next morning, after Bouchaib and the other heads of families went to the police station to plead for his life. Khetab was badly shaken and bruised from being hit and shoved, but he was lucky. Another friend of the family, who had been picked up while sitting in a café in the days after the riot, was sentenced to seven years in prison. The government set the death toll at 66 people, but the opposition and labor unions reported that the number was 637, nearly ten times the government figure. Thousands were arrested, 2,000 were tried, and hundreds, including teenagers, were jailed for up to ten years. The International Monetary Fund denied responsibility for the riots and deaths, saying that it hadn't forced Morocco to adopt its structural adjustment program or end the food subsidies.[3] Although Mamdouh sympathized with protestors, the dangerous atmosphere kept his political role down to an occasional rally. He largely focused on studying.

It was hard to keep going to school when the family's fortunes were so tight. By the time of the riots, the highway was finished and a seven-foot white wall now separated the road from their shantytown. The shop was virtually closed by then, and most of the family was unemployed. Mamdouh spent many afternoons sitting on the highway wall wondering where all the cars were going and whether he himself would ever leave. Trying to move them out to new housing, the government offered mortgages to families to move to new brick apartments about six kilometers away. These apartments were the equivalent of a new urban public housing development.

The move and the house were presented as voluntary, but there was clearly no other choice but to take it. Eventually the neighborhood wouldn't exist at all. They moved out in the mid-1980s, the very last family to do so long after all the shanties but their own had been razed. The move itself happened suddenly—the boys and parents were simply forced out one day while the girls were away in the country. Mamdouh stayed behind—someone had to be there to tell his sisters Lakbira and Saida that it was time to leave. Late that night, Mamdouh held Lakbira as she cried for their home.

Most prospective immigrants are part of a family chain, encouraged to search for a better life by a relative who took the first steps. Mamdouh was no different. Hassan, his youngest brother, began their generation's pattern of leaving Morocco entirely. He had carved out a niche as the family's maverick, the unpredictable one who always went his own way without asking permission. He and Mamdouh were hanging out in the street one night when they saw one of their neighbors getting into his small Honda. He had found steady work delivering cash and goods for a Saudi prince, mostly from hotels to his house and back, and that night he told Mamdouh and Hassan that he had just transported a lot of money that day. Hassan, only sixteen at the time, got the destination address of the deliveries. The next day, when the neighbor came out of the dropoff point, Hassan was waiting, asking for a chance to work. He shadowed this neighbor on his rounds, and three days later accompanied the royal party hunting gazelles in the Sahara. And just like that, after dropping out of high school at fifteen, Hassan had talked his way into a job guiding and doing errands for a Saudi prince. After a year of these kinds of trips, the Saudis told him to get a passport and gave him 1,000 dirhams for the family. He left with his Saudi sponsors and was sending money home to his family within a week.

For his part, Mamdouh started at university studying physics and chemistry and got an offer to study in Brussels. But his mother, devastated by Hassan's emigration, wept and wept over the prospect of Mamdouh's accepting the offer. Not wanting to hurt her, Mamdouh stayed put. Hassan was at the same time working to bring his brothers over to Saudi Arabia. He first tried to get a work permit for Mohammed, the eldest, but Mohammed's poor health led to a rejection. In 1985 Hassan finally called to say that he had a job for Mamdouh. One of the princesses wanted a "manager" to handle her family's affairs. In the way of mothers and sons, Aicha cried, but a little less hard this time, and Mamdouh was a little more determined.

"Cry all you want, Ma," he said, "but I am going."

Many immigrants are forced into much lower-skilled jobs than their educations or ambitions would indicate. In this way, too, Mamdouh was like most. He managed his first migration as a guest worker in a system that was designed to give employers complete power. He was lucky, though, to get a fairly easy assignment through his brother's connection to the most powerful family in one of the world's wealthiest countries. Even though Mamdouh had never imagined living anywhere but Morocco while he was growing up, once he left he found that he wanted more than just material things—he wanted to feel a sense of belonging and he wanted to have an interesting, independent life.

Mamdouh arrived in Saudi Arabia in 1986. He was twenty-five years old, with a full head of thick curly hair and a bushy mustache, but his body was in the state of borderline emaciation rarely seen outside the developing world. He was one of 11,000 Moroccans living and working in Saudi Arabia that year.[4] He earned $400 per month. His employer controlled his status and kept his passport. Mamdouh couldn't travel even within Saudi Arabia without his employer's written permission; if he lost his sponsor he would have had to return to Morocco. He knew people who actually had to pay their sponsors in order to stay in the country.

It wasn't quite the exciting life he had expected, even though it was the first time he had gotten a close look at extreme wealth. Although he quickly became used to material comforts—having a large bedroom to himself and anything he wanted to eat—he found that it wasn't enough to make him happy.

Mamdouh lived in a small mansion with nothing to do but sleep and read the newspaper. "It is just in name that I'm a manager," he thought. Eventually, the princess for whom he worked assigned Mamdouh to be a companion to her nine-year-old son; his life then consisted of taking the boy to school, then doing homework, skating, and playing. Mamdouh earned plenty of money, but he rebelled against the boredom and lack of independence. After two years, he began asking the princess for permission to go home, but she always refused. Finally, she said she would not release him from his contract, but she would allow him to work elsewhere in Saudi Arabia. He left the palaces and found a job selling cold cuts and cheese in an upscale supermarket with a large French clientele. He moved into a group house with fourteen other men from Europe, Asia, and the Middle East, getting his first taste of an international community.

Several weeks into the new job, he began to think about the possibility of going to the United States, again a move that Hassan had been the first to make. Hassan was now in New York working in restaurants. Mamdouh's first application for a visa to the U.S. was denied. When a casual friend offered to get him one, Mamdouh handed over his passport. One morning as he opened the grocery store at 7 a.m., the princess called, wanting him to accompany the family to Disney World—the young prince refused to go without Mamdouh. The only problem was that they were leaving the next day and Mamdouh didn't have his passport. Another friend drove him all over town in a frantic search for the man who did, finally finding him at noon.

Early the next day, Mamdouh was at the airport with a family group of about forty people, including servants. Stepping off the plane in Orlando, he felt an immediate and inexplicable sense of belonging. Nothing in his life had prepared him to be in that place, and he had spent his whole life in countries with large secret police forces. Yet as he looked around at the palm trees and sweated in the Florida humidity, he thought freedom seemed to have a smell to it. It might in fact have been the absence of scent, namely the sulfuric odor of coal-burning fires so thick in the air at home, that made him think so.

"This is my place," he thought.

The family rented four mansions for $3,000 a day each, two for the family and two for the servants. Mamdouh spent a month playing in Orlando's theme parks and racing golf carts with the young prince. One day the whole family went to a restaurant, a huge chain outfit that used beepers to let waiting customers know when their tables were ready. Looking around, Mamdouh saw that people were leaving money on the tables after paying their bills. He asked the British chauffeur why they did that and learned about the concept of tipping. That struck him as the feature of a very fine job.

As the family prepared for the trip home, Mamdouh faced a life-changing choice. He could either return to Saudi Arabia, where he would continue to live under the yoke of his guest worker contract, or he could join his brother in New York City. He didn't intend to stay forever in New York, and it wasn't completely clear to him that he would have to look for a way around his lack of a permanent visa, but he knew that Hassan would help him figure those things out and assist him in finding a job so that he could stay for a time. Mamdouh asked the princess for his passport so he could visit his brother. She refused, sure that he planned to run. In fact, there seemed to be a tacit understanding that everyone who got to the United States would choose to stay rather than return to the restrictions of life in Saudi Arabia or to the poverty of their home countries. Craving more than this limited set of options, Mamdouh secretly decided that he would go to New York with or without his passport. That would have made life hard. He wouldn't get very far with no ID at all. But he was willing to try it if necessary. He was relieved when he eventually got the passport from the princess's son-in-law, who handed it over with the equivalent of a wink and a nod.

When Mamdouh got to New York, Hassan told him to enroll in school and change his status from tourist to student, which he did by taking English classes at Baruch College. He also tried to get into aeronautics school, but was unsuccessful.

Instead of becoming a pilot, Mamdouh got a job in a restaurant.

The Restaurant as Port-of-Entry

By moving into food service, Mamdouh was following a time-honored immigrant and worker tradition. The first high-end restaurant in the United States was founded in New York City by John Delmonico when he opened Delmonico's on William Street in 1831; he provided businessmen with hot meals in the middle of the day, cooked by a real French chef, in a luxurious atmosphere with "prompt and deferential" service. The concept of the restaurant was itself imported from France, where the "liberated" chefs of former aristocrats had been forced to find a new clientele after the Revolution.[5]

The first American restaurant unions also sprang up in New York City. In 1885, German-Jewish waiters and bartenders organized the first culinary workers union in hotels, the direct antecedent of the Hotel Employees and Restaurant Employees (HERE) Local 100, the local that Windows workers would join a century later. Dozens of independent unions stepped into the industry, including the Industrial Workers of the World, which organized a series of wildcat strikes in 1912 demanding an eight-hour day, a $20 weekly minimum wage, and the banning of "vampires," agencies that charged a month's wages in return for finding someone a job.[6] HERE was one of only two unions to offer membership to black workers in those days.

But the unions were also roiled by infighting and corruption, competing to represent the same workers, refusing to support each other's strikes, and rushing to offer employers sweetheart contracts. In the 1920s, Prohibition attracted racketeers, including the famous bootlegger Arthur "Dutch Schultz" Flegenheimer, who bullied his way into the leadership of some HERE locals. Businesses had the choice of paying for labor peace or having Flegenheimer cause labor trouble, occasionally forcing a union election at gunpoint. Again, it was immigrant workers at another local who beat back organized crime, and the union's international office started a massive cleanup campaign in New York.

By mid-century more than 50,000 restaurant workers belonged to the union. That figure shrank through the 1980s as the union was hit with a combination of union-busting policies and corruption investigations. By 2000, the number of unionized non-hotel workers had shrunk to about 1,500, or 1 percent of the restaurant workforce.

While the power of workers to bargain collectively has declined, the supply of restaurant workers has exploded, thanks in large part to the influx of millions of immigrants. By the beginning of the twenty-first century, the U.S. restaurant industry had become a gateway of opportunity for immigrants from all over the Third World. People from almost every ethnic group work in restaurants as their first job in this country. Roger Waldinger's book *Still the Promised City?* describes how manufacturing jobs started to leave New York City in the 1950s, with the most severe job loss coming in the 1970s. Government and white-collar jobs boomed, however, including communications, transportation, and advertising, with many national headquarters of major firms remaining in the city.[7] There was great demand for high-skilled workers, and eventually, for lower-skilled workers to serve them.

During this period, New York City experienced an influx of blacks from the South, an outflow of whites to the suburbs, and three decades of immigration, with 80,000 new immigrants coming every year. These workers filled the demand for service jobs. While high demand should have resulted in high wages, the labor surplus among the rising immigrant and migrant populations kept job competition intense and wages low. The difference between the high rate of white-collar compensation and the low rate of service sector pay contributed to dramatically growing income inequality in the city.

Windows on a New World

Mamdouh's experiences as a waiter reflected these historical realities: large numbers of immigrants used the industry as a gateway and many were deeply abused by their employers, which drove them to organize for political change during the height of labor organizing in this country. Mamdouh worked in some of the city's fanciest restaurants, although he started out as a delivery man and busser like everyone else. He quickly rose from busser to waiter in a series of high-end French eateries, where his fluent French helped him break into front-of-the-house jobs. He was extraordinarily lucky to get these jobs, given how few immigrants of color generally are hired for them. He worked with all kinds of people, but he spent little time focused on the racial division of labor—he himself was at the front of the house, he was fortunate to have considerate bosses, and he was so enamored of life in New York City that it was hard for him to see beyond himself. He felt no need to look out for the secret police, as he had in Saudi Arabia, and he had only the most occasional, vaguest sense of discrimination. He read about blacks and sometimes Asians bringing discrimination charges, but never really believed that anything untoward could have happened.

By 1991 Mamdouh was working at Madison Square Garden, where he served meals worth thousands of dollars to star athletes. He joined the union there, but he had little interaction with it. His relationship with his employers was so good, in fact, that when his manager at the Garden moved to run the Hudson River Club, Mamdouh moved as well. The Hudson River Club was not unionized, but Mamdouh felt that management liked and respected him enough to give him a lot of flexibility. While he worked there, an Egyptian friend who felt that he had been passed over for promotion because of race subpoenaed Mamdouh as a witness to his Equal Employment Opportunity Commission claim. Mamdouh testified, but inside, he did not believe that such a thing had ever happened to him. It would still be some time before he understood restaurants as workplaces that needed to be reformed.

The only thing troubling Mamdouh was his lack of documented immigration status. He had been living on his student visa, but knew he couldn't do that forever. All around him, immigrants were talking about the amnesty that had been passed in 1986. Someone told him about a lawyer in Florida who was faking papers for immigrants to get legalized, and Mamdouh decided to try that. He knew that this was all against the rules, but he couldn't see a way around it. He justified it to himself as the only way he could stay in New York. His remittances and those from his brothers were supporting the entire family in Morocco, but he also had become attached to the city itself. If he went home and waited for legal entry, he thought it very unlikely that he would be able to return. So he flew down to Orlando again, looked up the lawyer, signed papers saying that he had been in the country before 1986, and got a temporary work visa that he had to renew annually. The visa didn't get him a green card, but it did allow him to travel for emergencies. Every year, he created such an emergency, a dying or sick family member, so that he could get permission to go home. He felt especially guilty about claiming those events, afraid that fate would catch up with him and someone in the family really would become deathly ill.

On the bright side, Mamdouh was enjoying a series of phone conversations with a young woman named Fatima who had emigrated to New York from Sidi Kacem, an industrial town not far from Casablanca. She regularly called the Brooklyn house in which Mamdouh was living with four other Moroccans to speak to her cousin. Fatima was tall and slim but sturdy—just slightly taller than Mamdouh himself. She had curly waist-length hair and a straightforward manner. Fatima had grown up an only child whose father was mostly absent, working as the head groundskeeper for a resort in France. She had come to New York intending to take English classes at New York University, only to be discouraged by the expense—and instead of school she started work as a housekeeper at the Essex House.

Their phone conversations often consisted of Mamdouh giving her advice. For one thing, NYU was too expensive. She had to check out Baruch College, as he had done. One day when she visited the house Mamdouh opened the door but didn't identify himself as her telephone friend. The next time Fatima called, Mamdouh said, "I'm the one who answered the door." For their first date, he took her to dinner in the West Village, where he worked and she lived.

In 1995 Mamdouh and Fatima married. As he prepared yet again to make up a story and get permission to travel to Morocco, she said, "Why do you keep putting yourself through this?" She had a green card, and he could get one as her husband, she thought. Mamdouh's machismo was activated for a while—he was loath to have his wife sponsor him, since the world was always meant to work the other way around. He eventually gave in, however, and found a lawyer to help him. Together they applied for his green card. In his application, he admitted that he had lied in order to get the temporary work permit and paid a penalty for having done so. He had been paying taxes all along, through his temporary work authorization.

When the vice president of the Hudson River Club moved to Windows on the World after its reopening in 1996, he encouraged Mamdouh to apply there as well. Windows opened as a massive luxury restaurant taking up some 50,000 square feet on the 106th and 107th floors of the World Trade Center's

North Tower and was well known for its floor-to-ceiling windows overlooking the Manhattan skyline. Given its tourist-attraction status, the restaurant's owners had always been committed to having an extraordinarily diverse and integrated workforce to match its international clientele. The restaurant had been destroyed by a bomb blast in 1993, and huge celebrations accompanied its redesign and reopening in 1996.

Mamdouh's hiring process was long and convoluted. He interviewed first with the company that was contracted to hire new staff, then with the woman who managed club lunches, then with the banquets manager. After three interviews, Mamdouh was allowed to enter the two-week Windows training program, where he practiced putting in orders and checking food and wine quality. Windows was run by the general manager, the floor managers, the maitre d', and the hostess, and was divided into thirteen sections, each with its own captain, waiter, and busser. Runners brought the food from the kitchen to all the sections. As he started the training, Fatima was about to give birth to their daughter Iman. Mamdouh told the manager who had placed him in the training that he might need to respond to a page from his wife about the baby. The manager responded by telling him that he would be fired for answering a page. Luckily, Iman was born in the middle of the night while Mamdouh wasn't at work.

On the final day of training, this manager told Mamdouh that he had failed, that he was too slow in entering orders into the computer and that he would never work at Windows because of that. Mamdouh tried to argue, but had no real standing and so gave up fairly quickly. He had gotten to know the bar manager, who offered him a job there, but the training manager changed her mind a week later for unknown reasons and Mamdouh finally started at Windows as an à la carte waiter. It was by far the most expensive and exciting restaurant he'd ever worked in. He looked forward to going to work and gazing out the windows at the weather and the city lights every night.

The Windows workforce was stable and tightly knit. The staff formed strong social bonds, checking in about their children or meeting in the stairwells for Muslim prayers. It was a good job, so the turnover was low and people tended to do well and stay for a long time. Most of the workers had significant experience in restaurants, so they recognized Windows' unique position in the industry, felt a lot of ownership of it, and looked for ways to take care of it. Mamdouh himself was earning more than he ever had before—within a year he was at $50,000. Even he was shocked that he could earn so much. Windows, however, was the most profitable restaurant in the country, and one of the most famous in the world. He worked hard for that money, too; there were no slow nights and the customers were rich and demanding. His earnings would leave him the lasting impression that restaurants could constitute a working person's lucky break.

Mamdouh enjoyed the company of his co-workers. Sekou Siby was a line cook and chef who had emigrated from the Ivory Coast. Siby spoke four languages and was studying for his certificate to teach French in the public schools. Mamdouh was not Siby's shop steward, but they used to meet in the large stairwell for daily prayers. Abdoul Traore was also from the Ivory Coast and the kind of quiet union leader who spoke rarely but always to great effect. Mamdouh also met Utjok Zaidan, an Indonesian waiter; Shulaika La Cruz, a pastry chef from Curaçao; and Jean Emy Pierre, a sous-chef who had come from Haiti as a child. He had good relations with most of the managers. When he and Fatima had their second child, a boy they named Zackaria, all his co-workers congratulated him. Family life suited him perfectly, and the restaurant schedule allowed him to help Fatima at home during the day, where he became an active diaper changer and reader of stories.

Windows' management had agreed to unionization, with Local 100 to begin representation January 1, 1997. Mamdouh gave that little thought until he focused on the manager who had hired him, a woman who was singularly abusive to the workers. Considering the manager's inordinate amount of power, Mamdouh began to look forward to the union's arrival. He was terrified that she would fire him before the union was set up, since managers went on what he saw as a firing rampage during the last days of 1996, the final period in which the workers lacked representation and a contract. They fired the last person one hour before the final New Year's Eve dinner shift. He felt lucky that they didn't pick him out for termination, and some relief that the union would come in and protect them. He ran for and became a shop steward, responsible for sixteen waiters and bussers in his unit but free to represent anyone who came to him. He quickly gained a reputation for being brave and dogged, challenging the management almost every day not to fire a particular worker and to make sure they all got fair schedules. And when people who had made mistakes came to him, he helped them work out a way to make it right with management.

Mamdouh quickly learned the value of the unions he had paid no attention to before. Like most union contracts, this one included a no-strike clause, but the workers really needed to deal with their abusive manager. For three years people had individually complained that she arbitrarily changed their schedules and disciplined them. The company never responded to these complaints. The workers didn't necessarily want to get her fired, but they certainly wanted her to have less power over them. On Thanksgiving Day 1999, the Windows workers decided to break the no-strike clause in their contract and force the company to act on their grievances. Mamdouh and other shop stewards went into the employee cafeteria that afternoon and spoke to the workers gathered there.

"Listen all," Mamdouh said, "we are going to sit down today. We are not going to work until the company agrees to deal with this manager."

With 1,200 reservations booked, the workers pulled a work stoppage and demanded a meeting with the general manager in the main dining room, where they insisted that he do something about the abusive manager. She was taken off the floor that day, and gone from the restaurant within four months.

But Mamdouh learned quickly not to take for granted the good will of his co-workers. At one point, more than a dozen bussers sent a petition to Human Resources claiming that Mamdouh pushed them too hard and perpetually wanted them to take on increasing amounts of work. The company began an investigation. Mamdouh, who had defended many of these bussers' jobs, furiously cornered each signer and asked them directly what was wrong, only to find that several couldn't say why they had signed such a petitition. Mamdouh suspected that the whole thing was set up by a captain whose seniority claim he hadn't supported. The investigation uncovered nothing and was eventually dropped.

In the spring of 2001, his eldest brother Mohammed, who had suffered from emphysema most of his life, told him to come home. Now he was dying, and he wanted to see Mamdouh one last time. Mamdouh took a month off and spent every day with Mohammed, taking him out of the house for the first time in months. He also started to build a new house in Casablanca, a 2,500-square-foot "villa," or detached home, in a new housing development going up at the southern edge of the city. He imagined that his parents would live there, along with his own family when they visited Morocco. Mohammed died on Mamdouh's fortieth birthday, and Mamdouh again returned to Morocco for the funeral and other rituals.

When he returned from Morocco the second time, the union was preparing to renegotiate the Windows contract. In committee meetings, the workers talked about their need for a pension plan and their willingness to strike for it. Windows was the most profitable restaurant in the country at that point, registering a profit of nearly $37 million.[8] The workers there were making good money, but they were concerned about their futures. He had just started doing his part to survey workers and to determine how well they would stick together through a protracted contract fight. His heart, though, was still grieving for his lost brother. If Mohammed had been in the United States instead of in Morocco, Mamdouh thought, he might still have been sick, but with better medical care he might not have died, or his passing would at least have been more comfortable.

Democratic Vistas

Mamdouh's immigration story is typical in some ways and highly unusual in others. Like many immigrants, he was pushed out of his country by a combination of government repression and lack of economic opportunity—the latter at least partly conditioned by the neoliberal policies imposed by the IMF and World Bank. Like most other immigrants, he found his first work at the lower end in restaurants, and he struggled to legalize his status, living on the margins of legality for more than six years. He certainly hadn't dreamt of being a service worker; he had studied hard his whole life so that he could work in the sciences. But that dream turned out to be impossible. In Morocco there weren't enough jobs, and in Saudi Arabia and the United States he couldn't get access to professional jobs. These are common enough experiences.

In other ways, however, Mamdouh was extraordinarily lucky. Lucky to never be cheated out of his wages, lucky to never be caught without immigration papers, lucky to marry a woman who herself had a green card, and lucky to be earning more money than many other people in the United States, not to mention Morocco. While he could take credit for any or all of these things, in truth his life circumstances were shaped by forces he couldn't control, such as where he was born, what his parents had, and that he'd arrived in the U.S. at a moment when people weren't asking many questions about how he had come to be in the country.

Like many immigrants who work in service industries, Mamdouh's jobs exposed him to a great deal of wealth. Seeing it didn't make accumulating money his primary concern, but it did show him what kind of lifestyle was possible. He also saw that many of the people who had all this wealth hadn't physically earned it themselves—they had inherited it, or they got it from investments—and that some of them were no kinder, smarter, or more creative than he was. This new view of the world gave him a sense not only that he deserved more than a life of penury, but also that the resources for a good life were far from scarce. They were just inaccessible to him. Both emigration and service work brought these resources within reach.

It wasn't just material wealth that attracted him, however. When he got to the United States, Mamdouh was able to experience living in a democracy. He had literally been too afraid to take up political activity in Morocco, and being a shop steward had given him his first taste of collective power. As he came to understand that poverty begets more poverty unless a person gets some proximity to wealth, he also began to understand that participating fully in the life of his community was important to him. With every such insight, the chances that he would return to a life of deprivation and limitation dimmed a little more.

Chapter 2

US AND THEM AFTER 9/11

On September 12, 2001, Mamdouh went to the headquarters of Local 100 of the Hotel Employees and Restaurant Employees at 10 a.m. for an emergency meeting attended by more than 200 people. Family members held photos of their loved ones. The morning before, Windows catering employees had prepared and served breakfast for the Risk Management Company in the banquet space on the 106th floor. Seventy-three of them were lost in the end, a number that would forever stick in Mamdouh's head. The "falling man," reportedly seen jumping from the top floors of the North Tower, was thought to have been from Windows.

The union was in a state of pandemonium, needing three full-time secretaries for a solid week just to handle the phones. Mamdouh spent that first week searching for his co-workers. He felt all their losses keenly. He felt particularly terrible about Telmo, the very young Mexican busser who had made a tight and optimistic unit with his even younger wife and tiny baby. Mamdouh's days were dotted with funerals.

The union negotiated with the Red Cross to set up a separate office to process union members and families that would supplement the official support center at Pier 94 at West 54th Street. HERE and two other unions established the Immigrant Workers Assistance Alliance (IWAA) to create a system for helping immigrants navigate the process and asked Mamdouh and three Windows co-workers to help staff it. Immigrants and family members poured into the office, usually seeking cash benefits for rent, clothing, and groceries.

Mamdouh took the Red Cross training for caseworkers and was officially certified. He translated for the French-speaking immigrants, most of them Africans, and guided many from the IWAA offices to Pier 94. Mamdouh found the family assistance center intimidating, with National Guardsmen surrounding the area. People were pushed into take-a-number-style lines with vague boundaries that snaked around the perimeter and could easily require two hours of waiting. There was an entire wall with hundreds of pictures of missing people put up by their desperate relatives. The Red Cross set up separate sections for those who had lost family members and those who were simply financially broken, creating one of the many distinctions among September 11 victims. It was nearly impossible to find a coordinator among the thousands of people.

Being there made Mamdouh worry about his race and religion. One day as he accompanied a worker, an encounter justified his anxiety. As his companion stood in line, Mamdouh sat down on a chair at the edge of the tents. Before long, four white police officers approached him, along with an older white woman.

The cops asked him why he had a Red Cross ID. "We need to know how you got this, sir."

"What do you mean, how I get it?" Mamdouh replied. "I'm a case manager."

"Would you come with us, please," the cop said, before taking him inside to the Red Cross office.

For an hour, Mamdouh explained his association with the Red Cross and the union and how he came to have the Red Cross ID. The woman who had reported him left for a time and then came back. He thought to himself, "She's so proud—she thinks she's found a terrorist."

He explained to the police, then to the site manager, who then phoned the Red Cross office in Brooklyn, giving Mamdouh's name and ID number over the phone. After that call, the manager told Mamdouh he had been cleared. Once he knew he could go, Mamdouh's anger rose. Unable to let go of the opportunity to say something, he told the volunteer that she had been completely out of line. She said she was sorry, but he rejected the apology.

"Your 'sorry' doesn't mean anything to me."

"I'm just doing this to help, I don't need any problems," she said, walking away.

Sacralization and 9/11

Collective traumas always take place within a larger context, and that context influences the collective response. Optimists expect survivors to band together, to help each other, and to unearth the event's larger lesson for humanity. Survivors do indeed band together, but the nature of their bonding is heavily influenced by the political and social context.

In times of globalization, when the reassuring anchors of national identity lose their grip, the dominant response to group trauma is to create a sacred memory of the event in ways that seem to restore that identity. Philosophers call this "sacralizing" a memory. The formation of a community of survivors—which can take place on scales both large and small—often constitutes a closing of ranks, building a wall around those who experienced the trauma.

The sacralization process relies on storytelling. The tale is told often enough to be frozen into the status of the sacred, unassailable by contradictory, or even just more complex, accounts of or reactions to the original event. The group forms around the act of remembering as much as it does around the memory itself, and one's relationship to the trauma becomes core to one's identity. Joining the group means passing a series of litmus tests, usually defined by recalling the event in a particular way.

Cultural critic Barbara Misztal says that this reaction tends to require obedience to the interpretation from other people: "This type of memory ... is characterized by the sacred and fixed vision of the past and demands loyalty and regulates obligation...."[1] When a group formed through this process attempts political action it often focuses narrowly on its own self-interest, isolating itself from others or even demanding that others subordinate themselves to the group's interests.

Inevitably, there are people who are left out of this sacralized narrative, or worse, unfairly vilified by it. These people might form a counter-memory, interpreting the event through a different story that extends rather than withholds the sympathy of survivors toward others: "In contrast to [the] uncompromising position of the first type of memory, the second type of memory does not impose such exclusive practices and assists people to articulate wider meaning and to cultivate links with a larger community," writes Misztal.[2] The counter-memory group will keep some elements of the dominant narrative—grieving for the dead and maintaining the innocence of individual victims, for example. But other elements get a new treatment, as the counter-memory group fights for an interpretation that allows more people into the community.

For forty years before 9/11, American identity had been increasingly challenged by global trends. Economic globalization had made many people less financially secure, while migration trends have changed the country's demographics. Policies that freed corporations to move around the world in search of the largest profit margin, along with advances in technology, had transformed our industrial economy into one focused on its information and service sectors. After our immigration laws removed national preferences for Europeans in 1965, immigrants of color began to arrive and settle in large numbers, not just in big cities, but also in rural and suburban areas. While we can see a less racist immigration policy as a more positive development than economic globalization, these things together nevertheless had a profoundly destabilizing effect on American communities.

September 11 is now the collective trauma of record for the United States. The attack itself was brutal enough to break thousands of families and destroy one of the most prominent elements of New York's cityscape. Manhattan took on the character of a disaster site, with toxic dust flying across rivers and into neighborhoods. New Yorkers, disturbed by the sight of the hole in the ground where the World Trade Center had stood, struggled to return to their customary collective self-confidence. The event also had an enormous economic impact that stretched from New York City throughout the nation.[3] The mainstream national response sacralized the day, relying on trusty, racialized archetypes of Americans as white and native-born, and foreigners as a dangerous, dark threat. The sacralization process, complete with racist stereotypes, merged with the immigration debate, pitting Americans and foreigners against each other and bolstering the idea that the United States should limit the entry of other people.

These archetypes, so prominent in the post–September 11 political discourse, had a narrowing effect on the subsequent immigration debate.

The ubiquitous narrative of that day is one of outsiders wanting to destroy all that generations of innocent Americans had built. "They hate us because of our freedoms" became an accepted mantra. The nation fixated on defining these outsiders, and on seeking out those who resembled them inside our borders. The characteristics of the insider group became more clearly defined. For one thing, insiders did not question the notion of U.S. innocence and suffering in this story, and they assumed that all Americans were affected by and reacted to September 11 in the same way. This story shaped both government and private action, and both sectors justified their actions in terms of nationalism. President Bush vowed to hunt down those responsible, driving the country to war in Afghanistan in less than six weeks. Congress passed the U.S.A. Patriot Act, expanding the government's power to suspend civil liberties in terrorism investigations.

Despite President Bush's proclamation that Americans should not blame all Muslims for the attacks, the line between insider Americans and outsiders became bolder, defined by the Patriot Act, hate crimes, and talk of ragheads on the Internet. A vigilante group called the Minutemen posse'd up to patrol the Mexican border. Conservative commentators like Ann Coulter associated Muslims with extremism. Coulter famously defended racial profiling when she wrote, "It is preposterous to assume every passenger is a potential crazed homicidal maniac. We know who the homicidal maniacs are. They are the ones cheering and dancing right now. We should invade their countries, kill their leaders and convert them to Christianity."[4] Sales of American flags grew exponentially; in immigrant communities, their presence reflected a mixture of patriotism and desire to deflect violence.

Even the most compassionate responses to the crisis reinforced economic and racial hierarchies. The intention to discriminate isn't necessary—the pull of the dominant story, and the existing context, will create the effect. A good example was the September 11 Victims Compensation Fund, which Congress established to support the families of those who had died. Their motivation was financial rather than political: Congress would pay for suffering and lost income to save the airlines from thousands of bankruptcy-inducing lawsuits. The fund's sacralizing effect was due to its huge scale and its unprecedented nature, distributing $7 billion to 5,000 families in grants ranging from $350,000 to nearly $4 million. No such fund was created after the 1995 Oklahoma City bombing that killed 168 people and was masterminded by two white men. By putting a price on the lives taken on September 11 but not on those killed in Oklahoma City, Congress unwittingly gave the impression that it was worse to have been killed by a foreign Muslim terrorist than by a white American one. The distribution of money raised questions of hierarchy among victims. Should the children of firefighters get less or more than those of stockholders? What about those of the dishwashers, janitors, and delivery drivers? Should the children of undocumented immigrants get anything at all?

Mamdouh began his work helping immigrants navigate the relief system as the country sacralized, and racialized, the memory of September 11. Experiencing the effects of that sacralization on himself and others, he began to develop a counter-memory. The fact that he, like many of his immigrant co-workers, had known the traumatic effects of poverty and political repression long before 9/11 gave him a broader perspective on the event's meaning. The fact that he was an immigrant, accustomed to having his national identity shaken up, gave him the capacity to embrace a diverse community.

Being Undocumented After September 11
The relief process highlighted the marginal position of undocumented immigrants. An estimated 250 died on September 11. Countless others were injured or lost their jobs. Few such immigrants or their families applied for services. Some feared deportation, but others didn't want to appear unable to support themselves in the U.S., ruining their chances of obtaining green cards in the future. Still others couldn't figure out how to get around the circumstances of undocumented life—not having the apartment lease in one's name or having worked for cash and so having no pay stubs to prove employment. Mamdouh figured that 20 percent of his co-workers were undocumented. He extrapolated this from the figures of the dead: 16 of 73 is 22 percent.

Other organizations, like the Red Cross, just didn't prepare for undocumented victims. Red Cross volunteers tend to be overwhelmingly white, and most who served during September 11 were not from New York. It took Mamdouh's co-worker Mario Peña, an undocumented barback from Ecuador, two tries before he could trust that he would get help. The first time Peña went to Pier 94, he overheard volunteers asking for documents, including immigration papers. Scared, he slipped out of the line he had waited in for two hours. He went back days later after another friend told him that the larger agencies had agreed not to check for immigration status.

"Where are you from? Do you have your green card?" he was asked by a Red Cross volunteer who wore a pin indicating that she was from Nebraska.

"I think you are not supposed to ask me that," he replied.

"You're right," the lady said. "I just wanted to know anyway."

From the Red Cross, Peña got $300 a week for four weeks to help pay his rent. Beyond that, he had nothing to fall back on.

The idea that undocumented immigrants use up public benefits without paying taxes is widely accepted, but in truth the overwhelming majority, a good 75 percent, actually work on the books like Peña did.[5] Using fake Social Security cards, they pay the same payroll taxes as anyone else, including Medicaid and Social Security. Their taxes support Social Security for the elderly and disabled and go into the unemployment fund, as well as funding the military, schools, and other public services. But undocumented people themselves can't use most of these benefits because to do so means risking discovery. Peña never filed tax returns, although he surely would have received refunds, and he couldn't apply for unemployment. When he gets old or if he becomes disabled, he certainly won't be able to get retirement or disability benefits. Through this mechanism of taxation without return, undocumented immigrants and their employers are thought to contribute some $7 billion to the Social Security system that they never use; all immigrants together bring the figure to $500 billion.[6] Peña didn't bother applying for any form of public income support such as public health insurance or food stamps. The Welfare Reform Act of 1996 cut off even legal immigrants from welfare, food stamps, and Medicaid, with exceptions for immigrant elderly and disabled people. The federal State Child Health Insurance Program, for example, is totally closed to undocumented children, and closed to legal resident children until they've been in the country for five years.

Other advocates reported similar experiences of scrutiny among their un-documented members. A union staffer went to the Red Cross with a twenty-two-year-old Mexican woman and her three-year-old daughter. Their volun-teer grilled the woman about how she had entered the U.S. and where her papers were, all for the purpose of giving her a $50 grocery certificate. An Indian immigrant who had worked off the books at a café in WTC Building Two lost consciousness while escaping, only to wake up and find that possibly hundreds of people had trampled his left arm into uselessness. This man had no Social Security card, no pay stubs or W-2s, no green card, no letters from employers (who would be afraid of sanctions for hiring undocumented work-ers), no access to unemployment insurance or Social Security disability ben-efits. Dozens more examples like these were reported in Chinatown, which also had a large undocumented population and was hit hard by the aftermath of September 11. Many Chinese families ended up paying two rents for a time, keeping their New York housing while sending one member out of state on the cheap Chinatown bus every week to earn a living.[7]

The fund ultimately distributed money using a complicated formula that reinforced existing social hierarchies, which the press called "an aristocracy of grief."[8] In return, the recipients signed waivers promising not to sue the government or the airlines. Everyone received the same amount for pain and suffering, but the economic relief packages were based on the income of the person who had died.

On the high end, the financial services company Cantor Fitzgerald protested when the fund published projections assuming that no one made more than $231,000, since many of its employees earned far more.[9] The initial formula also estimated women's wages at lower rates than men's, applying outdated data reflecting work time lost to child-rearing and assigning no value to domestic work at all. Others complained that the formula assumed that what people earned when they died was what they would have always earned. "Every human life is precious," Frank Keating wrote in a *Washington Post* editorial, "and taxpayer dollars should not distinguish between those with and those without. The government authors official inequity when it compensates a dishwasher at the World Trade Center differently from the way it compensates the person whose dishes were washed."[10] The awards ranged from $300,000 to $3.9 million. Tensions grew when the fund announced that it would reduce awards for those who had insurance, but not for those who received private donations.

The impression that some people deserve more than others was reinforced by the private sector; charities collected $676 million overall—the most collected for addressing any single tragedy in the United States.[11] Private charities set their own guidelines, implicitly valuing certain kinds of victims over others. For example, the National Association of Realtors, which gave $8.3 million to more than 1,000 families for rent and mortgage payments, decided explicitly to check immigration status. "We wanted to support the families of people who were here legally," spokesman Steve Cook told the *New York Times*.[12]

For the undocumented family members of Windows workers, immigration status was the most pressing issue. Because the federal Victims Compensation Fund included them, undocumented families were in the ironic position of being eligible for hundreds of thousands, even millions, of dollars, but did not have enough ID to open a bank account. Mamdouh's former co-worker Sekou Siby, the multilingual teacher from the Ivory Coast, brought one such woman into the union within a few days of the attacks. Siby had realized that Hadidjatou Traore, whose Ivoirian husband Abdoul had helped Siby get his job at Windows, needed more than friends could provide. Mamdouh had known Abdoul as a solid member of the union's contract committee. They had sometimes prayed together in the stairwell or sat together for an occasional meal.

Hadidjatou was a small, neat woman who spoke very little English and seemed quite shy. She gave away little of her panic and grief, except that her leg shook throughout the group meetings at the union hall. When Mamdouh translated for her, he often had to ask his questions twice. Abdoul and Hadidjatou had married in Abidjan, where she had been a nurse's aide and he had owned a grain-and-beans stall in a large open-air market. When the shop started to decline in the early 1990s, Abdoul had convinced Hadidjatou that they should leave the country. He'd tried for visas to France and the U.S., hoping to be able to legalize his status once there. The U.S. visa came through first, and Abdoul left a pregnant Hadidjatou in Abidjan. She followed him without the child in 1997 on a three-month tourist visa; she would never have gotten one for both herself and her daughter.

By then, Abdoul had started to hope for a new legalization law and he convinced his wife to stay, thinking they would soon be able to bring the little girl to the U.S. Over the years, they had two more children in New York. They celebrated the younger one's first birthday on September 10, in a Bronx townhouse that they had just bought. At 4 a.m. on September 11, Abdoul had left for his second job delivering *USA Today*, which he did every morning before going to work at Windows. No one had heard from him since.

While Siby searched for Abdoul in the hospitals, Hadidjatou sat with Abdoul's cousin, whom she thought of as her brother-in-law, at the Red Cross offices where families waited for news. Mayor Giuliani was there, hugging people and sitting with the families. Several times each hour, someone called out and spelled the name of a survivor who had been found, and a cheer went up from some part of the floor. When she had heard more than fifteen names called and watched her brother-in-law weeping, Hadidjatou decided she would never go back to that place. She was sick over the thought that her daughter would never meet her father. When Hadidjatou called Abidjan that weekend, her daughter cried and cried for her parents.

Hadidjatou's inability to confirm Abdoul's death made it hard to concentrate. She was sick with diarrhea and her heart seemed to shake the entire first week. Both kids had fevers, and the whole family cried constantly. With each rare survivor story, she thought Abdoul's prospects worsened. She worried about waiting too long to conduct the customary death rituals. Normally, one started praying on the first day. And she knew that she had broken Muslim tradition by emerging from her home so soon after being widowed. She would say to the family's menfolk, "He was on the 106th floor. The airplane crashed into the top floor, how can he survive, even if he jumped? My husband is not there." But it took three weeks for her to convince them that they should begin mourning rituals of prayer and fasting.

Hadidjatou and the union then started the long process of bringing her daughter to the U.S. First they tried to get the State Department to issue the girl a visa. They got Senator Chuck Schumer involved, but found that the State Department was adhering strictly to its rule of not issuing visas to people, even children, who had no legal sponsor and who were likely to stay. Given the circumstances, Schumer wrote letters imploring the State Department to show more flexibility. "There ought to be some way that in very rare and unique cases an exception can be made,'" he told the *New York Times*. "It's unfortunate that they could not find one here."[13]

The union had helped another family through diplomacy, having persuaded the U.S. embassy in Ecuador to grant a temporary visa to the wife and three children of an undocumented Windows worker. The State Department declared that Hadidjatou's only hope was to get the Immigration and Naturalization Service to provide a humanitarian exception to the visa rules that would allow the girl to join her mother. Soon after that the union lawyer who had been helping Hadidjatou called to say that the girl should present herself at the U.S. embassy in Abidjan. The visa was granted the next day, and in January, Abdoul's cousin flew to the Ivory Coast to bring the eight-year-old back with him. Hadidjatou bought a doll and took a small procession of people to greet her daughter at John F. Kennedy Airport. Getting this visa, however, was only the first step. Later, Hadidjatou would get a reprieve in the form of "deferred" status. Deferred status doesn't give someone a green card—it indicates that the authorities know that you are in the country, but would not pursue deportation. It essentially gives someone the chance to find a way to legalize their status, including waiting for a new law that would set the parameters for such applications.

Immigrants Create Counter-Memories

September 11 highlighted the aspects of immigrants' lives that already placed them at the bottom of New York's cultural and economic hierarchy, which they had been able to bypass momentarily while working at Windows. Their poverty, their vulnerability to violence, their problems with immigration status all played a role in how they ultimately interpreted the event.

As the IWAA reached the date of its planned obsolescence, it was obvious that Windows workers, their families, their friends, and their peers in the restaurant industry still needed help. The government treated the situation as a temporary emergency, but what Windows workers really needed was a political shift; the occasional job training or cash assistance would make no long-term difference in their unstable lives. While many Windows survivors accepted medical treatment for depression and anxiety following the attacks, they also needed jobs, housing, health care, and legalization—these were needs that therapy and pills couldn't meet.

For the immigrants in Mamdouh's community, their ongoing experience of hardship in turn helped them see the systemic nature of their problems, which would ultimately help them create a counter-memory. For example, Windows banquet server Ataur Rahman, who was forty-three on September 11, identified three major traumatic incidents in his life. After a bloody civil war that established Bangladesh's independence from Pakistan, he joined a movement to push for a secular, democratic state. His party held power for a time, but was overthrown in 1975 in a military coup. Although Rahman had already lost many friends and relatives to war and persecution, he felt the sharpest blow when the movement's leader was deposed and killed. "I was afraid that if I lived there, I would maybe not have any future," he said.

In 1979 Rahman came to New York and eventually found work at Windows. He was nowhere near the building in 1993, when Ramzi Yousef bombed the World Trade Center, killing six people and shutting down Windows for the next three years. Nevertheless, the bombing affected Rahman profoundly. He did not work for a year, believing that the restaurant would reopen quickly. He refused to let his wife work and incurred a large credit card debt. He didn't apply for unemployment or welfare benefits, and the government offered no compensation. Windows reopened after three years, but there was a protracted fight to get all former workers hired back.

When a relative called Rahman in 2001 to say that a plane had hit the towers, he felt as though fundamentalists were following him. "I left my country because of that," Rahman thought, "and now I'm seeing this thing."

This time, he reacted intensely. He lost his will to work and felt constant anxiety. He went on antidepressants, frequently switching prescriptions because of the side effects. He slept too much or not at all. He had nightmares. He couldn't concentrate. He felt unable to plan or even take basic next steps toward recovering his livelihood. Surrounded by therapeutic options, Rahman used some of the counseling offered to victims of September 11, feeling better for only a couple of hours after each session.

Other workers affected by September 11 had lived through poverty and the dangers of crossing the border illegally. While increasing the number of Border Patrol officers had no effect on the numbers of people crossing every year (that number remained steady), deaths at the border nearly doubled after 1995 as migrants took increasingly long and dangerous routes to the United States.

Manuel Guttierez,[14] who worked at Ranch One near the World Trade Center, grew up in Nezhaqualcoyotl, Mexico, in a two-room house that his construction worker father had built. All his siblings worked starting as teenagers and gave about half their earnings to their parents. In 1998, he decided to go to the United States, persuaded by his cousins who had already made the trip and had connections with a *coyote* who would charge only $1200. Guttierez had heard stories about people who died trying to swim across river channels or crossing the desert, and others who died because they were shot by border police, but he made himself think positively. Guttierez, whose stocky build belied his talent as a jewelry designer, traveled with a friend and a cousin; the three had vowed to stick together. They flew from their little town to a bigger city, then took a taxi to Naco, at the border, where they met sixty other migrants and an assistant *coyote* who guided them across the desert. Guttierez carried a gallon of water, *tortas*—Mexican sandwiches that his mother had made for him—and some fruit. There was a tense moment at the beginning when one man tried to bargain for a lower rate.

The group left at 8 a.m. to walk in a long single-file line across the desert to Arizona. The *coyote* told them not to talk, just to follow. Guttierez and his companions started at the middle but dropped to the back because his portly cousin was slow and tired quickly. They had to go through seven barbed wire fences (put up by farmers and the Border Patrol). Each time they had to help his cousin pull the barbed wire wide enough for him to squeeze through. At 10 p.m., they were the last of the group to run across the highway to the waiting point where vans would take them to a hotel.

Until then, things had been fairly smooth. But the van Guttierez was in—the last of three—broke down after only a few minutes. The driver used his cell phone and a four-door car arrived to take them to the hotel. Fifteen people crammed into that car, lying on top of each other. Guttierez lay across two men in the back. The driver got a call saying that the police were following them, so he sped up, erratically swerving all over the road. At one point, Guttierez looked up to see a big truck coming right at them. He had heard stories of people crashing and prepared himself to die at that moment. The driver lost control of the car, which almost flipped over, but Guttierez was lucky. He hadn't paid much for the trip, in money or in safety. The minimum price charged by *coyotes* is $1,000 and the maximum is $4,000. He'd heard of Ecuadorans and Chinese paying up to $10,000 to cross the border. He

Much has been made about how undocumented immigrants had broken American law and so shouldn't be rewarded as criminals. Mamdouh thought of this argument in light of his own experience. He felt that all the hand-wringing about "the law" was somewhat overwrought. Many people from poor countries simply can't get legal immigration, even if they are well-educated professionals. Such so-called law-breakers had worked for years at Windows, and been excellent employees and good people. He could imagine the conditions that had made otherwise honest people lie to ensure their own and their families' survival, having experienced some of those conditions directly. Mamdouh knew that but for a stroke of luck, any Windows worker could have died that day. If the planes had hit at 4 p.m., he too would have been dead. Others had come even closer. Two days before the attacks, Siby had given his morning shift to someone who had wanted to drop the Sunday shift because he played in a mariachi band on Saturday nights. Mario Peña had gone to work late so he could pay his bills. It was a matter of luck that all of them were still alive, and all felt that they somehow had to express gratitude for that good fortune.

Mamdouh knew that restaurant workers had had problems before that day, and that those problems would continue. What he didn't know, however, was that the most vilified of those workers, the undocumented, had had a decent chance at changing their status on September 10. That possibility had been swept away by the emerging September 11 narrative. He had little idea that this drama was taking place because it was happening far away, in Washington, D.C.

Chapter 3

CRIMMIGRATION

On September 10, 2001, Cecilia Muñoz walked into the White House with a half-dozen other immigration advocates. Known for having good relations with Latinos, President Bush had recently directed his domestic policy staff to meet with the advocates and begin hammering out a new immigration policy. Throughout his tenure as governor of Texas, Bush resisted English-only bills and recruited a good portion of the Latino electorate to the Republican Party. A friendlier, more respectful Immigration and Naturalization Service was among his presidential campaign promises. In 2000, he expressed the benign view of immigration that most Americans have taken when he told the League of United Latin American Citizens that "Latinos come to the U.S. to seek the same dreams that have inspired millions of others: they want a better life for their children.... Immigration is not a problem to be solved, it is the sign of a successful nation. New Americans are to be welcomed as neighbors and not to be feared as strangers."

In supporting a more open immigration system, Bush was responding to competing political pressures. Both the business community and the Latinos who had formed such a large portion of his electoral base wanted expanded legal immigration—but advocating immigration would put Bush in conflict with the restrictionist arm of the Republican Party.

Muñoz was well aware of these clashes as the vice president of policy at the National Council of La Raza (NCLR), a thirty-three-year-old nonpartisan Latino organization with hundreds of local affiliates that provided services to

Latinos and to low-income people. Her job was to limit the bad and maximize the good in the immigration measures coming out of Congress from year to year. Two months earlier, the *New York Times* had broken the news that President Bush and Mexican President Vicente Fox were crafting a plan to legalize 3 million Mexicans living in the United States without documents.[1] Although Muñoz had since had to push the administration to follow through on that commitment, this meeting gave her some hope that the process would move forward with presidential support. The White House domestic policy staff had pulled in the Departments of Labor, Education, and Health and Human Services.

It quickly became clear that the White House aide, sharply dressed in very high heels and a tightly tailored dark suit, was more interested in ending illegal immigration than in working out a legalization plan. Each time the advocates proposed specific ideas about how to legalize undocumented people, the aide redirected the conversation to discussing enforcement measures that would keep out future migrants. Muñoz had dealt with the woman before, and had found her singularly lacking in any desire to support legalization. The meeting lasted less than two hours and produced nothing.

Unsurprised, Muñoz prepared herself for what looked to be a more promising meeting the next day with the staffs of Senators Tom Daschle (D-S.D.), Ted Kennedy (D-Mass.), and Dick Gephardt (D-Mo.), who had already released a policy manifesto calling for legalization for any immigrant who had worked in the U.S. at least ninety days within the last eighteen months. This included a guest worker program, which the business community wanted, but it also allowed those guest workers to unionize, which the business community opposed. In addition, the proposal reduced the backlogs on family unification visas for current legal immigrants. Muñoz planned to negotiate the introduction of the bill that Cassandra Butts, Gephardt's chief of staff, had drafted.

Muñoz was in fact amazed that members of Congress were meeting with members of the immigrant rights movement about legalization. She had been talking quietly with colleagues since the late 1990s about the need to move another legalization program. The 1986 Immigration Control and Reform Act had last provided such a program, giving 3 million undocumented people a path to citizenship. In twenty years, the undocumented population had grown again to about 9 million. Before Bush's statements, she had thought it would be impossible to bring up another legalization plan in Washington until there had been at least five years of organizing to demand it.

That September 11, 2001, meeting, optimistically planned during what had been a decade-long economic boom, never took place. It would be a full year before Muñoz could return to the legalization issue, and the five years that she thought she could take off the timeline would be added back on before legalization could again gain any traction in Washington. She would spend the intervening time working fruitlessly to separate the image of immigrant from that of terrorist in a nation that had gone from the shock of September 11 to a state of war in what felt like an instant.

An Open Door—For Some

The idea that "America is a nation of immigrants" is one of the world's most resonant stories. It hides a great number of wrongs, depicting the settlement of this country as a matter of volunteerism rather than violence, and masking the forced land contributions of the indigenous people and the forced labor contributions of enslaved Africans. This image endures, however, because it has been true for so many Americans whose ancestors came here to escape the hierarchies of other countries, from serfdom and autocracy to pogroms.

Although immigration policy has always favored entrants from some countries over others, the U.S. has welcomed and integrated tens of millions of immigrants over the course of its history. There have been plenty of clashes, but over time the United States has come to see itself as a multicultural society—a melting pot in which many different kinds of people live and work together, contributing parts of their own cultures to a new American culture. In the large cities where most immigrants initially established their communities, people became accustomed to seeing and being with other ethnic groups. Because virtually everyone had immigrant roots, the principle of welcome was important to the American self-image and led many ordinary Americans to see immigration in a largely positive light. Mamdouh himself benefited tremendously from this open posture, generally receiving a kind welcome from New Yorkers when he arrived in the late 1980s.

This attitude of acceptance was, however, often more aspirational than real. U.S. history is full of attempts to exclude people who did not seem at the time to conform to the image of a "real American." And the treatment of immigrants has always been racialized. Over the years racial hierarchies have shifted and racial definitions changed as European immigrants gained status while Mexican and other Third World immigrants did not. Through a combination of straightforward exclusion, bureaucratic exceptions, and the creation of different mechanisms for entering the country, federal law expanded or reduced immigration based on labor needs, economic anxiety, war, and xenophobia.

Differential treatment was justified by constructing the image of an ideal American identity as white, Anglo-Saxon, and Protestant. In fact, not all Europeans have always been considered white: the flood of Irish famine emigrants during the 1840s sparked a strong nativist reaction, which viewed the Irish as both physically and culturally similar to blacks.[2] It took a generation or more for the Irish to gain secure status as whites in America's racial/ethnic hierarchy. The new immigration of the late nineteenth century was dominated by Italians, Poles, Hungarians, Jews, and a range of other groups from southern and eastern Europe, and again it was widely argued that these new immigrants were inferior to native-born whites.[3] The charges against them sound familiar: they were reviled for their refusal to speak English, for their political and economic demands on American corporations, for being so poor that they became "public charges" or undercut the wages of the native-born workers, and for their immoral sexual behavior. Then, as now, undesirable immigrants were equated with criminals who could not be rehabilitated.

The growing U.S. dealt with its labor needs by constantly switching preferences between different immigrant populations. Chinese workers were brought over as contract laborers throughout the 1800s to build up the West, particularly its railroad systems. For almost a century after the Mexican-American war in 1848, Mexicans could travel freely within the United States, and in the early twentieth century tens of thousands of Mexicans crossed the border looking for work, especially after the Mexican Revolution began in 1910. In 1907, the Dillingham Commission identified Mexican workers as the best solution to the labor shortage in the southwestern U.S., but warned against immigrants from southern and eastern Europe as a serious threat to American society.

No one was safe from nativist attack, however, and the immigrants who looked most unlike other Americans made easy targets for xenophobes. A series of laws were enacted to limit the mobility of Chinese workers.[4] In 1882, for example, the Chinese Exclusion Act, a huge victory for the era's restrictionists, suspended Chinese immigration for ten years; unauthorized Chinese immigrants could be deported and the Chinese were prohibited from naturalization. The ban was eventually broadened to cover the entire Asia/Pacific Triangle.

Both World War I and labor unrest increased public willingness to restrict immigration. The Immigration Acts of 1920 and 1924 limited the numbers of immigrants to 150,000 per year, less than a quarter of the immigration rate until then. This was the most restrictive set of immigration policies the United States has ever had. These laws crafted large quotas for England, Germany, and Ireland while limiting immigration from countries like Russia and Italy. Illegal immigration was so common among Italians, for example, that an urban legend grew up around the origin of the derogatory term *wop*. Its real etymology is from the Spanish word *guapo*, applied in Spain to denigrate Italian agricultural workers, but to this day many Italian Americans believe it was an acronym for "without papers."

In 1929 Congress made it a misdemeanor to enter the United States without documents and a felony to remain in the country. Thousands of southern and eastern Europeans, however, continued to come in just that manner.[6] As immigrants were detained and deported for violating the quota policies, social reformers began to take up the causes of longtime residents who had committed only minor offenses. It was wrong to separate people who had longstanding ties to the United States from their families and communities, these reformers argued. Rather than punishing them for the poverty and alienation that was forced upon them by the immigration laws, the country should find ways to alleviate their situation, starting with reversing their deportation orders. They won a series of changes that gave immigration officials the ability to change someone's status.[6]

Mexicans were left behind by this liberalization, not so much because they were explicitly excluded, but because they had little access to the mechanisms through which they could change their status. While programs that affected Europeans were increasingly liberalized in the 1930s and 1940s, those affecting Mexicans remained restrictionist. Europeans could come to live permanently, but Mexicans could come only to work temporarily through guest worker programs, such as the Bracero Program, created during World War II. This temporary worker program recruited 4.5 million Mexicans before it was cancelled in 1964. Braceros were intensely abused by their employers, and once the country decided it didn't need their labor anymore, they became vulnerable to deportation.[7] Undocumented immigration from Mexico rose in this period—by some estimates as much as 6,000 percent—and Operation Wetback in 1954 was the first massive deportation sweep in the U.S. On its first day alone, 4,000 people were captured for deportation.[8] The development of this hierarchy created the enduring image of the Mexican as an illegal immigrant, ignoring the large numbers of Europeans who had also held that status.

The civil rights movement and other progressive movements of the 1960s changed the national political scene, and blatant discrimination in immigration policy lost favor among public officials. In 1965, Congress changed the Immigration and Nationality Act and the Immigration Reform and Control Act to remove the national quotas left from the 1920s. Congress also raised the absolute numbers of immigrants who could enter. As a result, immigration increased, both in absolute numbers and in the movement of people from previously excluded parts of the world. The new law included other preferences that weren't explicitly racial, but they had a racial effect that followed the established pattern. The identity of the preferred immigrant changed some, but the fact of preference didn't. The new laws sought to recruit professionals, which disadvantaged the poor. They also privileged family reunification, which continued existing racial patterns. Only people who were already in the country could sponsor family members to come. People thus continued to immigrate without papers. As the underfunded immigration bureaucracy built enormous backlogs of people trying to get in legally, the number of undocumented immigrants grew as well.

The Right to Be Present

The 1986 legalization program reflected the Reagan Administration's pragmatic attempt to deal with the reality of undocumented immigration. Muñoz herself had helped thousands of people change their status while working at Catholic Charities in the late 1980s. She was surprised and thrilled to hear in July 2001 that President Bush was negotiating with President Vicente Fox of Mexico to legalize undocumented Mexicans living in the United States and seemed poised to extend the "right to be present" to Mexicans. Muñoz got word of it during NCLR's annual convention, which was in Milwaukee that year. The next day, Senator John McCain (R-Ariz.) said he understood the reality that people were already here and that provisions needed to be made.[9] The *New York Times* and *Washington Post* wrote editorials supporting legalization.[10] Within weeks, Bush had raised the possibility of legalizing other immigrants as well. "We'll consider all folks here," he said.[11]

Bush's campaign platform thus seemed to be a remarkable step in a progressive direction. The excitement about his promises to come up with a legalization plan proved premature, however, with the White House spending some weeks backing away from fast action. By early August, a White House spokesman was saying, "Let me do everything I can to downplay your expectations.... I don't think I'm in a position to say where we'll be in September."[12]

At the end of August, Bush told reporters that he and President Fox would come out with principles but not a full-out plan during Fox's September visit.[13]

Feeling the opportunity slipping away, Muñoz chased down all these statements. She warned that it would be unwise for Bush to abandon expectations that he had raised, and she pushed back against the notion that legalization amounted to amnesty. "We had a legalization program under Ronald Reagan, and the sky did not fall," she said to reporters. "Everybody understands and winks and nods at industry. Who are the real lawbreakers here? There is a general understanding that businesses hire these folks and bring them up here, or at least encourage them to come. We need to shift our laws so there is a rationality to them."[14]

Although there is a great deal of talk about the criminality of undocumented immigrants, the way things worked in real life suggested that many Americans didn't really want to stop illegal immigration. The laws that were designed to deter illegal entry were largely symbolic. People continued to come without documents, and in spite of employer sanctions most employers looked the other way unless they needed to use the law to control their employees. The immigration system as a whole was underfunded and outdated. While the national debate focused on how to keep criminalizing immigrants, Muñoz and her colleagues had been unable to reform the system itself to make legal immigration easier.

Even so, the debate was moving at a much faster pace than Muñoz could have predicted.

As Muñoz sat in Senator Tom Daschle's waiting room on September 11, watching the planes hitting the Twin Towers, Cassandra Butts ran in.

"Turn to Channel 5," she said. "I hear the Pentagon's been hit!"

As they changed the channel, Butts said, "I've got to go." For the next two years, Muñoz would feel guilty about letting her return to the Capitol. As Muñoz herself started leaving the building, a security guard announced that another plane was headed toward the Capitol, so she and her colleagues ran to the closest offices, at the National Immigration Forum. In the midst of the chaos her mother called, and Muñoz was surprised to hear her crying. She reassured her mother that she was all right and decided to find her husband and head home. She found a cab that took her across town to where he'd been waiting for a meeting, and they picked up his car and drove home. Muñoz's mother-in-law, who had been visiting and meant to return to London the next day, was glued to the television in the recreation room. Muñoz took out her rosary and used the beads to meditate. The couple then picked up their two daughters, then six and nine, from school, which had closed early. It was a spectacularly beautiful day, and they didn't want the kids in front of the television, so Muñoz took the elder one out for a long-promised bike-riding lesson. "This way, you'll always remember a happy thing about today," Muñoz told her daughter.

At 4 p.m., Muñoz's mother called again to say that her friend Josh Rosenthal had been in the South Tower and had not been heard from. Muñoz had met Rosenthal when she was nine and he had become her elder brother's high school debating partner and best friend. She'd grown up playing poker with the two boys, winning quite often, as their families became increasingly integrated. Rosenthal had informally moved in with the Muñozes when his mother had surgery, had passed on his college mentor to Muñoz, and they had grieved together when Rosenthal's brother died unexpectedly of a heart condition. She had last seen him at her parents' fiftieth anniversary party. As time passed, it became increasingly painful for Muñoz to hear the government invoking the 9/11 victims to justify racial profiling as a national security measure.

Nevertheless, Muñoz's own family history motivated her to keep trying. Slightly built with wavy light brown hair, Muñoz was born in Detroit and raised in its middle-class suburbs, ensconced in a tight Bolivian immigrant community that was largely comprised of her own extended family. Her paternal grandfather had attended the University of Michigan in the 1920s before returning to La Paz to build the only house with a front porch in that city. Her own parents had come to the U.S. as newlyweds in 1950 so that her father could finish an engineering program that he had started but never finished in the 1940s. Disturbed by political unrest in Bolivia, the couple decided to stay in Michigan. By the time things stabilized in Bolivia, Muñoz's father was working in the auto industry and the family had four U.S.-born children. After listening to President Kennedy's speech about the Cuban Missile Crisis, Muñoz's father turned to her mother as they watched their children sleeping.

"Should we go back?"

"This is our home now," her mother replied.

Muñoz grew up in the supremely segregated suburb of Livonia, essentially in a white family that spoke Spanish, exotic in nothing but language. Her mother was of Spanish descent and light skinned, and her father, though he had more Indian heritage, also happened to have blue eyes. They had few direct experiences of racism. The most dramatic incidents were funny and pathetic rather than violent. In her parents' first apartment, the landlady heard them speaking Spanish and chastised them for "talking Mexican" in her house, which they found hilariously ignorant. All of the Latinos Muñoz knew as a child were related to her, and Thanksgiving dinner at her house included forty people eating turkey with Bolivian music playing in the background.

Muñoz had heard about the civil rights movement, which her parents told her was also their struggle. But she didn't feel a part of it until one day in high school when her boyfriend was over at the house listening to her father express his horror at the Central American wars, including the role of the United States.

"Well, you know, Cecilia," her boyfriend said, "if we do end up in a war, it seems like your parents should be interned. I couldn't know where their loyalties lay." Muñoz was astonished that anyone could think her family was anything other than fully American.

Merging Immigration Law and Criminal Law

The 1965 Immigration and Nationality Act removed national quotas, opening the United States to immigration from all the countries that had previously been restricted. These new immigrants in turn slowly began to change the demographics of the United States, fueling a new, but familiar, nativist backlash. Modern nativists came up with contemporary ways to criminalize and alienate immigrants. They made it illegal to hire undocumented workers, expanded the list of crimes for which legal immigrants could be deported, and cut off both legal and undocumented immigrants from a wide range of public services. Even before September 11, they had tied the threat of terrorism to immigration, a strategy that legal scholar Juliet Stumpf has dubbed "crimmigration."[15]

Under crimmigration, states and the federal government created a number of new laws throughout the 1980s and 1990s to punish border crossers and visa violators, a policy direction that recasts immigration law as criminal law and immigrants as lawbreakers.

The crimmigration impulse has waxed and waned over time; when it surfaces, it always has a strong racial component. The racial agitation prevalent in crimmigration-friendly eras raises the temperature all around the table and makes it less likely that policymakers and citizens will be able to think straight about what policies make sense. September 11 fueled that impulse, making it much harder for Muñoz to do her work. The national day of mourning followed, and it took a week for Muñoz to be able to focus again on work. It took even longer for her to realize that the possibilities of winning legalization for the undocumented had changed forever, that she would never again be able to speak about immigration policy as separate from national security.

The crimmigration approach, however, creates significant new problems that are often invisible to the general public. First, it makes citizenship a requirement for basic civil and constitutional rights, even such very basic ones as the right to due process. Second, the distinctions between those who deserve rights and those who do not are intensely racialized. They are unevenly applied among immigrants themselves and they rely on racial stereotyping—how else can you tell whether a person is deserving other than by looking at them? The main effect of crimmigration is to pit Americans and immigrants against each other; it has not, however, slowed down either undocumented or legal immigration at all. Moreover, it results in a profoundly, and racially, divided community that is incapable of solving its problems. When Americans face hard times, it's easier to target a particular group of people as the cause than to address the larger system. Casting foreigners as criminals protects that larger system from critique, and at the same time diverts communities from seeking real solutions.

These trends were exemplified in employer sanctions, increased border security, expanded criminal deportation, others suspending the rights of terrorism suspects and laws excluding immigrants from public services. The 1986 Immigration Reform and Control Act (IRCA) legalized millions of undocumented immigrants, but it also established sanctions, such as fines and jail time for employers who knowingly hired undocumented workers. It's unclear that employer sanctions truly deter rogue employers, since only a minuscule number of employers are prosecuted each year for hiring undocumented workers. Research suggests that sanctions may have far greater impact in preventing immigrant workers from resisting exploitation. Because there was so much more focus on routing them out, undocumented immigrants were reluctant to report wage or safety violations to the Labor Department. As the demographics of entire industries shifted to become dominated by immigrant labor, employers frequently used the threat of deportation to bust union organizing campaigns.[16]

Unions complained that employers called the immigration authorities themselves to report an undocumented workforce in an organizing campaign. It was cheaper for employers to pay the resulting fine than to improve the wages and working conditions a union contract would have required.[17] Congress also increased funding for the Border Patrol significantly. Between 1986 and 2002 the number of officers tripled and the number of hours they patrolled the border grew about eightfold, but the rate of apprehension actually fell from 33 percent in the early 1980s to an all-time low of 5 percent in 2002. Restrictionists argued that fewer people were crossing the border illegally, but it is more likely that they just found new ways of avoiding capture. These new ways were undoubtedly more dangerous, but the numbers of undocumented people continued to rise.[18]

Another school of restrictionists focused on fiscal anxieties, the idea that immigrants had to be prevented from using up finite public resources. These attacks echoed those of earlier generations against immigrants as being "liable to become a public charge." Undocumented immigrants became ineligible for virtually all federal and state benefits, except for emergency medical care, immunization programs, and disaster relief.[19] The notion of ending the immigration drain on public funds was encoded into the Personal Responsibility and Work Opportunities Act of 1996, which radically changed the welfare system overall, and which cut legal immigrants off from food stamps, Medicaid, and Supplemental Security Income (for the elderly and disabled), generating threats of suicide among elderly immigrants around the country. Only under great pressure did Congress restore Social Security benefits for those populations.

Since the late 1980s, federal policies for criminal deportation have made it easier to treat immigration violations as crimes, while also adding to the list of existing crimes that could trigger deportation of legal residents and people who were in the country waiting for their papers. The problem with this list wasn't so much that these acts were not crimes, but that the government set a pattern of creating increasingly harsh punishment for an ever-growing list of decreasingly important crimes. For example, the Immigration Act of 1990 defined an aggravated felony as any crime of violence for which the sentence was at least five years, even if the statutes under which immigrants were convicted defined the crime as less serious.

This trend created a secondary class in the eyes of the law: this class, comprising foreigners, some of whom had been in the country for a very long time, had fewer rights than citizens. In some cases, they were never tried and convicted, but simply deported without having had access to an attorney. (Since immigration courts are administrative rather than criminal courts, they do not guarantee the right to an attorney.) Deportation amounted to exile for immigrants who had built families, businesses, and communities in the United States. Those ties were the most important consideration in the

1965 reforms that removed many of the 1920s restrictions. As the color of the immigrant population changed, however, consideration of family ties was abandoned.

Finally, the Antiterrorism and Effective Death Penalty Act of 1996 was a series of laws to "deter terrorism, provide justice for victims, provide for an effective death penalty, and for other purposes." It allowed the government to suspend the writ of habeas corpus in terrorism cases. Although it didn't explicitly target immigrants, it would be used later to suspend the civil rights of thousands.

Ultimately, the growing list of deportable offenses reinforced the impression that foreigners, whether legal residents or not, did not deserve even basic constitutional rights, further separating them from American citizens. This pattern helped accustom Americans to the idea that it was all right to deny rights to some people, and to create life-long punishments for even petty crimes. Collateral punishment—serving one's sentence not only in prison, but through a restricted life afterward—is something immigrants share with other marginalized communities. African Americans, for example, suffered badly from this trend as states passed laws that doubly punished ex-prisoners by making it illegal for them to vote, live in public housing, or receive state licenses for certain kinds of work. Activists were also affected after September 11, when numerous civil liberties were suspended. Once you create a class of not-quite citizen, the possibility that government will add more people to that class grows and grows.[20]

With these policies, the merging of immigration and criminal law—the essence of "crimmigration"—became essentially complete. Under crimmigration, legal immigrants have fewer constitutional rights than citizens, and unauthorized immigrants have virtually none. The government's burden of proof is lower for immigration matters than for criminal matters, so it has increasingly used immigration law to arrest and detain terrorism suspects.[21] Immigrants have fewer rights, and so law enforcement can get around the need to respect the right to privacy, the right not to incriminate oneself, and, in some cases, the right to due process, by engaging the immigration courts rather than the criminal justice system.

The Impact of 9/11

Although it took Muñoz a long time after September 11 to accept that the legalization debate had ended for the moment, Mark Krikorian realized it right away. Krikorian is the executive director of the Center for Immigration

Studies (CIS), a think tank whose motto is "Pro immigrant, low immigration." Despite the neutral name of his organization, Krikorian was a central figure in the restrictionist movement. Even with a small staff, CIS produced prodigious amounts of research justifying immigration restrictions, and Krikorian himself was widely quoted in the press. His style was less shrill and more intellectual than many of the other restrictionist leaders, but his point was nevertheless the same—immigration on a large scale had no place in today's United States.[22]

Surprisingly, Krikorian is himself the grandson of Armenian immigrants who escaped being killed during the Turkish genocide of the early twentieth century. His grandfathers had emigrated before the genocide started. One of his grandmothers had been sold into slavery, eventually escaping and working as a domestic servant in France before coming to the U.S. Krikorian grew up speaking Armenian, although he wouldn't call himself fully bilingual. After attending the Fletcher School of International Relations and spending two years in Russian Armenia he tried to get a job at U.S. English, Ron Unz's anti-bilingual education lobby organization. U.S. English had no jobs but referred him to the Federation for American Immigration Reform (FAIR), where he became the editor of the organization's newsletter. After a stint with a news service in Virginia's Shenandoah Valley, Krikorian moved to CIS, an immigration-control outfit looking for a media-savvy director.

One of Krikorian's central arguments against immigration was that current immigrants were not engaged in the Americanization processes available to his grandparents and parents. He frequently cited the fact that his mother had to memorize the Gettysburg Address in school, wondering if the big-city school systems that are available to immigrants today, so influenced as they were by multiculturalism, even taught the Gettysburg Address at all. To his mind, the technological features of modern life—easy travel and global communication—made it harder for new immigrants to break ties with their home country and develop loyalty to the United States.

On September 11, as Muñoz waited for her meeting to start at the Capitol, Krikorian was in his office. Everyone left, which struck Krikorian as foolish since they would then be sitting in gridlocked traffic. He stayed, transfixed by the television, until a reporter called him that afternoon. The reporter had already concluded that the attacks would bring an end to Bush's legalization plan, and Krikorian agreed with him. On September 17, he was quoted in the press as saying, "The issue of amnesty for illegal Mexican aliens is out of the question. It's defunct."[23]

Because six of the nineteen hijackers had overstayed tourist and student visas, the movement to limit immigration found fertile ground in linking foreignness to the threat of terrorism, even though visa issuance is not an immigration matter.[24] Muñoz's chief rival organizations, FAIR and CIS, both found their stars rising. Krikorian pulled up data on the number of Muslims entering the country and argued that, rather than racially profiling them, the nation should cut legal immigration altogether to reduce the pool of potential terrorists.

People who had traditionally been in favor of immigration began switching sides. Ron Unz, who had opposed bilingual education but was supported immigration, changed his position. American Jews, with their long history of refugee immigration, discrimination, and assimilation in the United States, felt particularly challenged. Muñoz was shocked to get a call from the American Jewish Committee, which had always been a staunch ally, asking if the AJC should reconsider its support of family reunification policies. Before 9/11, Krikorian had been talking with the policy director of the American Jewish Committee, though with little hope of actually converting him. After the attacks, however, the same person sent Krikorian an analysis of the effect of current immigration on American Jews in the context of September 11 and in the larger context of synagogue vandalism and anti-Semitic attacks in Europe. Krikorian was invited to speak to the board of directors. He sensed the organization's ambivalence; its members were clearly proud of their history of supporting open immigration, but wary of the large numbers of Arabs entering the country. Krikorian thought, however, that an immigration policy aimed at limiting Arabs would be impossible in today's multicultural political climate.

A growing number of Americans, though, did support singling out Arabs and Muslims. Polls showed renewed support for racial profiling as a security measure and emerging support for limiting immigration. A CNN/USA Today/Gallup poll taken a few days after the attacks revealed that a majority of Americans backed proposals targeting people of Arab descent. Fifty-eight percent supported more intensive security checks for Arabs, including those who were citizens; 49 percent favored special identification cards for such people; and 32 percent thought "special surveillance" was justified.[25]

Government action followed suit. Between mid-September and the end of November, the FBI visited thousands of Muslim homes for "voluntary" questioning, developed a watch list of 5,000 Muslims, South Asians, and Arabs, and held some 1,200 Muslim men indefinitely in secret detention facilities without notifying their families or allowing them access to attorneys. Only a tiny number of anti-terrorism charges were brought, however, and there have been no convictions as a result of this process. Untold numbers of people, many waiting for their immigration cases to be adjudicated in the backlogged system, were deported or left voluntarily. All refugee admissions were immediately suspended—even though none of the 9/11 attackers had gained entry to the U.S. as refugees.

Racial Profiling

Cecilia Muñoz spent the rest of 2001 formulating a workable argument to prevent the conflation of immigration policy and national security. To temper the development of anti-immigrant and repressive regulations in the USA Patriot Act, she drew distinctions between visa issuance and immigration, hoping that the State Department would then figure out how not to issue visas to the wrong people. She argued that encouraging mass scrutiny would drive immigrants, both legal and undocumented, deeply underground, and that pulling people out of the shadows would reduce the size of the haystack within which police sought potential terrorists. Advocates managed to keep many of the worst provisions out of the act, but could not prevent a substantial expansion of the government's power to spy on, detain, and suspend due process for U.S. residents in the name of fighting terrorism.

One night in October, Muñoz sat in the green room at CNN preparing to debate conservative commentator Pat Buchanan. As each sat for makeup, Muñoz could easily hear Buchanan chatting animatedly with his makeup artist, crowing about the effect that 9/11 had had on the immigration debate. While Buchanan congratulated himself for taking advantage of the opportunity to stir things up, Muñoz's head filled with images of Sikhs, South Asians, and Muslims being attacked.

The first murders resulting from 9/11 hate crimes had received scant press attention. Sikh-Americans' turbans made them an identifiable target for racists and they suffered numerous assaults, including at least two murders that took place on a single day, September 15. First, Balbir Singh Sodhi was shot outside his own gas station in Mesa, Arizona, by a man who had bragged hours earlier that he intended to "kill the ragheads responsible for September 11." That same day a Pakistani convenience store owner was shot to death in Dallas. His killer had days earlier murdered an Indian man nearby and later admitted to having blinded a Bangladeshi as well. "I did what every American wanted to do after September 11 but didn't have the nerve," he had said.

Overhearing Buchanan in the chair next to hers, Muñoz thought of these men and her own South Asian husband. Being a solicitous husband and father, he insisted on having Muñoz and the girls sit aside while he checked all their luggage when the family traveled. She had had many opportunities, particularly during the first Gulf War, to observe other passengers giving him suspicious looks; she imagined them wondering why he had so many bags and whether they should get on a plane with him.

On the show, Buchanan, who started first and interrupted Muñoz enough to take up two-thirds of the segment, argued that the U.S. should reduce the immigration limit to 250,000 per year from the current rates of about 900,000. He wanted future immigrants to pass a test proving their loyalty to the United States—the kind of test that had just been outlawed in the 1996 Immigration Act. He soon turned to legalization.[26]

"The president and Mr. Fox said before September 11 amnesty for 3 million, the Democrats said for 11 million.... That is insanity.... It was a different world pre-September 11 than we live in right now," Buchanan said. He advocated getting Americans to "run down" people from the countries that harbored terrorists, specifically Iraq, Afghanistan, and Saudi Arabia. Americans would have to spy on these populations, particularly when they encountered people they didn't know, if they wanted to be secure. He wanted Mexico to militarize its side of the border to prevent 500,000 Mexicans from "invading" the United States every year. He equated those "wide open borders" with free trade and globalization, while also invoking the image of the World Trade Center in ashes to override Muñoz's objections to Americans spying on each other.

Although there was no connection between terrorism and immigration or the southern border, Buchanan used the emotional grip of the September 11 attacks to create one. His language, Muñoz argued, would have a lasting impression that would lead to the vilification of and violence against immigrants. His argument for racial profiling and automatic suspicion of certain people was the same one that had been made during other wars, the same one that had justified internment of Japanese Americans during World War II and the widespread civil liberties violations of the McCarthy era. All these laws had ultimately shamed the United States and had been reversed, although not quickly enough.

In connecting September 11 with "free trade," Buchanan revealed how the attacks provided a touchstone for anxiety over the effects of globalization on American national identity. The event gave him a platform from which to object, not to focus on the effects of economic globalization on working people, but to ratchet up fear of the Other by mischaracterizing economic globalization as being about open borders. Those borders had opened only for corporate investment—for dollars, but not for people. Fear would keep the public from realizing that the connection between immigration and terrorism was specious, and that making immigration policy more restrictive would do nothing to actually prevent terrorism.

"That's exactly the kind of talk which leads to policies that make us feel better for a short time," said Muñoz, desperately hoping to encourage some common sense. She held it together long enough to leave the studio, but cried all the way during her drive home, imagining her gentle husband encountering someone infected by Buchanan's brand of patriotism.

Unintended Consequences

On September 11, 2002, Muñoz found herself in a meeting with many of the same advocates she'd been with in 2001. They had debated the appropriateness of meeting on that day. But when they got together, Cassandra Butts set the tone.

"We're together because we were together a year ago," she said. "This is what we do. We do it because it's important, and we're all going to keep on doing it."

A month later, the government started the Special Registration program, requiring Muslim men from a list of countries believed to harbor terrorists to turn themselves in for fingerprinting. The list eventually grew to thirty-three countries, including Morocco and Bangladesh, before the government abandoned it as less than useful. On November 26, 2002, President Bush took another step in conflating immigrants with criminals when he signed a new law creating the cabinet-level Department of Homeland Security, into which the Immigration and Naturalization Service was relocated and renamed the Bureau of Immigration and Customs Enforcement (ICE).

Crimmigration brings to bear the harshest elements of the criminal justice and immigration systems. It will inevitably result in an ever-growing population of people who have strong ties to the United States but are nonetheless alienated from it. That alienation will damage U.S. society in ways that far outweigh the psychological benefits of feeling that we have isolated criminals from the society. There's no rational connection between immigrants and terrorists, and no significant indication that immigrants, even the undocumented, commit crimes at a higher rate than citizens.

The combination of "secure the borders" talk, war, and racial profiling is meant to make Americans feel safer, but it's likely to backfire in dangerous ways. The Migration Policy Institute noted in a June 2003 report that "the post 9/11 crackdown on immigrants has actually put this country at greater risk by alienating and intimidating communities that could help with terrorism investigations."[27] The report also noted that even under the strictest immigration laws, the hijackers would still have been able to enter the country with visas from European countries.

Although Mamdouh wasn't privy to the negotiations between politicians, he could still see the results of the post–September 11 dragnet playing out in New York City. A close friend's asylum claim was delayed when refugee admissions were suspended. Others told him about hundreds of South Asian and Arab Muslims being held without access to their lawyers or their families in Brooklyn's detention center. Undocumented Mexicans and Bangladeshis continued to fill the kitchens of New York City restaurants, with little hope for legalization of their status.

A restrictive policy prevents immigrants from asserting their full presence in the United States. It does not, however, keep them from coming. Because the conditions they are escaping are worse than the conditions lawmakers are creating, the population of undocumented immigrants has continued to grow. Although their attempts have made life miserable for many immigrants, restrictionists have not significantly stemmed the flow.

In mainstream media and politics, restrictionists now seek to close these doors, or at least to shut them for most people most of the time. Their proposals are accompanied by hundreds of rationalizations. They focus on illegal immigration, but their arguments are ultimately directed toward restricting all immigration. They argue that undocumented people have broken the law, that they drive down wages and take jobs from native-born workers, that they use public services but don't pay taxes, and that they enter the country to commit terrorism.

Some of these assertions hold a grain of truth—undocumented immigrants have indeed broken immigration law, for example—but they hide a great number of important facts. Others are patently false. Immigration law was discriminatorily created and applied; wages are driven down largely because the United States won't enforce its own labor laws; immigrants, even the vast majority of undocumented immigrants, do pay taxes. And there has been no sign that restricting immigration will have any effect on preventing terrorism. True or not, however, these arguments shape the public debate by playing to the worst fears and racial prejudices among Americans. While making an effort to appear rational, the restrictionist movement amounts to people whose own ancestors escaped hardship to make good for themselves in the United States now pulling up the ladder behind them.

Chapter 4

LEARNING TO ORGANIZE

By the time Mamdouh was wrapping up his work at the Immigrant Workers' Assistance Alliance, he was beginning to see that restaurant workers needed political power far more than temporary relief. Hotel Employees and Restaurant Employees Local 100 decided to help start a new organization to support the thousands of restaurant workers who faced daily exploitation. Local 100 couldn't invest any money, but it could offer advice and office space for a few months. It was clear that the Windows workers, especially Mamdouh, had the leadership instincts, networks, and industry knowledge necessary to build a permanent organization, but they would need an experienced organizer to facilitate the process. The union had heard of the work of a promising young Indian American woman, and one of the organizers left her a voicemail message in early October.

Saru Jayaraman, then twenty-six, was a first-generation Indian American who had grown up in a working-class suburb outside Los Angeles. Her computer technician father, unable to find work that matched his skills in India, had emigrated to Rochester, New York, in 1973. Saru's mother and elder sister had followed a year later, and Saru was born soon after the family's reunion. When she was in sixth grade, the family moved to Whittier, a small city southeast of Los Angeles. During most of her childhood, Saru's father earned a good salary working as contractor for Honda, but the job had no security. He was laid off when she started college and had been mostly underemployed ever since. Saru's mother worked as a part-time school aide and was the couple's chief source of income. Saru's most dramatic feature was a pair of large, perfectly almond-shaped light brown eyes. Her otherwise delicate jawline thrust out slightly, hinting at her strong will. She was the family rebel, but was also a family leader, regularly gathering everyone up to teach them something, usually a handicraft she herself had just learned.

Saru was active in high school, volunteering at the local hospital and serving on the student government. Although a straight-A student taking Advanced Placement and college preparatory classes, she was also in a school that was 90 percent Chicano, frequently hearing from teachers and counselors that all the students were bound for early pregnancy, prison, or, at best, community college. The school had a massive ROTC program, and many of its students went on to join the armed forces. She was keenly aware of not being white. In her valedictorian speech, Saru urged her class to show the world who they really were, to prove the predictions of crime and promiscuity wrong.

Her college and graduate school years made Saru into a very smart, highly educated service provider. While still an undergraduate, she started a leadership development program for low-income girls that now operates in ten cities. Admitted to Yale Law School, Harvard Law School, and Harvard's Kennedy School for Public Policy, Saru crafted her own joint program by convincing Yale to let her leave law school after half the program, spend two years at the Kennedy School, then return to law school for eighteen months to finish. This arrangement, too, is now a formal joint program between Yale and the Kennedy School.

In law school, Saru became exposed to political activism. That exposure intensified at the Kennedy School, where she had much more sustained contact with organizers and professors of organizing. She began to understand, still academically at that point, that people needed collective power to change their situations, that individual actions alone—avoiding pregnancy, studying hard, saving money—would never really make a difference when a whole system was working against you.

Returning to Yale with a new outlook, Saru helped public housing tenants in New Haven organize against Hope VI, a federal program designed essentially to privatize public housing. She also researched farmworker organizing for Jennifer Gordon, an adjunct law professor who was thinking about starting the Workplace Project to build a political community for the growing population of immigrants, especially undocumented people, on Long Island. By her last year of law school, Saru was living in Brooklyn, working for Gordon two days a week on Long Island, and commuting to Yale the rest of the time. Gordon is widely recognized for establishing the Workplace Project as an innovative program providing legal services to help get immigrants organized. Saru started out working for the legal program, but eventually redesigned it along with the project's political education programs to encourage self-organizing rather than dependency on the staff attorney.

When Local 100 called her about organizing restaurant workers, Saru had left the Workplace Project and was teaching at Brooklyn College and writing about her experiences dealing with the polarized immigration politics of Long Island. She ignored those calls at first, having had to fight to make Long Island unions inclusive of immigrants and having no desire to be on any union's staff. But the calls kept coming and Saru finally agreed to go to a meeting. She met Mamdouh for the first time at the IWAA offices late one afternoon in February. The staff was taking out a cake for a Windows co-worker's thirty-fifth birthday. Saru had no way of knowing that it was a particularly poignant birthday for this person, who had survived September 11 because of a last-minute shift change.

Mamdouh kept up a steady stream of jokes, mostly about their recent visit from Denise M. Quiñones, the reigning Miss Universe ("Oh, now we are so famous!") and smiled constantly. His happy nature seemed to bring a feeling of lightness to the little group, and she could see that he served as their leader in fact if not in name. When it came time to pack up the party, he both directed and pitched in. The group was extremely multiracial—African, African American, South Asian, Latino, Arab. She was struck by an intangible sense of their intimacy and kindness toward one another. She had loved being at the Workplace Project, but in such a monoracial setting, she'd sometimes encountered more irony than sympathy for Muslims and Arabs caught up in the post-9/11 dragnet. As they were formally introduced after the party, Saru asked Mamdouh what he was planning to do after the IWAA. He didn't mention that the union had offered him the job of building this new organization. At that point, he was rejecting the $34,000 annual salary as inadequate for his family of four.

Intrigued by the possibilities of building something new and so multiracial, Saru decided then that she wanted the job. The union, however, kept her waiting while asking for workplans and ideas. She wrote memos describing how she would define the new organization's strategy and developed a chart of its potential structure. At one point, her union contact asked Saru how she would feel about being co-directors with Mamdouh. She replied that she would be fine with it, but that in her experience such arrangements—a partnership between a middle-class professional organizer and a worker—often turned out to be a sham. The professional wielded too much unacknowledged power, while the worker served as window dressing. In the end, Saru was hired as the director and Mamdouh as a job development coordinator with a salary of $53,000, less than he had earned at Windows. Saru earned $47,000. Beginning to reveal her formidable fundraising skills, she put together enough funding to keep the project in business for six months to a year. None of this money came from the union; it served only as a fiscal agent, holding and disbursing funds until the new organization received its nonprofit designation.

Mamdouh had actually intended to go into computer networking when the IWAA finished. Even before September 11, he had been taking classes from another Moroccan who had pledged to help countrymen get into the field. He signed on to this new project mostly out of curiosity and a bit of post–September 11 inertia. After meeting Saru, he figured that he would stick around and see what broke. He hadn't yet taken the exam for computer technicians, and he was otherwise unemployed. He wondered how it would be to work with this earnest, intelligent young woman who spoke fluent, idiomatic Spanish.

On April 8, 2002, Saru and Mamdouh set up shop in borrowed space at Local 100's pension offices in midtown Manhattan. Two weeks later, they would move again, to an office downstairs, and again after another month to 99 Hudson Street in Tribeca, near what was now Ground Zero. On the first day, Saru and Mamdouh met privately in the union president's office.

"What do you think we're going to be doing in this new organization?"

"We're going to be doing what we did at the IWAA," Mamdouh said, "getting people jobs and cash to get through."

Saru began to talk to him about organizing. "It's the only way for people to get enough power to change their situations," she said.

"But how can you organize people who can't even pay their own rent?" In spite of his experience fighting for his co-workers at Windows, to Mamdouh power meant nothing more collective than that.

"That's the best time to organize, when people have nothing to lose."

She told him the story of César Chávez, widely considered the most important Latino leader in U.S. history. Chávez had grown up in a migrant farmworker family, sleeping by the side of the road and attending thirty-eight schools until he gave up in eighth grade. For much of his early adulthood, he dreamt of changing the lives of farmworkers. He learned how to do that in the 1950s as an organizer for, and eventually president of, the Community Service Organization, but when that group refused to take up farmworker issues, he quit to start a new organization in Delano, California, using the principles of nonviolent direct action. He deliberately didn't build a union because of the bitter feelings broken union promises aroused in farmworkers. Chávez insisted that members pay dues, even though a good part of the strategy was to emphasize their poverty—for many years, every organizer and volunteer, including Chávez himself, earned $5 a week. The National Farm Worker Association organized strikes in Delano where the grapes were grown and boycotts in the cities where they were sold, bringing public attention to farmworkers for the first time. In 1969 the Delano growers signed historic contracts with the United Farmworkers Organizing Committee, which would later become the United Farm Workers Union (UFW). Mamdouh, who had never heard this story before, was suitably inspired.

"What you were doing as shop steward was organizing," Saru said, "but now you'll be doing it with workers who aren't union members."

Over the next month, he and Saru had more long, rambling conversations in the office, about September 11, terrorism, and their families. Slowly, Saru let go of her secret apprehension that Mamdouh, like other immigrant men she had known, would dismiss her leadership role in light of her youth and gender.

"So what should we be called? What are we going to be doing?" Saru asked the team at their first staff meeting.

"We're organizing restaurant workers."

"We're the Restaurant Organizing Center."

"Of New York."

"Hey, that works out to ROC New York." The team loved that acronym, imagining themselves turning the city upside down.

But when Saru ran the new name by a union ally, he urged her to reconsider using the word "organizing." He said people thought it was too confrontational, and that it aroused the hostility of foundations, employers, and government. Saru went back to the group, and they replaced "organizing" with the all-American "opportunity."

Early on, Saru led a political education session with her new staff, using a game she had designed to help people understand corporate globalization. In the game, two groups each represented a country that would negotiate to attract a multinational shoe manufacturer to set up operations. In each country, someone played the role of labor, someone else the government, and a third person the subcontractor who would actually manage the factory for the corporation. Each team had to come up with a price to offer the corporation, which would then choose the most profitable place. The group could then see the three in-country parties deciding how much money would go to the workers, how much to the subcontractor, how much to the government in taxes and fees. To get the corporation, they of course had to offer as high a profit margin as possible.

At the end of the game, Saru asked the staff what would have made it easier to offer the company a good profit. Someone who had played the government said it would have been easier if they were a dictatorship and they could just tell the workers and the subcontractors what they were going to get. In an instant, Mamdouh connected Morocco's poverty to globalization. "I always thought all those companies coming into Morocco was really a good thing," he said. "I never realized how it really worked." The staff discussion turned to all the dictators that the United States had supported over time, the corporations that had done business in those countries, and the immigrants from those countries who were now working in New York restaurants.

Mamdouh set about recruiting former Windows workers into the new organization. He brought in Mario Peña, the undocumented immigrant from Ecuador and Ataur Rahman, the Bangladeshi who had fled a civil war. He also recruited Utjok Zaidan, whom he ran into one day looking for a job and who eventually became an organizer at ROC-NY. And Jean Emy Pierre, a gruff Haitian immigrant with shoulder-length dreadlocks who had been a sous-chef at Windows. By then, Sekou Siby, the multilingual Ivoirian, had put his dream of teaching on hold to drive a cab. He came around to the protests, but not all the time.

Over the first year and a half of building ROC-NY Mamdouh would learn how to fight, not just by himself *for* one worker at a time to resolve a specific employment problem, as he'd been doing at Windows, but *with* many workers together to change the rules, both explicit and unspoken, that shaped their relationship to the industry. As his work changed, Mamdouh had to confront the tension between providing a space for Windows co-workers and building an organization for all restaurant workers.

The organization had four sets of activities. Three of them amounted to a strategy, and the fourth kept them deeply connected to Windows. They brought in restaurant workers by providing a network that connected them with training and good jobs. They started campaigns against owners who exploited their back-of-the-house workers. They began a research project to analyze conditions across the industry, looking to craft new public policy, and started reaching out to employers who were trying to do the right thing. Mamdouh began to see that what was going on at the bottom of the restaurant hierarchy was connected to making things better for other people as well— for restaurant owners who were trying to follow the law and for customers who were trying to get a good meal. Undocumented workers from Windows were some of the most active people in the new organization. Partly, that was because they had time, being largely un- or underemployed. But the new organization tapped into their keen sense of the system's unfairness as well.

These three things moved them forward from September 11, but their relationship to Windows didn't end, and was expressed in two projects. For one, they remained committed to helping the undocumented survivors of Windows workers to legalize their status. Second, Mamdouh came up with a plan to build a new restaurant that would memorialize Windows while employing restaurant workers suffering the economic effects of September 11. As time went on, however, the distance between the Windows experience and memory and the expanding role of the organization grew. Their first campaign would be closely tied to Windows, but subsequent ones had to tackle issues beyond getting Windows workers hired elsewhere.

Mamdouh had to learn many new things during this period. Some he took to easily, but others were harder. First, he had to learn how to connect people who had immediate needs to each other, and then how to lead that group to make a public intervention against the industry's conditions. He had to learn the nuances of campaign planning, how to craft and make demands, and how to pressure employers to negotiate by confronting them with their own illegal practices. In addition to these hard skills, he also had to get used to being an organizer, with the obligation to think beyond himself and with a new schedule that disrupted his life as a family man.

Although Saru had laid out the organizing mission of the organization, the initial work was very service oriented. Nearly six months after September 11, the number of workers filing for unemployment insurance was still 20 percent higher than the year before. Surprisingly, the restaurant industry turned out to be somewhat more resilient than others. It lost 12,300 jobs in October 2001, but gained 4,600 over the next two months. Still, that was a total loss of nearly 8,000 jobs, and the former Windows workforce felt it.

Mamdouh's official title was "Job Developer," and his early work focused on finding resources and new jobs for his former co-workers. One of the first projects was to distribute funds collected by the union and administered by the Judson Memorial Church near New York University to support Windows workers and their families. Saru and Mamdouh helped the fund's administrators set up a special unemployment benefit for undocumented workers who couldn't get benefits from the state. The fund ultimately also paid for workers' health insurance for two years. With that money, Mamdouh set up a stipend program for workers who participated in ROC-NY's earliest activities.

To begin helping people find jobs, Mamdouh relied on the workers themselves. He built two job-sharing groups, one for the back of the house and one for the front. He named the front-of-the-house group after one of their lost colleagues, the Mexican runner named Telmo. "This is the Telmo meeting," Mamdouh declared. Building the jobs pool was a matter of getting a few people into a room together where they all shared information about which restaurants were open and hiring. Ultimately, Mamdouh helped more than 100 of his former co-workers find jobs in this way. He also started new training programs for restaurant workers to develop their skills, including a bartending class and a computer class. Recruitment was no problem—former Windows workers were constantly stopping through anyway, and their needs were great.

ROC-NY's first campaign opportunity emerged in these job-sharing meetings. Even before ROC's official start, the conversation among Windows workers had revolved around Noché, the new Latin-themed restaurant and night club that former Windows owner David Emil was planning to open in Times Square. By early 2002, Noché was hiring staff. The restaurant would have three levels, each with its own bar, and a smaller dining room on the third floor. Emil had hired some of the managers from Windows, but only sixteen of the line staff, and those were largely white, even though the Windows workforce was so international. Mamdouh knew this because a friend of his at the union kept him abreast of who was getting hired and who wasn't. The union had met with Emil, asking him to hire more of his former workers. He had agreed to set up a dedicated time and place for his Windows employees to apply and interview.

So it was that on his first day at ROC-NY Mamdouh received a letter from Emil at home. The invitation to apply to work at Noché was buried between disclaimers:

> My family was the owner of Windows on the World, but we have only a small interest in Noché.... Nonetheless, in light of my family's relationship to Windows on the World, ownership has agreed to accept applications for

employment from former Windows employees before accepting applications from other people.... Because Noché is much smaller than Windows,
many of the positions which existed at Windows will not exist at Noché.

Dozens of other Windows workers waited for their interviews at the Van-
derbilt YMCA between 10 a.m. and 3 p.m. on April 19, but several days later
all had received rejections. Although he was committed to ROC-NY, Mamdouh applied for a job to see how the former Windows workers were treated
and what would happen. He was well known by the former Windows managers who were now doing the hiring at Noché, and his interview lasted only
five minutes, but he too received a rejection letter. At that point, the union
said it didn't know what else it could do, but ROC-NY asked for a follow-up
meeting with Emil. They got one with his lawyers at the firm's offices, where
they were told again that there was nothing more they could do.

Back at a raucous, angry membership meeting still fueled by post–September 11 emotions, Saru proposed demonstrating in front of Noché to demand
that Emil hire more Windows workers. No one expected Emil to rehire hundreds of Windows workers at a much smaller restaurant, but they felt that he
had picked and chosen out of the Windows workforce, taking all the white actors and students but leaving behind the immigrants and the people of color.
They speculated that he had avoided hiring Windows line staff because he did
not want union leaders coming into the new restaurant. At this early stage in
the organization's development, they also needed to take collective action
so they could start building that capacity, like developing a muscle—hence
Saru's suggestion to take the protest public.

ROC-NY began to prepare for its first demonstration. Two weeks before
the restaurant's scheduled opening, about fifty former Windows workers
picketed Noché. Mamdouh led the chanting, surprised to feel perfectly at
ease. The chants reinforced their Windows identity.

David Emil, we worked for you
Now let us feed our families too!!!

We are Windows on the World
We will be seen, we will be heard
Until our jobs are returned!

Mamdouh enjoyed yelling into the bullhorn and leading such a large group. The protest was covered in the *Daily News* and the *New York Times*, to whom Emil presented himself, not completely unreasonably, as a beleaguered victim of people with no business sense. "The truth is, a restaurant of this scale can't possibly have jobs for all of our former employees," he said. "Unfortunately, there are a number of former Windows employees who feel that they are entitled to a job at Noché, whether or not they are qualified or even whether a job exists."[1]

There were some people he couldn't hire, he said, because they didn't have table-serving experience or proper immigration papers. But Mamdouh knew that some of the people rejected, including himself, were highly successful waiters at Windows, handling $10,000 bottles of wine and serving food worth hundreds of dollars. As for immigration papers, he knew that many of those same people had worked for years at Windows with no trouble, a signal of how much things had changed since September 11.

The group decided to prepare for another protest on Noché's opening night. Mamdouh spent hours on the phone every day with former co-workers asking them to come. The day before the opening, as the team made picket signs and copies of song sheets, Emil called the union and asked the local to arrange a meeting with ROC. It was set for the next morning, at the restaurant.

Saru and Mamdouh went, along with a union representative. Saru wore a bright pink skirt with Indian-style embroidery.

"That's a very attractive skirt," the union rep said to her, "but I think you should know that it has a hole in it."

As they took seats around a dining table on the restaurant floor, in front of its small stage, Saru tried to sit strategically to hide the hole. She quickly forgot her embarrassment, however, when Emil said that he had decided to hire an additional fifteen Windows workers, to make the total thirty-one, adding a banquet service to occupy the new hires.

Mamdouh was stunned. Although he'd been happy to go along with the plan, and had even enjoyed the protest, he hadn't really thought that they would win jobs for fifteen people. It wasn't everything they had wanted, but he began to see that fighting together was different from his advocating alone for one worker at a time. After the meeting broke up, Mamdouh and Saru found themselves alone on the dining room floor. "My God, we did it! We did it!" he said to Saru, and they gave each other a spontaneous hug.

That afternoon Saru and Mamdouh stood in front of Noché turning away dozens of ROC-NY members and union leaders from the cancelled protest.

When Emil appeared, though, Mamdouh couldn't resist heckling him. His temper, often hidden under all his charm, was riding high. Mamdouh was happy that Emil had done the right thing, but thought he should have done it without all the protest. "This is bullshit," he said to his former employer's back. A rabbi who organized religious support for labor struggles pulled Mamdouh aside and chastised him.

"Listen, if you've accepted the settlement, you shouldn't say anything more," the rabbi said. "You have to let it go." Letting go was hard for Mamdouh in general, but he immediately quieted down and never forgot the rabbi's lesson.

Noché was a logical first action for ROC-NY, but it wasn't really a campaign, just an intervention, and heavily tinged with September 11 emotion rather than clear industry analysis. Emil was far from the worst employer in New York City. Still, the victory had helped to give everyone a taste of what it meant to act together, and, more important, consolidated the fledgling staff into a team.

Bolstered by the Noché victory and press coverage, members began bringing in friends and relatives. The next campaigns clearly established the organization as a defender of the rights of undocumented workers. One member brought in his friend, an undocumented Mexican dishwasher at a West Village restaurant and bar called Pangeae who hadn't been paid for several weeks and who was peremptorily fired for demanding his back wages. He presented his case to the ROC-NY membership, which, optimistic after Noché, voted unanimously to start a new campaign.

In short order, a committee formed, drafted a demand letter, and planned a noisy protest in front of the restaurant when it didn't respond within the deadline. This protest attracted far less press, but when a reporter for a Spanish-language television station went in to interview the owner, he sent her back out with the message that he wanted to settle the issues immediately. Saru went in; the owner wrote a check for the full amount, and she walked back out with it.

Enormous coverage in the Spanish-language press followed, attracting more Latinos. As reporters asked about undocumented workers, Saru and Mamdouh developed a clear reply. Labor law guaranteed workplace rights, even to undocumented people. They had to be paid minimum wage and overtime, be provided with health and safety equipment, and be able to take breaks and receive workers' compensation payments if they were injured on the job. They also had the right to unionize. Their general lack of work authorization still made them vulnerable to exploitation, of course, but denying un-documented immigrants these basic workplace rights would give employers a class of workers who were little more than slaves who could be paid at any rate and treated in any manner, undercutting labor rights for every worker in this country. In particular, exploiting the undocumented undercut other res-taurant workers, giving employers total power so they could easily fire work-ers and find new ones. It also created unfair competition for those employ-ers who tried to follow labor law—their prices would have to reflect higher wages, overtime, workers' compensation, and other costs of doing business honestly. Employers who didn't grant workers sick leave were obviously not concerned about the safety of the food they served. The larger problem, of course, was that these workers couldn't become legal in the first place, but that issue would have to be resolved elsewhere.

Word of the new organization spread. A member brought in Josue Ca-banas, an undocumented Mexican immigrant in his fifties, who had worked "effectivo," for cash under the table, at Giant Farm, a deli and small corner gro-cery store in Brooklyn. Cabanas had been hospitalized for respiratory illness for two weeks. When he returned to his job with a doctor's note saying that he could work only forty hours per week, the owner insisted that he'd have to work sixty, threatening to replace him with a younger worker if he could not. ROC's review of his situation revealed that the owner owed Cabanas and his co-workers more than $100,000 in minimum wages and overtime. Saru helped Cabanas recruit the other deli workers, and five out of the six eventu-ally joined the campaign. When one was fired in retaliation for organizing, they all walked out in solidarity.

The Giant Farm protests began in October 2002 and continued weekly throughout the winter with dozens of former Windows workers attending each one. Eventually, the owner agreed to meet with ROC-NY, but when he came to the center he suddenly fell ill and left without finishing discussions. With the assistance of the Puerto Rican Legal Defense & Education Fund, the five workers initiated a lawsuit. The combination of protests and litiga-tion ultimately led the owner to agree to a meeting with Saru and Mamdouh facilitated by a mediator; the case was settled for $50,000 and reinstatement of the workers. Cabanas was relieved to keep his job. He had crossed the border without documents in 1991. It was much harder to get a new job after September 11, and he thought it was now much more dangerous to cross the border, so he would have been out of options if the campaign hadn't been successful.

However, Giant Farm wasn't even a restaurant. ROC was in danger of moving away from its mission of transforming the industry. The team needed to move toward larger restaurants, and it didn't take long for another opportunity to appear. A Mexican kitchen worker came in from the Park Avenue Country Club. The Club was a glorified sports bar at the corner of Park Avenue and 27th Street. It featured a restaurant and banquet hall, along with 50 televisions, live radio and television broadcasts, and the presence of sports stars most days of the week. It had 600 seats and had been listed as Best Sports Bar by *New York Magazine* in 2002.[2] Owner Stephen Schmeelk is the son of Lehman Brothers founder Richard A. Schmeelk.

The worker brought in eighteen months' worth of time sheets and bounced paychecks. After talking with Saru, he recruited five more current and former workers from the restaurant, to whom Schmeelk owed a total of $60,000 in unpaid overtime. The organization made a slight but important adjustment in their action plan. Rather than jumping straight to a protest, they quietly delivered their demand letter in a group, without signs, chants, or other accompaniments. They gave the employer one week to respond. Any response offering to talk about the problem would postpone protest, litigation, or other actions. Those would be justified by no response or by opposition.

It was important to give the employer a chance to do the right thing, but it was also important to make the problem public from the very beginning, hence group delivery of the demand letter rather than mailing it. These employers, after all, had been operating without public scrutiny for years. The fact that no one could see their abuses gave them cover. Moreover, the organization had to consolidate itself with the start of each new campaign. Old and new members had to integrate the idea that they were in it together, not just into their heads by sitting in meetings, but into their bodies by preparing for and conducting actions.

Schmeelk didn't respond to the demand letter, which thirty members delivered during a dinner service. They began weekly protests and started talking with the New York University Immigrant Rights Clinic about filing a federal lawsuit. They also got a major insurance company to cancel two parties at the Club, worth an estimated $30,000 in lost revenue. Schmeelk then called and scheduled a meeting at the ROC-NY office. He negotiated the payment down to $45,000 and signed an outline of an agreement. Then he left and they didn't hear from him again. Soon after, though, he fired one of the workers who had joined the campaign. ROC-NY continued its protests and filed the lawsuit alleging labor abuses and retaliatory firings.

On a Thursday afternoon that June, Mamdouh called the company, fruit-lessly trying to get a meeting. He had to berate the receptionist. "Is Stephen Schmeelk there? Tell him this is Mamdouh from ROC-New York. He's not there? This is Mamdouh ... HALLO? You were going to hang up on me with-out taking a message?" Although the receptionist was clearly doing what she'd been told, Mamdouh knew he couldn't let the company avoid them. He had to make every interaction count to keep the pressure rising. "Tell him to call Mamdouh at ROC-New York. Tell him if he doesn't call, he knows we're go-ing to protest."

A week after this phone call, Schmeelk also fired Delfino Réal, one of the workers most active in the campaign.

Réal stood up at the next membership meeting to tell how he was fired only for defending his rights. Saru described Schmeelk's stalling tactics, saying that "it might be necessary for us to go demonstrate." The group's reaction—one man slapped his forehead as though frustrated with all the demonstration demands on his time, while a smile snuck over his lips; a woman cheered out loud and pumped her left fist in the air—indicated that the demonstrations provided a highlight of being in the organization. Saru was pleased with that reaction. She felt no guilt whatsoever about going after a man who had cheat-ed his workers of tens of thousands of dollars and then reneged on a deal.

The campaigns not only attracted undocumented current workers, but also those who had come out of Windows. Mario Peña, the Ecuadoran barback, was one of Mamdouh's co-workers who had been active in the new organiza-tion. Peña, who wore his straight black hair in a longish crewcut, was core to the protest team that took on the Park Avenue Country Club. During one such event, he took tiny steps around a protest pen that the police had set up inside six wooden barriers.

"It's illegal, it's a crime, pay your workers overtime!" he chanted in the direction of the Park Avenue Country Club, while others handed out explana-tory flyers.

Peña felt that he had the right to protest, just as Delfino Réal had the right to get paid for working. After September 11, though, risk became a compli-cated thing, always easier in a collective. After the demonstration, Peña made his way home carefully. He crossed every street only when the light was green and he didn't litter. Although five cops stood a yard away while he chanted and sang with the others, he wanted no police contact when he was alone.

Mamdouh thought it was surviving September 11, a sense of having little to lose, that gave Peña courage. "Even if they are undocumented, they have rights. When they know they have rights, they stand up," he had said. "They say, so what if they deport me, at least I'm not dead, and they can't deport all of us."

A year and a half after September 11, Peña was still undocumented and only occasionally employed. Instead of returning to Ecuador, though, he was taking English classes at Baruch College and computer, bartending, and wine classes at ROC-NY. His parents had died, he spoke English, and he had no children to support. He was no longer waiting for some kind of amnesty to transform his status. He knew he would find enough work here and there to support a single man. His student ID card had replaced the one from Windows, although he still carried that one in his pocket. He wore the new one on a chain around his neck, tucked into his shirt between two buttons. It lay flat just below his heart.

"This is the million-dollar ID card," he said. "I'm going to use it for everything now."

Three weeks later, Schmeelk had still not come through on his promises, so ROC-NY organized a Friday evening protest meant to start at 7:30. Things started badly. It isn't that easy to turn out big crowds for Friday night protests week after week in New York City. Even the most committed get bored. For forty minutes, 7 members occupied a pen designed for 200. Most passers-by refused to take flyers. More than one said, "What are these people complaining about?" The manager stood casually at the side door on Park Avenue, smiling but not wanting to make a statement to the press. A friend of the organization went in with a small group to take a table, tip the server—and leave without ordering after telling Schmeelk to pay up.

At 8:10, however, 150 students arrived. They were in New York for a meeting of United Students Against Sweatshops, and this protest benefited from their boundless energy. Their chants were far hipper than ROC-NY's, mostly because they used songs from the 1970s rather than the 1930s. They especially liked this one to the tune of KC and the Sunshine Band's *Shake Your Booty*:

Pay, pay, pay
Pay, pay, pay
Pay your workers!
Pay your workers!

Now the corner drew spectators. Cabbies hit their horns in support. People took flyers all the way around the block. The restaurant sent out two bussers with opposing flyers that said: "These protestors do not work for the Park Avenue Country Club. They are paid hourly wages by this organization to harass the restaurant and our customers. Most of our workers do not work more than 40 hours per week."

Comments on the street shifted in tone. A tall blonde who stepped out of the Club to smoke almost joined the picket line. "I'm impressed that people have the wherewithal to do this, and I'm embarrassed to be inside drinking," she said. "I don't think I'll be coming back."

The manager moved to the main door; he looked stressed while hanging halfway outside while smoking a cigarette. Inside, a waiter and a busboy gave the frilly white curtain, which had been hanging down to block the view, a couple of quick pulls. The protesters cheered this as the equivalent of a solidarity honk.

Stephen Schmeelk continued to hold out despite the protests. Their lawsuit, however, was decided in the workers' favor, and Schmeelk was forced to pay. In an emerging custom, ROC-NY made a three-foot-by-two-foot replica of the check and presented it to the workers at a membership meeting in October 2003.

After this, their fourth victory in less than eighteen months, the members and staff of ROC-NY felt invincible. Although they had far fewer resources than their union counterparts, they seemed able to win just about anything they wanted, including vacations, sick days, back pay, lunch breaks, a proper time clock, retention agreements for the workers who had organized, and the right to follow up on the agreement for one year. But there were important differences between them and the union. Unions had to go through a much more stringent process, usually an election, to establish themselves at a workplace. If a union won that election, it could then create a collective bargaining unit that would negotiate a contract with the company, setting everyone's wages and benefits at once and replacing individual negotiations. Unions were also allowed to automatically collect dues from all the members of the bargaining unit, which gave them a stable source of direct funding. Because a workers center is not a union, ROC-NY could neither define a bargaining unit nor collect dues.

The organization was following in the footsteps of earlier waves of immigrant workers both inside and outside formal unions. European immigrants had fueled the Industrial Age with their labor, and they had good cause to unionize.

The Hotel Employees and Restaurant Employees, to which Windows workers had belonged, was formed by immigrant workers and was among the first to include black workers, who were barred from many other unions. In other industries, immigrants, including a large proportion of Jewish women, built the International Ladies Garment Workers Union (ILGWU) and conducted a series of strikes with its 100,000 members in Chicago, Boston, Cleveland, and other cities. One of these, still the largest in U.S. history, involved 23,000 textile workers in Lawrence, Massachusetts, in a spontaneous walkout for a $6 per week minimum wage. The funerals of the 146 women who died in the Triangle Shirtwaist Factory fire of 1911 drew 100,000 mourners. Sixty percent of the factory's workforce were Eastern European Jews who had fled pogroms, and reaction to the fire sparked labor reforms in New York State that eventually helped shape the New Deal. These work stoppages, strikes, and marches to improve wages and working conditions led to the most fundamental labor rights still in play, including the eight-hour day, the five-day work week, the minimum wage, and the right to form unions.

After the Park Avenue Country Club campaign, Saru and Mamdouh proposed a set of rules that would guide future campaign investments, hoping to avoid turning these small campaigns into a service, and to avoid being used by workers who just wanted their own cases resolved without regard for further organizing. Any worker who wanted support had to attend at least three political education sessions. They had to be willing to fight for more than money, and they had to still be working in the restaurant. The group's goal, after all, was to reform restaurants from the inside and to change the power dynamics between workers and owners. Finally, Saru codified an eleven-step process, from getting membership agreements to negotiating the final agreement, laying out all the points at which workers would have to make decisions about their situations. The eleven steps were designed to make change not just for the workers active in the campaign, but for all those employed in the restaurant.

With these rules in place, ROC-NY continued organizing largely Latino back-of-the-house workers, adding antidiscrimination demands for the first time. Two Mexican kitchen workers came in from The 3 Guys, an upscale Greek diner on the Upper East Side where then Attorney General Eliot Spitzer and other luminaries were known to breakfast regularly.

The Mexican immigrants who worked in The 3 Guys complained of problems somewhat different from the straight wage-and-hour focus of earlier campaigns. Rather than missing back wages or overtime pay, these workers said that discrimination kept Mexican workers from getting the better jobs at the front of the house. The company allegedly provided vacations for the Greeks but not for the Mexicans, with the exception of a former Mexican army officer who looked quite Greek. One Mexican worker told the ROC-NY membership that he had been told he was too dark and ugly to ever become a waiter. The hostile environment had produced a fight in which a waiter had clipped one of the bussers behind the ear. After the first ROC protest, the owner agreed to a meeting, which took place at the ROC-NY offices. Over several more months, they negotiated a settlement with payment for past discrimination, promotions, paid vacations and sick days, and a grievance procedure.

Two years later, Anthony DePalma wrote a story for the *New York Times* comparing the life of The 3 Guys founder and owner John Zannikos, who had also been an undocumented immigrant, with that of one of the kitchen workers, and investigating whether the opportunities that had placed earlier generations of undocumented people squarely in the middle class would be available to today's undocumented immigrants.[3] Zannikos had arrived in New York without papers in the 1950s. Other Greeks gave him jobs and chances, and he eventually opened The 3 Guys, and then a dozen other diners over the years. Illiterate and starting with no more than $100 in his pocket, he had built the restaurant to defy Greek stereotypes—he refused to call it a "diner," put no posters of Greece on the walls, and forbade the employees to chew gum or call customers "honey"—and used it to propel himself to economic security, even after being deported and making his way back into the United States in 1956.

By contrast, Juan Manuel Peralta, at thirty-four, had already spent fifteen years working in minimum-wage jobs. His father, who had always dreamed of going to the United States, was never able to afford it. He had borrowed the money to send his son, saving him from a future of fixing flat tires. After working for years at The 3 Guys and having a good relationship with Zannikos, whom he called "Babba Yuni," a Greek term of respect, Peralta was fired over an altercation with another worker, with dozens ready to replace him and no access to unemployment compensation without documents. In 2004, according to the article, he had earned $24,000 to feed his wife and two children, with whom he lived in a Queens apartment that they shared with two other Mexican families.

Experts disagree on whether people like Peralta will ever be able to assimilate well enough to move into the middle class. Today's economy has fewer

high-mobility jobs for the uneducated, low-wage worker, and the sheer numbers of undocumented workers creates tremendous competition for those
jobs. Others, however, say that legalization would make all the difference,
and could enable Peralta to see the day that "his children will someday join
the millions who have lost their accents, gotten good educations and firmly
achieved the American dream."[4] There's a cyclical relationship between illegality and bad jobs—the status of undocumented workers helps employers keep
the jobs poor and feeds the surplus labor pool that creates uneven competition. If the workers were legal, they would have far more ability to negotiate
not just higher wages in all jobs, but also to create a career ladder, gradually
moving to the more lucrative front-of-the-house jobs that pay better.

These larger issues informed much of ROC-NY's other work. Saru and
Mamdouh also realized that they wouldn't be able to get a hold on the entire industry by campaigning against one employer after another. As their
third major project, they started researching the city's restaurant industry as
a whole, wanting to explain how it all worked and to create the analysis that
would help them develop new public policies. Encouragement came from
Bruce Herman, the director of the Consortium for Worker Education, which
had funded Mamdouh's position as job developer. Herman, a white man in
his forties who often wore a closely cropped beard or goatee, was a student
of labor movements who had worked for various institutions of the AFL-
CIO, but never for a union. He was an expert in sectoral organizing, in which
a union takes up an industrywide strategy rather than moving through one
workplace after another. From their initial meetings, Herman quickly recognized Mamdouh's keen knowledge of the industry and his deep social networks among restaurant workers.

Herman helped them develop a plan to research and analyze the industry
from top to bottom, explaining that new policy options would emerge from
their findings. He had used such a process to analyze the garment industry.
Struck by the potential benefits of such a project, Saru and Mamdouh reached
out to researchers at the Urban Justice Center (UJC) and the Brennan Center for Justice. UJC agreed to conduct interviews with employers, while the
Brennan Center helped design a survey for restaurant workers. Mamdouh
recruited members to go out on the street with surveys. They had to produce
at least 500 for their study to be taken seriously. Simultaneously, they started
reaching out to other restaurant employers, trying to develop relationships
with "high-road" employers who might work with them to control "low-road"
employers.

With a comprehensive study, ROC-NY could make a place for itself at the center of the restaurant industry. The only collective voice, besides the union, which really represented cafeteria and hotel workers, belonged to the New York State Restaurant Association. Its president, Charles Hunt, was committed to the position that the industry operated fairly. It was still the only one, he said, in which you could start as a dishwasher and end up owning the restaurant. Low profit margins, he said, made demands for higher wages unreasonable. "Restaurants across the country are fortunate if they can make five to six percent net before taxes," he told the *New York Press*. "Just because a restaurant is big and does a lot of business doesn't mean they make a fortune." But Mamdouh and Saru knew that the average profit margin for a restaurant in New York was 10 percent, and that the industry's profits and jobs had grown by 250 percent over twenty years. Workers' wages, however, had stagnated, and most earned less than $20,000 a year.[5]

Although the campaigns were exciting and moving quickly, ROC-NY's Windows-related work was more troublesome and less successful. Their effort to redefine the significance of September 11 clashed with the narrow nationalism of mainstream responses to the attacks. In 2002, when the group began a tradition of commemorating the anniversary, they decided to organize their own memorial rather than participating in any of the city's official events. They wanted to recognize the contributions of their lost colleagues, so many of them immigrant workers, without competing with those of firefighters and police officers and stockbrokers. They had to get a city permit to conduct a memorial elsewhere, and were shocked to encounter bureaucratic resistance, which only hardened their determination to have their own ceremony. Hundreds of Windows friends and survivors gathered at the Hudson River Park in Tribeca, about half a mile from Ground Zero. As different people read out the names of the victims, others threw a flower for each one into the river. Mamdouh took his son and daughter to the memorial.

The Windows workers were also angry about the Bush administration's drive to war in Iraq. The federal government was using their loss, they felt, to justify a war that had nothing to do with them or with preventing terrorism. Despite their still tenuous financial situation, workers pooled their money three times in 2002 and early 2003 to rent minivans and go to anti-war rallies in Washington, D.C. Although many were undocumented and feared participating in massive rallies that might draw police action, they still felt obligated to show that September 11 survivors did not see the invasion and occupation of Iraq as a remedy.

The emerging national story of September 11 had terrible effects on un-documented Windows families. ROC-NY was committed to winning legal status for the undocumented family members of people who had died at Windows, but this project would be far less successful than their other work. Shulaika La Cruz, a former pastry chef at Windows, was assigned to recruit families into the Amnesty Committee. There were sixteen such families, made up of widows, siblings, and children, including some born in the U.S. Hadi-djatou Traore, the widow who'd fought to bring her daughter over from the Ivory Coast, was among the first to join. La Cruz set up meetings with lawyers from the Urban Justice Center to explore legislative and legal options for the families.

The lawyers first tried to get a member of Congress to sponsor a private bill. Private bills are exceptions to immigration law that grant legal residency un-der extraordinary circumstances, often having to do with illness or death. In 1999, for example, Congress passed seventeen private bills, sponsored evenly by Democrats and Republicans. Senator Fred Thompson (R-Tenn.), whose later presidential campaign was among the most vitriolic about undocument-ed immigrants, sponsored a mother and three children who had come to the United States seeking cancer treatment after the father and another child were killed in a car accident. After the Persian Gulf War, Representative Nick Rahall (D-W.V.) introduced a private bill to legalize fifty-four families who had evacuated from Kuwait during the Gulf War, arguing that the shelter they had given Americans when the war started had made them targets of the Iraqi government. The Amnesty Committee and the lawyers spoke to all of New York's congressional representatives, but could not find a sponsor.

A colleague told Saru that they needed to look at the administrative device of the UVISA, an idea that had also occurred to Haeyoung Yoon, a newly minted Korean American lawyer at the Urban Justice Center. Created for victims of crime, UVISAs allowed immigrants suffering domestic violence to stay in the U.S. so they that could testify against their abusers. ROC-NY considered the possibility of naming the September 11 attacks as a crime, and having all of the families apply for the visa as survivors of a murder. Saru's ideological analysis that U.S. foreign policy was related to September 11 made her wonder about calling the event a crime, but Mamdouh thought it was absolutely clear. "They were murderers, they killed innocent people, so of course it is a crime," he said.

UVISAs, which should have provided legal residency and a path to citi-zenship, had been authorized in 2000, but the federal government had never released guidelines for their use. People could still apply, but they would get only deferred status without having their cases adjudicated. With deferred status, one can get a work authorization, so it would definitely be worth going through the process. To make it succeed, however, they had to get an investigator to say that he needed these particular witnesses, who would then certify the families, which would allow them to stay in the country. Yoon convinced the federal prosecutor on the Zacarias Massaoui case, who was looking for people to testify at the sentencing, to examine twelve applications, including those who had lost family, were injured that day, or had lost their jobs.

As lawyers, Yoon and Saru both felt conflicted about going this route. They had no idea whether Massaoui was guilty, but the unprecedented suspension of his due-process rights, combined with the harsh detention of thousands of South Asians, Muslims, and Arabs, cast a pall over the whole UVISA enterprise. Having few other choices, however, they moved ahead. The special prosecutor found only three of the cases compelling enough to certify, and in the end he used none of those statements. Hadidjatou Traore was lucky to be among the three. All this did, though, was allow her to *apply* for the UVISA. It could not be granted until there were guidelines and her application went through the system. Still, that was enough to get her deferred status, which Yoon renewed annually.

In spite of this somewhat contradictory record of victories and setbacks, the organization treated the amnesty campaign with its characteristic optimism. ROC-NY's fall newsletter had the committee's report. "CONGRATU-LATIONS! Amnesty Committee Moving Forward!" it said. They celebrated the three applications that had been made and vowed to pressure the assistant attorney general to certify the others. They had gotten a story in the *New York Times* and held a successful press conference at Ground Zero. The report ended: "With the public's help we can surely be celebrating the successful applications of all of our eligible members before New Years!!!"

In fact, this campaign was the only one the organization would not see through to the end. The national climate simply made it impossible. Members of Congress had become so much less tolerant of undocumented immigrants after September 11 that no one was willing to step forward with a private bill or significant intervention. As conservatives carried on about the link between America's so-called open borders and the hijackers, it is doubtful that a private bill would even have passed Congress.

On the Way

Within 18 months, ROC-NY claimed nearly 1,000 members and was on its way to being fully independent of HERE Local 100. They raised their own money, largely from foundations. They had applied for their own tax status so they could leave behind the fiscal sponsorship of the union's nonprofit arm. They had moved into their own overcrowded office—seven staff jammed into a ten-by-fifteen room with every inch of wall space covered in notes, posters, and photographs.

In this first year and a half, Saru and Mamdouh developed a smooth and synergistic working relationship. Their interactions reflected a growing friendship in its early stages, marked by a blossoming respect for each other's skills and way of being, as yet devoid of significant disagreement. To the extent that Mamdouh pushed the group to take a fighting stance toward the system that produced their circumstances, Saru pushed him to do the same. Had she not entered the picture, he thought, he would have done his six months at the IWAA and then looked for a regular job like everyone else. The two of them got into the habit of leaving the office and walking to the subway together. As they walked with another co-worker one night Mamdouh said, "Saru is the poorest," meaning the least paid, "among us, yet she fights the hardest."

But the group struggled with staffing and racial issues. Shulaika La Cruz had moved to Florida, and the new organizer hired to work with the families was hampered by her lack of relationship with them. Another organizer, still suffering from guilt and shock after accidentally surviving September 11, had quit. Although Mamdouh and Saru got along fine, other staffers, especially men, were offended by Saru's directness and her habit of working sixty-five hours a week and expecting others to do the same.

The organization became increasingly Latino, though Saru and Mamdouh struggled to keep it multiracial. When Jean Emy Pierre, the Haitian sous chef at Windows, applied for an organizing position in the spring of 2003, he was rejected by a largely Latino panel of members comprising whoever happened to show up that day. "I was discriminated against," he said. "I had been volunteering four days a week, but they chose someone else because that person spoke Spanish. ROC-NY had turned into Latino New York." Hurt and still unemployed, Pierre pulled back for a time until Mamdouh cajoled him into returning.

Mamdouh later recruited Sekou Siby. Siby, also still grieving and unable to work around many other people, had been driving a cab and appreciating the isolation.

"Siby, brother, driving a cab is a very hard job," Mamdouh told him over the phone. "It's not something you can do forever. I am asking you to come and work here. It will be fun."

Siby said no, but a conversation with his wife changed his mind—she would much prefer him in a stable position than driving a cab—and he joined the staff in October 2003. A short time later, they would give an internship to Rekha Eanni, a law student of Indian and Italian descent in search of placement in a political organization.

As the organization grew, it developed a somewhat schizophrenic relationship with the memory of Windows. On the one hand, they still needed the Windows base to remain significantly multiracial. Windows was unique in having had a global workforce, with many different kinds of immigrants working in both front- and back-of-the-house jobs. The rest of the industry was much more segregated, and most of the low-wage workers were Chinese, African, Latino, and Bangladeshi. For the most part it was Mexicans, activating their substantial social networks, who had been coming into the organization. It was largely because of the Windows base that a typical ROC-NY membership meeting included four Venezuelans, two Colombians, two Ghanaians, three Indians, one Bangladeshi, two Moroccans, and a Haitian, in addition to eight Mexicans.

But there were limitations to being a Windows organization, not the least of which was that Windows no longer existed and couldn't keep providing them with new members. The emotional connection with September 11 could last only so long for so many people. To move forward, ROC-NY had to generate equally strong emotional ties on the basis of fighting for the future rather than on a sacred memory of the past. This also seemed to be true for the families of those who had died at Windows. They never got involved in other ROC-NY activities, trying hard themselves to move on. At a staff and board retreat, as the group discussed the possibility of engaging the families in the policy committee, one staffer noted, "The families don't want to come around us. It makes them too sad."

Their last major project of this period would highlight this tension between the future and the past in unexpected, sometimes hurtful ways. In ROC-NY's early days, Mamdouh asked Saru what she thought about starting a new restaurant to employ displaced Windows and other restaurant workers. He and his friends had always dreamed of opening their own restaurant, and he was now seeing that many of the families had received substantial money from September 11 relief funds. Maybe some of them would be interested in investing in such a business. Saru found the idea "cute" but wasn't interested in an economic development organization, which she perceived as working within the system rather than trying to change it. The only way she would entertain the idea was in the form of a cooperative, to which Mamdouh agreed.

Just after the first anniversary of September 11, Mamdouh added a third meeting to the organization's weekly roster, one for members interested in starting a cooperative restaurant. Ataur Rahman, Magdi Labib, and Jean Emy Pierre were among the first to join, along with twelve other former Windows workers. The project ran on the memory of Windows for a long time, but that same memory generated obstacles at least as often as it did energy.

Mamdouh's self-image had changed significantly over this period. At a staff retreat, listing his five-year goals, he used words and ideas that had never before been in his mind. In that time, he said, he imagined ROC-NY providing good restaurants with a seal of approval that would be as coveted as a five-star Zagat rating. They would have won amnesty for all the undocumented survivors of Windows co-workers and they would now be talking about amnesty for everybody. And for his personal goal, "I speak Spanish now." For the first time in his life, Mamdouh had the chance to make full use of his charisma for a purpose other than earning money, and he was happy.

He enjoyed many aspects of the work. He did find the protests fun, and he liked constant interaction with people; instead of serving the city's luminaries, he was often attending meetings with them. The press coverage brought him significant notoriety among his friends, and he loved going home at night to tell Fatima about the things they were winning. But the time wasn't without adjustment. The life of an organizer differs hugely from that of a waiter with only one job, and Mamdouh found the long, unpredictable hours difficult. He was used to being a real family man, and he missed his full weekends and long bike rides with his son and daughter, who were growing up fast.

Mamdouh made one other change in his identity. On the morning of July 13, 2004, he went to the U.S. District Court, pledged his allegiance to the United States of America, and became a U.S. citizen. He had begun the naturalization process soon after September 11, wanting to have the same nationality as Fatima and his kids, and also thinking that he would be safer as a citizen than with a green card. He didn't cry during the ceremony, but he felt the weight of the moment nonetheless. He had changed everything in the course of two years, from his citizenship to his profession. His new life was taking on a permanence that he hadn't intended, but that he was prepared to embrace.

Chapter 5

BUILDING A COOPERATIVE RESTAURANT

Mamdouh's idea of building a cooperatively owned restaurant started out as an innovative project with great emotional appeal, looking both to the past and to the future for inspiration. Looking back, it would provide a memorial tribute to the fallen Windows workers, many of whom had dreamed of owning their own restaurants. It would provide employment with an ownership stake for former Windows workers and others who had become unemployed after September 11. Looking ahead, the cooperative would prove that a high-end restaurant could operate without a racial hierarchy; it would allow invisible restaurant workers to shift into the owner's role, thereby giving them equal standing with other employers when the time came to comment on labor issues. A portion of the restaurant's profits would be used to fund more co-ops over time.

Many people invested huge amounts of time, money, and energy in pursuing this agenda, not least of all Mamdouh and Saru. More than fifty members worked for several years to raise money and organize themselves. A group of Italian cooperatives invested hundreds of thousands of dollars. Attorneys, chefs, and students donated their time to work out an unending series of details. However, although the effort attracted lots of support, it got too little of the conventional kind—it was never fully financed and executive chefs were hard to recruit.

Ultimately, the two different motivations grounding the project clashed. The conflict between ROC-NY and a dissident group of members focused on this question: Who was this co-op really for? Was it solely for the benefit of Windows workers who had survived September 11? Or was it meant to benefit restaurant workers as a whole? The argument centered, as such arguments so often do, on the future distribution of the restaurant's profits. The clash, along with the predictable challenges of opening a new restaurant in New York City, nearly brought down the entire project. Even though the dissident group repeatedly evoked Windows to justify its demands, the remaining players, including Saru and Mamdouh, were not fully prepared for the challenges inherent in the project they had taken on. Their desire to build something that would make a political point, combined with the urge to build something as close to Windows as possible, tied them down, blocking the kind of flexible creativity the effort needed to succeed. They would learn these lessons and make adjustments, but some blood would be spilled along the way.

For Mamdouh, the conflict caused the biggest emotional crisis since September 11. He lost more than one close friend over it, and, for a time, also lost his position as ROC-NY's resident hero. His relationship with Saru became marked by arguments in which he regularly threatened to leave the organization. He was forced to confront in a personal way the same question that plagued the project as a whole. Why had he become an organizer? Was it because inertia had propelled him straight from Windows to ROC-NY, or was it because he now had a larger agenda to pursue? Was it the past or the future that kept him going to work every day?

Expansive Dreams and Cold Realities

The enterprise started with plenty of enthusiasm. Mamdouh's weekly meetings for people interested in starting a cooperative restaurant initially attracted about fifteen members: nearly all had worked at Windows. The group imagined something that evoked the aesthetic and importance of Windows, thinking of the entire project as a tribute to their fallen co-workers. They wanted it to be high end, with a fully multiracial staff. They wanted a space near Ground Zero. They talked about using it to change the industry. They were deeply attached to the idea of being owners, of reversing their position on the ladder, and of creating a workplace in which no one person was "the boss." They had expansive dreams, vowing to invest a portion of the business's profits in a trust that would provide startup money for new cooperatives.

The first significant reality check came as the group searched for a model to follow. They discovered the Industrial Cooperatives Association (ICA), an organization based in Boston that supported cooperatives across the country. The ROC-NY staff visited the ICA, who took them to an Ethiopian restaurant that had been started by three women who were the only owners and the only workers. The place was tiny and dark, more of a takeout than a restaurant, and the ROC-NY group constituted its sole customers at the height of lunchtime. The ICA representative told them about the endless number of decisions the women had had to make, and how difficult it had been. The ROC staff was discouraged. If it was so difficult to start an enterprise with only three people and no other employees, how could they hope to build a high-end place with dozens of worker/owners? "This has nothing to do with us," thought Mamdouh, convinced that they were building something entirely different. It had been many years since he had worked in anything other than a high-end restaurant, and he was as attached as anyone else to this concept.

The aspiring co-op members decided to pay the ICA $15,000 to conduct a feasibility study for their idea, starting a catering business to raise the money. Soon they had a busy schedule working events for small nonprofits, student groups, and unions. Serving spaghetti at ROC-NY and at antiwar events and getting a small grant, they raised the amount they needed in only three months.

The results of the study gave them pause. The ICA reported unequivocally that a cooperative restaurant would not work unless ROC-NY had a wealthy and experienced restaurateur as partner. Manhattan's restaurant revenues had declined by nearly $1 billion over the past two years. "Given the current economy and the prevailing conditions in lower Manhattan," the study said, "an independent restaurant venture sponsored solely by ROC would be a difficult and probably unfeasible undertaking." The ICA urged the group to build a catering business instead.

But the members dug in, saying that their connection to September 11 was too special and too serious to allow them to give up on their dream. ICA's response was that, if they insisted on moving ahead, they would have to find an experienced restaurateur to guide them through the process of restaurant formation. The members called all their personal contacts among chefs and owners, as ICA suggested. None was willing to commit much time.

The project floundered until Mamdouh called Bruce Herman, the director of the Consortium on Worker Education, who had become a consistent adviser, especially on the industrywide research project. Herman had spent years in Italy, where, far from being exotic, cooperatives dominate the food processing, construction, and transportation industries. Herman spoke to one of his Italian mentors. Oscar Marchisio was a modern Renaissance man. He had a number of socially responsible business interests, including marketing the products of Italy's largest food cooperative. Herman told Marchisio about ROC-NY, the Windows workers, and their idea for a restaurant cooperative. Marchisio pledged his help.

Three months later, Herman met Marchisio and Ivan Lusetti, the head of the Italian cooperative, at their hotel on the Upper East Side and prepared to take them over to ROC-NY for a day and a half of meetings with the members. Lusetti, a small, white-haired man in his sixties, had founded the Cooperativa Italiana di Ristorazione (CIR) food Group in 1977 with nine people, the minimum number required to build a co-op as written into the new Italian constitution adopted after World War II. They started with each member contributing the equivalent of $30 and had strong ties to both the public schools and local government. CIR had since grown into a €350 million company that included restaurants, school food contracts, cheese factories, wineries, and subsidiary operations in France, Belgium, and China. CIR had 7,500 cooperative members in Italy alone.

ROC-NY showed Lusetti a potential restaurant space in Tribeca, explaining that they were hoping to locate the restaurant close to the World Trade Center site, since the association with Windows on the World had great meaning for the venture.

Lusetti was moved. As an Italian leftist, he was interested in doing something positive in relation to 9/11, in contrast to the Bush administration's drive for war against Iraq. Although Lusetti never said so, Herman got the impression that he was thinking, "This is our chance to stick it in George Bush's eye." Lusetti was intrigued by the notion that he could help to bring the cooperative model to New York City, and he was always in search of opportunities to create new markets for CIR products. But the biggest draw for Lusetti was the global diversity of the Windows workers.

CIR has its headquarters in Reggio Emilia, near Bologna. The province is now home to the largest concentration of immigrants in Italy, who have come primarily from North Africa and Eastern Europe. Observing the huge breadth of people involved in New York—Latin Americans, Indians, Moroccans, Africans—he wondered if CIR could learn something from their effort that would help him understand how to integrate immigrants into the Italian system. Immigration to Italy is a fairly recent phenomenon, beginning in the 1980s. Above all, cooperatives are a collective venture, easier to build when people share a common history and culture. Lusetti hoped to learn from the ROC-NY experience of building a co-op with such diversity.

He invited the members to visit Italy so they could present their plans and tell their stories to his colleagues. He told them to bring as many workers as they could, but that they would have to fund their own transport. Within four months the group had raised enough through a small grant to fund travel for eighteen members, three staff, and an intern. They bought Herman a ticket to come along as their translator.

The New Yorkers arrived in Reggio Emilia to great fanfare for a week-long meeting. The Italians had rented a small bus to transport them and announced that they would cover their room and board. They were fed sumptuous meals—CIR is a food cooperative, after all. Local newspapers covered their visit. Each day they visited individual cooperatives, including cheese factories, vineyards, and cafeterias. In very long meetings that ran until nine every night, the Italians described the details of building their businesses, not just the mechanics of production, but also how they handled the social relations, salaries, and hierarchies. The New York group came to understand that CIR was first and foremost a remarkably profitable business. Mamdouh and Lusetti found that they could communicate in French, and they had long talks about capitalism and revolution. They also had spirited discussions about the treatment of workers in U.S. restaurants. Mamdouh was not surprised to find that Italian unions included very few Moroccans, nor to see Moroccan men, clearly unemployed, standing on the side of the road in the middle of the day.

For his part, Lusetti thought the New Yorkers had a rather individualistic sense of democracy. Among eighteen people, there were eighteen different ideas about their venture. Moreover, the CIR team focused heavily on the mechanism for buying in to a co-op—traditionally, members do just that, putting down money to finance the business and buy an equal share of decision-making power. They were shocked to hear that the New Yorkers didn't plan to do it that way. ROC-NY explained that Windows workers, and restaurant workers in general, didn't have enough capital to invest, so ROC-NY would contribute a large share, and the cooperative members would earn their shares through a sweat-equity system. Members would put in hours setting up the co-op, going to ROC meetings and protests, and catering to buy their way in. The Italians said bluntly that they did not think that was going to work, even if ROC invested cash to help with the hard-money costs of starting up. Lusetti warned that the presence of other investors required a high degree of accountability to them, which could be a complicating factor in an already challenging project.

The exchange started to surface some of the New Yorkers' internal challenges, which would emerge more forcefully later. There was the matter of eighteen different conceptions of how the co-op would work and what it would do. Although they debriefed at the end of each day, the language barriers and the newness of the subject matter had created a situation in which the less assertive members had little direct contact with the Italians, effectively sidelining them for large chunks of the discussion.

Before the New Yorkers left, Lusetti indicated that CIR might be willing to invest up to $500,000 in the restaurant if certain things fell into place—a location, other financing, a chef. As the New Yorkers moved forward, Lusetti worked to convince his own colleagues to involve themselves in an American restaurant. There was substantial resistance. He was the most positive about it, but even he had his doubts. Could the kind of restaurant they imagined— one paying very high wages relative to the rest of the industry, using a global menu, operating collectively—do well in the political, economic, and social climate of New York? The Italians found ROC-NY ideologically correct, but they doubted the project's feasibility. The business plan changed continually. In the end, CIR decided that it didn't want to provide money without having any other kind of influence. Lusetti created a consortium of cooperatives that would invest in the restaurant, but would also provide advice. They asked Herman to represent them among the co-op's financial partners.

Within a month of returning home, the co-op hired Stefan Mailvaganam, a fast-paced, straightforward Sri Lankan–Canadian who had worked for Danny Meyer, one of the top restaurateurs in New York. Mailvaganam was to staff the process. They wrote to Lusetti and invited him to visit and look at a proposed location. Their letter described two spaces, assuring Lusetti that previous restaurants had done well there and had closed for reasons other than location. ROC's lawyers, contributing their time from a nonprofit and a local law school, were ready to begin defining the relationship between ROC-NY, the Italians, and the co-op.

At this point, the co-op began to get major press. During its September 11 memorial in 2003, ROC-NY featured the new restaurant plan in its annual memorial at Hudson River Park. The media couldn't get enough of this part of the Windows story, which seemed to simultaneously critique and embrace American-style capitalism. While there was some discussion in the press of the cooperative model, the narrative was otherwise conventional—the downtrodden would triumph by owning a business, a hallmark of the American dream. Dozens of stories appeared, including a profile in *People* magazine, where it was reported that the new restaurant was tentatively named Windows on Tribeca, and that they had to raise $3.5 million and find an 8,000-square-foot space to realize their dream. The stories were intensely sentimental.

At the beginning of 2004, then, Mamdouh was just able to start putting together the mechanics of opening a restaurant. They projected opening in September, but then encountered a new round of difficulties: finding a space and recruiting other investors, keeping the members involved, and finding an executive chef. As these details became increasingly complicated and farmed out to professionals like Stefan Mailvaganam, members' participation faltered.

They had real trouble finding a space, and the restaurant's location was all-important to its chances of succeeding. In 2004 they had found a space on Greenwich Street, very close to Ground Zero. ROC-NY had agreed to a lease-to-own arrangement in which it would buy the space for $860,000 and to put down a 10 percent deposit upon signing an initial lease agreement, which it then did. Mamdouh had been negotiating with the owners of the restaurant that had been in the space. Before signing the final agreement, Mamdouh wanted documentation that the actual owner of the building approved the change of lease. The restaurant owners kept promising the documents, but in the end could not produce them when Mamdouh, Mailvaganam and their lawyers went to sign the final agreement. "If you don't like the deal without that paperwork," the restaurant owner said, "we can return your deposit, and you can leave."

Mamdouh asked for a few minutes of privacy to discuss the situation, and the other team stepped outside. The lawyer said the deal appeared shady, advising them to turn it down. When they regrouped, Mamdouh said, "OK, we want our money back. We decided not to go through with the deal." He could see their cashier's check in the other attorney's shirt pocket as one of the owners said that he wanted a signed document attesting that ROC-NY rejected the deal before they would return the deposit. Their attorney promised to have the document ready for a signature the next day. When Mamdouh called that office the next day, however, there was no answer. It would take them almost three years of litigation to get this money back.

Meanwhile, the implications of not having a lease on a restaurant space were immense. Every financing deal would require the lenders' confidence in the restaurant's future, and their financing deals included a lot of false starts. The project needed a minimum of $2.5 million to open, although $3.5 million would have been much better. Mamdouh had three primary leads for money—the private September 11 Fund, the quasi-public Lower Manhattan Development Corporation (LMDC), and private banks.

ROC-NY first applied to the September 11 Fund for $1 million to start this and future co-ops. The fund initially committed funding for a staff person if ROC-NY met certain conditions, but the conditions kept changing. First, the fund wanted a project manager hired. When they hired Mailvaganam, the fund then wanted a space determined. Once ROC-NY found a space, they wrote in to ask for the release of their grant and were shocked to receive a generic rejection letter instead. More negotiations followed. In the end, the fund gave them only $350,000 over two years for ROC-NY, not for the co-op, and $60,000 for Mailvaganam's salary.

The next source Mamdouh chased was the Lower Manhattan Development Corporation, a quasi-public entity that had been set up to revitalize the area after September 11. The LMDC never actually rejected the project; it simply never responded. Mamdouh was frustrated and very sad. He felt that these funds were denying them access to money that should have come to them because of who they were—survivors of September 11 who could clearly make restaurants work, but who would never be able to open one of their own through conventional means. Mamdouh told Errol Louis, a columnist for the *Daily News*, that it had been "very hard to access the money," which Louis called the understatement of the year. Louis criticized the LMDC's lack of transparency, saying that it had skipped out on a City Council hearing about how it was allocating its money. The LMDC claimed to send out every idea for public comment, a process consisting largely of erratic discussion with community groups, some by invitation only. "Nobody knows why particular ideas are included for funding or passed over," Louis wrote. "The TriBeCa Film Festival, for instance, got $3 million from the LMDC. The Windows workers, zip."[1] The workers went to an LMDC board meeting to get a final response to their request. When they approached the board chair, he waved them off to his deputy to schedule a meeting. They had the meeting, but again there was no response. Eventually, Mamdouh gave up.

The banks generally showed no interest at all. In the fall of 2004, when ROC held a Restaurant Industry Summit to release its comprehensive study of the industry, a representative from HSBC Bank expressed some interest but never followed through. Mamdouh took the business plan to bank after bank, only to be rejected by all of them. They didn't believe that the restaurant could succeed in the current economic climate. In the end, it was the non-profit lenders and grant makers that saved the project. Seventeen such lenders eventually contributed $1.2 million, bringing their total capital to $2.2 million. Catholic Charities also provided a wage subsidy grant.

Colors

In spite of these obstacles, the team lurched forward. Magdi Labib came up with the name of the restaurant: Colors, to represent all their diversity. The members decided to build a global menu based on their own family recipes. The tone of the 2004 September 11 memorial was somewhat lighter than in previous years, and the portion of the program highlighting ROC-NY activities was as long as the memorial ritual. As had become their habit, about thirty-six people met at Hudson River Park around 8:30 in the morning, preparing for 9:17 when the first plane had hit the South Tower. More people came over the next hour. Four or five children ran around, including Mamdouh's daughter Iman and son Zaki, and the picnic tables were loaded with food. People laughed as Mamdouh tried out a little "Todos, hombres," and someone corrected him, "Hombres y mujeres." Saru presented a blown-up check for $65,000 to two leaders of the Park Avenue Country Club campaign, which had just ended.

Labib gave the co-op's report, calling all its members to stand with him, telling them to "forget about the food!" About twenty people joined him. He said they had two needs: one was to be together again, the other to find a job after September 11 in which everybody had the opportunity to work with dignity and respect.

"This restaurant will be an example for other restaurants where workers don't get overtime or have health insurance," he told them. It would have an employee lounge, he said, with a TV and couches, so people could sit and read the newspaper or a book during their breaks. Worker/owners wouldn't be denied a day off if their wives were in the hospital. "Is this a good idea? Is this going to give people jobs?"

Labib asked the crowd, to a predictable response. "Let's go and do it, guys, we cannot delay this. I cry, I cry for every one of my lost co-workers. Thank God for this beautiful organization that has provided help. I look at this as a journey to freedom. Who said to all of us that restaurant workers must work seven days, fourteen, sixteen hours a day?" They projected opening the restaurant by the end of 2004.

Their final set of problems concerned keeping the membership engaged. In August 2004, a letter to the co-op membership exhorting them to come to meetings received virtually no response, and the staff planned to set up new committees to find a general manager and chef, and for fundraising, catering, and overall project management. In organizational life, a need for "new committees" most often signals that no one has been coming to the old committees. The catering business had been struggling for labor. It was difficult to sustain interest in a project that had already taken eighteen months and was still nowhere close to opening. Although the co-op had thirty-five members on the books, a few people did most of the work. In this period, Bezhad Pasdar, an Iranian American bartender and labor-relations student whom Saru and Mamdouh had invited into the co-op on the basis of a friend's recommendation, came into the organization, and quickly emerged as one of its most committed leaders.

As the work became more technical, such as writing bylaws and negotiating over money, the membership had to engage in unfamiliar and complicated discussions. The workers created a subcommittee to work with a law professor and a community development expert to go through the tedious process of drafting every aspect of the co-op's functioning, from how workers became worker-owners to how work teams would make decisions. They produced an agreement for all members, which required 100 hours of time invested to buy their way into the restaurant and pledged their commitment to the ROC-NY mission of restaurant worker justice. There was some concern that co-op members would eventually become wealthy, exploitative owners, and both the character of the sweat equity (you could meet the requirement by going to ROC protests and meetings, as well as by doing co-op–related tasks) and pledge were designed to test members' commitment.

Although members actively developed and signed off on those decisions, there was trouble over the investment arrangement. That arrangement had two complementary parts. First, the notion of sweat equity came under attack. Members resisted when they had to choose a date on which to start tracking people's hours. This of course benefited the people who had contributed little time over the years and disappointed those who had put in a lot of time to get things done since the beginning. Members got paid for their catering hours, but not for any other time they put in. One characterized this later as exploitation, "enslaving them to do things they don't want to do." Another member who was undocumented said that he was afraid to attend protests because he might get arrested.

The second element of the investment structure concerned how the restaurant's earnings would be shared down the line. Because the Italians and ROC-NY would each contribute $500,000 and the workers would individually be contributing no money, the two investors would normally have split the profit fifty–fifty. That would have given the worker-owners, well, nothing to own. ROC-NY convinced the Italians to donate 10 percent of their profit share to the workers, and ROC-NY would do the same, so that the workers would begin with 20 percent of the profits, leaving ROC and the Italians with 40 percent each. Over time, the workers would use their 20 percent profit share to buy out the Italians, ultimately winding up with 60 percent equity in the restaurant. ROC would place its 40 percent into a fund for future cooperatives.

The co-op voted its agreement to this profit-sharing proposal, but later people evoked the Windows memory to fight for a revision. Members asserted that the money ROC used to make its own investment in the restaurant had been donated specifically to support Windows survivors. If that were true, they should have full access to that investment without further contributions of money or time.

On the day the workers were asked to sign commitment letters, Saru presented the funding sources at the co-op meeting, showing that none of the money came from September 11 grants. Those streams had in fact long since dried up. She laid out ROC-NY's enormous investment of time and resources in the project, and she explained how that investment obligated beneficiaries of the project to continually contribute to the mission of the organization. One member refused to sign, stating that, as an owner, he might not want to side with workers in future ROC-NY campaigns. If you didn't sign, though, you could not be part of the co-op.

Sekou Siby, who had become a balancing voice on the ROC staff and who was friendly with many of the co-op's founding members, attempted a mediation. He and another staff member sat down with Mamdouh, Saru, and some of the disgruntled co-op members in what was known as the "green room" because it had long green tables. They asked the group to make a list of the positive things and the negative things about the co-op, trying to determine why it had not yet opened. On the positive side, members listed how hard they had worked and the entire project's orientation toward justice.

But they had issues over control. In addition to the sweat-equity and financing issues, the Spanish-speaking members had language concerns. Mailvaganam had said that everyone would have to speak English to work in the restaurant. When they complained to Saru, she backed up Mailvaganam. They had to hire a general manager, she said, and it would be virtually impossible to find one willing to translate instructions and other communications. ROC-NY itself had made major accommodations on language, providing simultaneous translation for every meeting, often in two or three languages. But the pace of a busy restaurant and kitchen was ten times faster and more dangerous than that of a membership meeting, and it would require a common language. As reasonable as this sounded to Saru and Mamdouh, it felt like an enormous betrayal to the Spanish speakers, who thought the English requirement was racist. Siby understood the importance of the common language. He thought there were ways to communicate this to members that didn't demean them, but it's unclear that anything would have mitigated the resistance. The conflict continued.

In the last days of 2004, the group finally caught a break. Mailvaganam heard about another restaurant location from a real estate agent. When he told Saru and Mamdouh, they knew it—it was the site of Pangeae, ROC's first back-wages campaign. On the last day of the year, Mamdouh signed a lease agreement.

Growing Tensions

Despite the challenges, the co-op retained a tough core of committed members, although their cohesiveness was shaky at the beginning of 2005. They included Jean Emy Pierre, the Haitian who had been a sous-chef at Windows; Ataur Rahman, who had escaped the Bangladeshi civil war; Leticia Rios and Nereyda Peña, two Nicaraguan women who were always together; Manuel Guttierez, who made jewelry; Howard Christiansen, an Italian American cook from Queens and the co-op's only white member at the time; and Grace Gilbert, an African American woman in her fifties who had watched the towers fall from her housekeeping job across the street at the Millenium Hilton. Utjok Zaidan, who had been a waiter at Windows and was now on the ROC staff, was part of the crew. The core group also included people who hadn't worked at the World Trade Center, such as Bezhad Pasdar, the tall Iranian American labor relations student, and Mohammed Khadiry, a Moroccan friend whom Mamdouh had recruited.

The atmosphere was tense. The staff planned to start ESL classes to establish English as the common language, but there were still bad feelings about that. There was a growing division between the co-op and the larger organization. Co-op members had stopped regularly attending ROC protests, leading one staff member to suggest that the policy committee regularly brief the co-op because some members were forgetting the ROC mission.

The staff and board of ROC-NY were very much aware of the importance the public placed on the Windows connection. As increasing numbers of Windows workers dropped out or re-raised issues that seemed to have been resolved, the ROC-NY staff and board worried about retaining the identification with Windows. If they replaced inactive Windows workers with new cooperative members, what would happen if the Windows workers wound up being as little as 20 percent of the whole? "What will we tell the press when they ask how many Windows workers there are?" asked one staff person.

By February, these conflicts had started to emerge in co-op and membership meetings. Two sides formed, with many people finding themselves in the middle. On February 14, 2005, some fifteen members dealt with several perplexing issues while sounding notes of urgency and resentment in equal measure. Mamdouh started the meeting with the problem of recovering the lost $86,000 deposit, then moved on to the catering business, which was understaffed. Asking for volunteers hadn't been working, and Mailvaganam wanted to set up a rotation system. Jean Emy Pierre called the question: "It's been two years," he said. "If you can't make it for the catering, how are you going to be there for the restaurant?"

Mailvaganam said it would be easier because they would create only two menus for each meal. And catering would pay $10 per hour, in addition to giving people sweat-equity hours.

"What do all the members think about that?" asked Zaidan, not clarifying the "that." "Any opinion?"

Someone piped up, "It's good."

A young man in the back timidly started to put together a question. "So what he say about the time, and you were saying about the sweat equity, those who have sweat equity accomplished, they ... " but he couldn't get it all out.

"Guys, just speak up if you don't like something," said Pasdar. The sweat-equity question was forgotten as the conversation moved into disagreements about a rotation system.

Just then Saru entered the room. It wasn't unusual at membership meetings for Saru's entrance to engender a round of applause, but on this day she received only a lukewarm welcome.

"That's not a ... that's not a ... what kind of hello is that?" she said.

Saru had come to do her thing, to plan the process by which the co-op was going to get its money back from the fraudulent landlord. For a time, focusing on a common enemy restored their sense of humor, although some of the co-op members continued to appear disengaged. Saru hoped, in part, that a campaign to recover the money would reconnect co-op members with the political mission.

"You guys know what we do?"

"Protest."

When it came time to list demands, people were well versed.

"Pay our legal fees."

"Pay us interest."

"Make a public apology."

"We want them to buy us lunch, too," Pasdar joked.

But no one signed up to deliver the demand letter.

"If nobody's interested in getting the money, then there's no point in doing this," said Saru.

"I thought it would be like, 'Me!'" said Mamdouh.

Four people raised hands.

"You need at least four more to be effective," said Saru, before moving on. "I think you are going to need a committee of people, permits, flyers."

"You got to bring out your friends, your sister, your cats and dogs," said Grace Gilbert.

Someone offered to ask for more volunteers at the general membership meeting, giving Saru an opportunity.

"But you know what they're going to say. We've asked you guys to come to our protests, but co-op members don't come. If the other members show up at your protest, they're going to expect you to come to theirs."

The growing distance between the general membership and the co-op came up again at the next membership meeting two weeks later. More than fifty members were crammed into a stifling hot room.

Mailvaganam started the co-op report with "We're going to need more workers. Make sure you put your name with office manager Rosa Fana." He thanked Saru and Mamdouh for their support. Zaidan got up to say that the people from the first space had taken their money and they needed every-body's help getting it back.

Pasdar said, "For some time I've heard about the general membership not being too happy. That's really bothering me. Every single person who's [in the co-op now] ... we started a lot of the stuff. Forty percent of what we make is going to go into ROC-NY. Please support us and understand that we're working very hard, putting in a lot of hours to make this happen. I want to put to rest any animosity between the general membership and the co-op."

Nereyda Peña moved on to report, in Spanish with a translator, on the location they had found in the East Village near the Public Theater. It is a beautiful space, she said, very wide and big. The team met last Friday with the architects. "I'm very happy because they're doing something that's very unique and interesting and beautiful. But the other members should keep coming," she said about the waiting list. "We're going to open more and more restaurants for other people. This is not just talk, talk, talk, it's a lot of work involved."

Pasdar again told the story of how the co-op came out of Windows. Other members commented on the little time until opening. Did they have a chef? What kind of food would they be serving?

"After the restaurant gets going, what are the co-op members going to give back?" asked a relatively new member.

Pasdar said he found it ironic that the members who had been there the longest were now being criticized for not contributing enough while they were concentrating on the co-op. "If our dream could come true, once the co-op begins, 40 percent of what we make is going back to ROC, we're going to be attending meetings, protests, holding the bartending classes, cooking classes, working with people who want to learn a new trade. I need the general membership to understand that the co-op opening up is one of the major things ROC can contribute to society. I feel we've given a lot."

Mamdouh and Saru jumped in together. "We have to clarify that 40 percent," Saru said. "That money is not going to go to ROC directly, but be put into a trust to start other co-ops in the future."

Mamdouh took on a stern tone that ROC members had rarely heard from him. "I just want to make a point," he said. "There are other committees, they do a lot of work. And they also come to end-of-the-month meetings. So there is no excuse 'We are busy.' We need everybody to participate."

Two weeks later, Zaidan and Pasdar called a special meeting of co-op members to discuss their complaints about ROC-NY, which seven or eight people attended. This small group then went to the ROC office to present demands. They had followed the eleven-step plan, including Step Three, "Locate Legal Resources," for which they brought in attorney Arthur Schwartz. They were upset about what they called a lack of democracy in the co-op's working arrangements with ROC, but their most focused demand was about the financial arrangements. They wanted a 33 percent share of the initial equity share, rather than 20 percent. Mamdouh and Mailvaganam left, angry, but

Saru listened for two hours, afraid that leaving would fuel their complaints about a lack of democracy.

At a follow-up meeting between Saru, Mamdouh, Mailvaganam, and five disgruntled members, the language and transparency issues seemed less intractable, but the finance issue remained. If the Italians wouldn't give up more of their share, it would have to come from ROC-NY. Saru explained, for what felt to her like the fiftieth time, that ROC's share of profits was intended to help other workers start restaurants, and that none of the money would go to the organization for operating expenses or staff salaries. One person responded that he didn't want to fund workers they didn't know to start new co-ops.

At an impasse, Saru proposed hiring a mediator, to which the group agreed. ROC hired one with thirty years of experience working in recently desegregated communities. The mediator began a process with co-op members to help them list grievances and define ground rules to keep things productive and to avoid personal attacks, but the disgruntled committee didn't attend most of these meetings. When they did come to the next regular co-op meeting, discipline broke down quickly, with Mailvaganam, Pasdar, and the member who didn't want to build future co-ops all yelling. Mamdouh had decided to stay in the office behind a locked door trying to avoid further escalation. The dissidents banged on the door, shouting for him to come out. Someone raised the issue of the sweat-equity agreement, and Pasdar yelled, "No one signs until I say they sign!"

The mediator tried to move the group to another room, but ultimately had to shut the meeting down. The next day, she quit the project. Their landlord told them they could no longer allow Pasdar to enter the building so disruptively. A month later, the ROC board voted to revoke his membership, the first time they had taken such a step.

The disgruntled members called Bruce Herman trying to get support from the Italians. Herman spent some hours talking with various players on the dissident side, feeling that none of them really understood the financing. He saw that they had a real problem with dedicating their profits to buy out the Italians or pay dividends. They wouldn't see any profits for some years, although they would be paid salaries far above the prevailing wage rates. Herman had heard one member say that he expected to purchase an apartment on Park Avenue with his share and knew that another planned to retire in Guatemala as soon as the restaurant opened, expecting dividends to be sent to him.

Herman had clear direction from the Italians that they considered the financing plan and many other things to be settled. If these issues were reopened, the Italians would walk away. The dissidents asked for phone numbers for Lusetti and others, which Herman provided with a warning that Italy was six hours ahead. One Italian called him later to report being woken up at 2 a.m.

Finding no support from the Italians, the smaller group then staged a protest in front of the ROC-NY office just before a regularly scheduled co-op meeting. The ROC staff prepared anxiously. At 1 p.m., Mamdouh was on the phone with a Haitian co-op member who would have come later in the afternoon for a meeting. "Come early, come earlier than three," he said. "Please try. Those guys are going to come protesting. And we might need you guys to talk to the media. We don't want to be talking to the media."

At 1 o'clock on a bright June afternoon Pasdar pulled up in a Mitsubishi SUV with signs pasted on its sides: "ROC-NY Lies." The dissidents had called three unions trying to get the giant inflatable rat typically seen on picket lines, but the unions refused the request. They set up the police barricades in front of the office at 99 Hudson Street, from which they floated one red, one yellow, and one orange balloon. Two Spanish-language TV stations stood waiting, but Channel 41 seemed prepared to leave before the protest even got under way. Pasdar stepped out of the car wearing his ROC-NY t-shirt.

The group had renamed itself the Cooperative Worker-Owner Power (Co-WOP) and written a list of demands, which included reinstating Pasdar and the member who first refused to sign the sweat-equity agreement; a stipulation that no rules or bylaws could be changed without permission of the members; reviews of the 20/40/40 operating agreement ("designed to enrich a few at the cost of the members"); an end to language and racial discrimination; and an end to what they called verbal abuse. Their press release claimed that the majority of the co-op members (although only nine people signed the attached demand letter) and five of the six elected co-op board members had spoken out and planned to file a lawsuit against ROC-NY. They alleged that Saru forced them to sign agreements and retaliated against those who didn't. "ROC negotiated a contract without the consent of the workers that doesn't represent their interests, where 40% of the profits from the multimillion-dollar restaurant will go to ROC and the workers will pay back 100% of all the debt."

In fact, because ROC and the Italians had agreed to donate 10 percent each, the worker-owners had to pay back only 80 percent of those investments. The undocumented member who had earlier said he was afraid to protest because of his immigration status was quoted on the press release and listed as a contact. Khadiry, Mamdouh's Moroccan friend, gave an interview. He'd been there almost since the beginning, he said, when the leaders were telling them they were one. "Now we are not one, we are separate. I don't know why." He blamed Mailvaganam—where had he come from? Why was he separating them? He wanted to know how much Saru earned, and he was against paying most of the loan. "People when they see money, they change," he said.

At 1:15, Pasdar got on the bullhorn. Their chants were impassioned, but somewhat disorganized.

"Down with ROC! Mamdouh lies! Saru and Mamdouh have got to go!" Then they started on Herman: "Bruce Herman sold us out!"

The Future of Colors

Saru and Mamdouh were faced with some critical choices, but their relationship had changed significantly over the last two years, and this conflict threatened to push them apart. Their easy camaraderie of the first two years had morphed into something both stronger and more challenging. Saru was increasingly integrated into Mamdouh's family, spending time with Fatima and taking the kids to an occasional movie. Nevertheless, the two had many conflicts, not so much over the major decisions, but increasingly over their style of work.

Saru wanted Mamdouh to put in more hours, make to-do lists, remember his appointments, and generally move faster. He resisted these things and had taken to leaving the office without her when he was upset, breaking their tradition of walking to the subway together. He did not want to put more hours into an organization that didn't seem to appreciate him, especially since his growing family needed him. He and Fatima had had a third child in 2005, a little boy they named Mohammed after Mamdouh's eldest brother. His son Zaki, who was then eight, had developed an irrational fear of terrorism and called Mamdouh constantly. If Mamdouh didn't answer, Zaki would ask Fatima if someone had blown up Baba's building again.

On June 11, Saru and Mamdouh met in the late afternoon at the Delhi Palace in Jackson Heights. Mamdouh did his best not to leave Queens on the weekends, so Saru made the long trek from Fort Greene and was half an hour late. The conflict was tearing up the membership, and people whom Mamdouh thought were solid turned out not to be. He had spent the morning with Khadiry. Fatima had told him not to go, and indeed, Mamdouh wasn't able to change Khadiry's mind. Their conversation ended with Mamdouh telling the other man, "Don't pray if you don't know the difference between right and wrong." Zaidan's adherence to the dissident side was also hard for Mamdouh to take.

The dissidents had been applying increasingly aggressive pressure on other co-op members to join their movement. One co-op member had reported someone calling his wife and intimating a relationship between him and Saru. They had pledged a noisy protest when Saru was scheduled to speak at a conference in Washington, D.C., the following week. She had turned down the engagement at the last minute. Everyone had been hit with intense paranoia, and Saru had spent several nights in Queens with Mamdouh's family.

Mamdouh and Saru entertained the unthinkable possibility of backing away from the plan.

"If we don't do it, we're going to lose a lot of money," said Mamdouh.

Saru wondered how they would drum up business with protesters in front, and whether their funders would stick by them. A minute later, though, she predicted that by September, when ROC-NY would host a gala fundraising event at the restaurant, the dissident group would have lost energy and disappeared. Saru then asked Mamdouh if he intended to file a police report alleging harassment. Mamdouh definitely did not.

"Saru, I told you I don't want to do this," said Mamdouh. "I don't want it to be me against a member. I'm not like you, I fell into it." Whenever they fought now, Mamdouh reminded Saru that she had chosen this work, but he was in it by accident, implying that he could just as easily fall back out.

"I've been asking you to do this. Other people have already done it."

"But they haven't said anything to me really."

"Yes, yes, they have, they've been making threats, they've been talking about your wife."

As they had done with another member, the dissidents had threatened to tell Fatima that Mamdouh and Saru were having an affair. Saru was cast as sleeping with virtually every man in the organization.

"I don't want to do this," Mamdouh told her. "I never want to do this, before I just have a happy life, I go to work, I spend time with my kids, I don't have no fights."

"That's not true, you were fighting!"

"I don't mind fighting employers, but when my own member comes in and fights with me, I don't want that." Mamdouh had never before been the target of such animosity, and he still couldn't accept that his leadership role had brought so much conflict into his life. He knew that criticism was an inescapable aspect of leadership, but so far most of the staff and membership complaints had been directed at Saru.

The meeting ended tensely, but they decided to move ahead with the restaurant, filling the rest of the slots with as many Windows workers as possible. Afterward, though, they took a walk, apologizing to each other for allowing the pressure to split them.

At this point, about thirty-five co-op members, only two-thirds of the required number of workers, set about expanding their group.

Their greatest immediate need was to find an executive chef—future financing depended on it. This proved to be as politically and logistically challenging as keeping the group together. Restaurant kitchens are notoriously hierarchical, and most head chefs answer to no one about how they run theirs. In July, a group met at Herman's brownstone in Fort Greene to taste the food of their third candidate. Labib was there, along with Gilbert, Pierre, and several others. Herman's kitchen was a gourmet's dream, with a marble-topped chopping island in the middle and a stainless steel counter running along the back wall.

The chef presented a creative menu that evoked the globe, if not always perfectly. The *amuse bouche*—just a bite of something that starts the meal—was pappadum and a mini baked samosa, garnished with beet tops. The appetizer was a round piece each of yellow and red watermelon with goat cheese, a sprig of basil, and a sprinkling of balsamic vinegar. Then the courses came out one by one. A roulade of dover sole wrapped around a kumamoto oyster, with a beurre blanc sauce that included a tiny bit of coconut milk. A Moroccan bastilla, filo dough wrapped around a too-large piece of chicken. Saru passed around the vegetarian plate of broccoli and cauliflower with a "Please don't use your oyster forks!"

After dinner, Pierre and the chef stepped outside for a smoke while the others moved to the dining room to prepare for the interview portion.

"I've got some tough questions," said Mailvaganam.

"Have to ask them," said Mamdouh.

Gilbert named the toughest one: "If we expect the chef to protest."

During the interview, the chef expressed great enthusiasm about the cooperative model. "Some people work in a restaurant to get a paycheck," he said. "Food is good, not good, they don't care if they're getting a paycheck. Here, everybody's going to care." He was attracted to the concept of the global menu, and he was willing to teach anyone who wanted to learn.

Gilbert asked the hardest question. "You know the mission of ROC. Just say … there's a protest over at another restaurant. Do you feel that you can go to protests?"

"For me to go out and speak, I'd be very happy to help. It's just about organizing the schedule."

"So then you will become a face and spokesperson for a movement. It's really important for you to understand what you're stepping into."

"Mmm hmmm."

"Not just for the food side of it."

"Mmm hmmm."

Mamdouh asked him how he would deal with the restaurateurs for whom he had worked before. They might try to discredit Colors.

"Yeah, it's not easy. You have to fight for that," said the chef just before leaving.

The group deliberated. They considered whose food they liked more, whom the press would pay more attention to, and who would be most down with the social mission. There was a clear tension between the latter two questions. People felt this chef would have the highest profile. Debate ensued about how much difference that would make.

"The press will be more into this chef, he will be more respected. It's a bias."

"They're just going to give him more credibility," said Saru.

"We're all going to be the face of the restaurant," protested Labib, nervous about ending up with an attention-hogging chef.

"But all the banks have been asking us who's the chef. Their background, their pedigree is going to have a huge impact on our restaurant," said Saru.

And then they came to the crux of the trouble they foresaw with the best-known chef.

"That's the problem, that this guy can throw down his apron anytime," said Mamdouh.

"He can basically say take this job and shove it."

"But I didn't like any of the food," Gilbert piped up for the first time since her initial question. "Only thing I liked was the watermelon and goat cheese. I didn't like the bastilla. The salmon, to me, it didn't taste done. But what I'm saying, I didn't like anything but the watermelon—and you know black folks always like the watermelon," she joked. It turned out others preferred another chef's food also, but thought this one would attract a wealthier clientele.

In the end, they chose the most prominent chef and made an offer that was accepted in principle. When the time came to negotiate the terms, however, Mamdouh's jaw dropped at his requirements. For each protest he attended, he requested a $5,000 bonus. For each press interview, $10,000. The team went to their second choice, who put in a month of preparation time before backing out, leaving them with their third choice. Aside from the chef, the co-op also had to find fifteen new members to replace those lost through protest or attrition. Every week throughout the summer they interviewed applicants. As people were voted in, they began to attend meetings and conduct interviews. By the middle of August, each applicant was being interviewed by at least twenty people asking questions that no other employer had ever asked them. The members struggled to find the correct balance of political and practical questions. On August 15, for example, the co-op interviewed a thin, dark young African man who had seen an article about ROC-NY in the newspaper. He had come to the United States to study sociology in Montana. He'd done the first semester but couldn't afford the second. He had moved to New York with no marketable experience, so he started as a dishwasher in a gourmet coffee shop.

After this interview, a member asked, "Are we going to ask if they've ever been arrested or anything?" A chorus of no's.

"No, 'cause I know a lot of people who've been arrested. You could get arrested," said Jean Emy Pierre.

A pushback. "We don't know if people have any record, misdemeanor. I don't care, but we don't know."

"Let's say he was in jail, that's discrimination," said Mamdouh.

"We're not a traditional restaurant. We don't care about all that stuff," said Pierre.

"Why don't you give me your Social Security number, and I'll tell you all about yourself tomorrow," said Gilbert.

The African was voted in.

A week later, a slim Chinese man applied for a job in the kitchen. He was so soft-spoken that it was nearly impossible to hear him, but it became clear soon enough that his English was just shy of basic.

"You cook American food, easy?" Pierre asked. The answer was inaudible.

Had he paid his ROC-NY dues yet? The man held up his membership certificate, drawing applause.

Pierre again: "So what do you want to see changed in the restaurant busi-ness? I know you worked in Asian restaurants, I know they work you guys hard." The man struggled to understand. They got through some questions about his computer skills, and then Howard Christiansen, the co-op's only white U.S.-born member, asked if he knew how to handle food according to health department rules. The man described another certificate he had received.

"Is this in New York City?"

"He doesn't need one. I just want to know if he has any experience handling food properly," said Christiansen.

"He speaks English, that's not a problem. He's probably shy around all these people." Pierre offered to train him if he would come to his job.

"In or out, in or out?" Gilbert called the question. Hands rose.

"Sure, why not?" said Christiansen. "Give everybody a chance."

Finally, the co-op gathered enough of a mass to staff ROC's gala fund-raiser on September 12, 2005, at the new restaurant. The real opening wasn't planned for several months, but this event would unveil the long-anticipated restaurant to ROC-NY supporters. The day of the fundraiser was hectic. Four hundred people were expected in a space designed for 100, the construction was incomplete, and the team had started three hours late because of miscom-munication about the key. By midafternoon, it was clear that the air condi-tioning system would be overwhelmed by body heat. But the place looked excellent, buzzing with the energy of fifty owners and their friends preparing for their first major test. The bar gleamed, with martini glasses stacked in the right corner. Photographs of workers lined the raw wall, as yet lacking dry-wall. Centerpieces including a yellow rose, a daisy, a white rose, and a bit of baby's breath sat on each table. A map of the world covered one large section of the south wall. Expecting an overflow crowd, they had set up fifteen round tables on the wide sidewalk of Lafayette Street, covered with a white tent.

At 4 p.m. Mamdouh gathered the crew together for a meeting outside by shouting, "Todos, todos." He then led the ROC-NY chant, which was done in four languages. The day before, he had gone to see Zaidan, whose father had just died; Zaidan had said he didn't know if there would be a protest. Saru had learned that the dissidents had set their police permit for the day before and then had had to change it. The meeting ended at 4:30 and Saru and Mamdouh bickered over the need for a dry run, which did not happen.

At 7:02 p.m., after the dinner crowd was already seated, six protesters ar-rived. Pasdar was on the bullhorn: "The leaders of ROC-NY do not support the workers. Do not support Colors.... It made the workers slave for three long years and then kicked them out. There is a lawsuit being filed against ROC-NY. ROC-NY is being sued and there is no democracy." The steady stream of talk behind the white curtain did not cease or even slow down.

At 7:09 p.m. Saru started the program and introduced Mamdouh.

"We started this restaurant," said Mamdouh, "to bring hope out of tragedy." He asked for a moment of silence to honor the Windows dead. Mamdouh then introduced the worker-owners, who were rewarded with a long standing ovation.

Outside, the protesters screamed, "Mamdouh is a thief. Mamdouh, you're dirt. Stop stealing from the workers. Mamdouh makes a hundred thousand dollars a year." And then, bizarrely, "The University of Toronto sucks, Stefan!" directed at Mailvaganam.

The space was overcrowded and hot, and the food came out very slowly, with some people not eating until close to 9 o'clock. But the diners were good-natured about it all, and things essentially went well.

"I feel excited. Even though they protest, I still feel excited," Mamdouh said as the post-dinner cocktail crowd arrived. "I wish they didn't protest, but I still feel good."

At 10:40, the members gathered for a photograph, cheering, shouting, clapping. They did the chant. ROC-NY's office manager administered hugs and kisses. Herman wore a satisfied smile. Christiansen and Pierre took a picture of themselves.

One of the kitchen workers sat down, took his shoes off, and rubbed his feet. "I feel happy because all my family is here. I work very, very hard. Wednesday, Friday, Saturday, Sunday, Monday," he said. The standing ovation was his highlight. "All the kitchens I work in before, never recognize our work, never. The owner gets the credit. When they recognize the kitchen, I feel so happy."

Pierre said to Guttierez, as the tall Chinese prep cook stood nearby, "Manuel, man, what did you think about the communication in the kitchen tonight?"

Guttierez shook his head.

"No good, huh?" said Pierre. "ESL, man, ESL."

On January 2, 2006, Colors opened for real, without incident. Frank Bruni's review in the *New York Times* praised the handsome décor and gave kudos to the creativity of the menu. He saw the design as a "hopeful symbol of harmony and unity, a counterpoint to the impulses and enmity behind

September 11." Bruni also listed some problems. They hadn't managed to put up a sign yet, and flyers covered the entranceway, a nice detail for the movie he predicted would never get made. There was a problem with slow delivery of cold or undercooked food, and he had difficulty getting his server's attention.

Over the long term, however, numerous other problems emerged. For one thing, the restaurant was underfinanced by at least $1 million. They had raised less money than they actually needed, opening with only $300,000 in cash, or about six months' operating expenses, far too small a cushion in New York's competitive market. They were paying salaries starting at $14.50 per hour, about five times the minimum wage for tipped workers. The combination of high salaries and other expenses forced them to charge high prices, putting a meal out of reach for many of their own supporters.

They had too few customers, and both the food and the service were gaining a shaky reputation. The numbers would rise after press attention such as a *New York Times* article entitled, "For Former Windows Workers, a Struggle to Fill Tables," but then it would slacken again. Within a year, the restaurant had racked up a $1 million debt and was consistently late in paying the rent and suppliers. The co-op board voted to cut salaries in 2006, and a slow attrition of worker-owners began.

These were exactly the problems that Ivan Lusetti had predicted. Lusetti felt that ROC should have started with a more humble effort, made that work, and then moved on to larger, more complicated projects. In the summer of 2006, he met Saru and Mamdouh at the Rockefeller Foundation's retreat center in Bellagio, Italy, where the two were on a three-week fellowship to write about their experiences building the organization.

It was a cordial but difficult conversation. Lusetti told Saru and Mamdouh that he wanted to transfer the Italians' interest to someone else. He could see that they wouldn't be getting any loan repayment for a long time, perhaps never, and CIR was, before anything, a profitable business. Not eager to lose their biggest supporter, Mamdouh and Saru returned to New York determined to regroup. They knew something had to change to prevent an otherwise certain closing.

Within another year, the restaurant had adopted a new strategy. First, they made a deal with the Consortium for Worker Education, Bruce Herman's former organization, to train and place restaurant workers during the day when Colors was closed. Five hundred students went through each year, learning skills during the day and bringing in new diners in the evenings. In addition, supporters, including a representative from the Italian investors, suggested taking off the tablecloths, reducing the prices, adding some late-night activities, and introducing locally farmed organic ingredients. They recognized that in chasing a Windows-like clientele, Colors was passing up its natural customer base: younger activists who worked in unions and non-profit organizations. These changes impressed Lusetti, who decided to put off the decision about transferring the Italians' interest, and revived Colors, in turn helping to attract an experienced general manager and chef as well as new customers.

From building and launching the cooperative restaurant, Mamdouh learned that the past only gets you so far. He had known this instinctively, often saying that people might come to Colors the first time out of nostalgia for Windows, but they wouldn't return unless they liked the food, the atmosphere, and the service. "They're not going to keep coming because they're sad," he would say. The sacred Windows memory still pulled on him emotionally. In the end, though, the Windows connection had nearly shut down the project. It gave the dissident group a club to use in revisiting every decision and attempting to discredit ROC-NY, and the sentimental attention Colors got from the media hid the lack of real commitment from traditional financiers and restaurant leaders to a new venture that would benefit many people beyond former Windows employees. By the same token, ROC's attachment to certain political ideals created additional problems. Ivan Lusetti had built his cooperative in a completely different political and economic climate. It wasn't so much that ideals had to be adjusted to a particular situation, but rather that ROC-NY had to creatively express them in a way that it could sustain in a more capitalist context.

The process changed Mamdouh, first making him question how much he was willing to put up with, later destroying two important friendships, and finally challenging his self-image as a "regular" person who just wanted to make a living. The most important aspects to keep from his time at Windows, Mamdouh felt, were the camaraderie, the multiracial character, and the sense of collective ambition. Whether those things found a new home in a high-end restaurant or a cafeteria didn't matter. The decisions that led to the broadest benefit for the largest community, including whether he himself would remain an organizer, had to be made in the present with the future in mind.

Chapter 6

SCALING UP THROUGHOUT
THE INDUSTRY

While Mamdouh was busy trying to create a new restaurant model, ROC-NY's other campaigns and projects focused on expanding the organization's reach upward. ROC wanted to have a larger effect on the industry by taking on bigger targets among restaurant employers and by recruiting allies among restaurant employers. By 2004 and early 2005, the group had two major projects to accomplish these things: its first campaign against an industry leader, and the Restaurant Industry Summit, where ROC released its citywide study of restaurant workers and employers to a packed house of industry players. Organizing throughout the restaurant field required speaking to the self-interest of other people who had a stake in it without abandoning those of ROC-NY's existing base.

The first project was a campaign to address conditions at the high-end steakhouse Cité, owned by Alan Stillman, the founder and CEO of a national chain, the Smith and Wollensky Restaurant Group. As usual, the Mexican kitchen workers sparked the campaign, the organization's largest and most ambitious to date. These kitchen workers represented the bottom of the industry. Many had been small farmers who were forced to migrate by economic crisis, including rising prices and falling wages after the Mexican government adopted the neoliberal policies that mark economic globalization. This trend had only worsened after the passage of the North American Free Trade Agreement in 1993, followed by the devaluation of the peso in 1994. Less than ten years later, there were over 275,000 people of Mexican descent living in New York, a great number of them undocumented and working in restaurant kitchens.[1]

If the restaurant industry was likened to a class hierarchy, we could think of the back of the house as the working, the front of the house as the middle, and the owners as the upper strata. Reaching out beyond the industry's bottom rungs brought new challenges and the possibility of new rewards to ROC-NY. While the campaign started with the Mexicans in the kitchen, an important element of their strategy was to reach into the middle class to recruit the restaurant's only Mexican waiter, with whom they had both discrimination and wage abuse in common, but who had a more individualistic approach than ROC-NY's.

Their second project, the Industry Summit, showcased their massive research project analyzing the entire industry, which had taken three years to complete. Including surveys with over 500 workers and interviews with thirty-five employers, the report outlined the way the industry was organized into good and bad jobs distributed largely along racial lines. ROC used the report to create a distinction between low-road employers who frequently broke the law to increase profits and high-road employers who tried to do the right thing. That distinction gave them the foundation to make common cause with those high-road employers, with whom they could work to create citywide policy changes to improve the rules for everyone rather than taking on one restaurant at a time.

Together, the Cité campaign and the Industry Summit complicated ROC-NY's image and made the organization harder to pigeonhole as tactically limited industry outsiders. By spring 2005, ROC was on its way to being able to speak to everyone involved in the industry, starting with kitchen workers and ending with employers and customers.

Cité was a luxurious and always packed steakhouse located on 51st Street at 7th Avenue. Its heavy glass door with a pewter lion's-head handle opened the way inside to two dining rooms and a substantial bar. A stone lion's head took up half the wall near the bar, its mouth open in a roar. The main dining room flowed around a massive mirrored pillar. The bathrooms had completely enclosed stalls with marble tile walls that muffled noises from the next stall. The surf-and-turf special cost $110 and featured a two-and-a-half-pound lobster tail. The bills included a discreet note: "Publicly traded on NASDAQ. Code: SWRG" for the Smith and Wollensky Restaurant Group.

Owner Alan Stillman was known as the father of the singles bar and a brilliant filler of entertainment niches. In 1965, Stillman, then twenty-six, had been selling essential oils to perfume companies when he thought of creating a space that would attract the young white professionals moving to the Upper East Side. He borrowed $5,000, bought a bar on First Avenue and 63rd Street, set up a burger-based menu and called it Thank God It's Friday (TGIF). He built a dozen more of these before selling the chain for $1 million in 1975, holding on to the original to sell for over $3.8 million in the late 1980s. Stillman opened the first Smith and Wollensky Grill in 1977, which he imagined as the "Tiffany of high-end steakhouses," then built fourteen more restaurants over the next twenty years into the Smith and Wollensky Restaurant Group, including Cité, which opened in 1989. By 1996 the average investor in SWRG was getting an annual return of 45 percent. In 2002, annual sales reached $140 million.[2] Reportedly, Stillman preferred to leave day-to-day matters to others. "I learned a long time ago to run restaurants as a business and not as a mom-and-pop organization," he told *Crain's New York Business* the year Cité opened. "My managers do a better job of running them than I do."[3]

His managers were "running them" by breaking labor law. The kitchen workers were typically forced to work without breaks, were not paid for overtime, and were unable to take sick days. Largely Mexicans, some undocumented, they were also subject to racist abuse from the chef, who repeatedly screamed at them and called them "fucking wetbacks." In April 2003, a worker made an anonymous call to the Department of Labor (DOL) to report that the company withheld five to ten hours of overtime pay each week and made them work double and triple shifts without additional breaks and wages. The DOL scheduled an inspection for two months later.

The Smith and Wollensky campaign started with a ROC-NY organizer who had once been a waiter at Cité stopping there in search of kitchen workers with grievances that the group could pick up. This outreach was generally the method ROC used to find new campaigns. The organizer immediately met Floriberto Hernandez, an undocumented Mexican who had been a Cité prep cook for fourteen years. Hernandez was a portly man with a broad, easy smile. He told the organizer that the restaurant had been withholding wages from kitchen workers for years.

Hernandez believed that the company knew about the DOL inspection in advance and changed the work schedule so that many of the "trouble" workers would be away during the inspection. Nevertheless, the DOL found that Cité failed to pay overtime amounting to more than $65,000 for a two-year period and violated labor law by not having a time clock. According to the agency's report, a company representative "explained that the company wanted to correct its mistake immediately and promised that all employees they were able to get in contact with were to be paid no later than 10/30/2003." Soon after that, a manager told Hernandez that the corporate offices had ordered the kitchen workers' pay rate reduced by 15 percent. The company then started paying for all hours due, but at the reduced rate.

When Hernandez met with Saru, she immediately recognized Alan Stillman's prominence and got very excited about taking on an industry leader. She told Hernandez that he had to bring in three other workers in order for ROC-NY to invest in their fight. Hernandez returned with sixteen kitchen workers, including his friend Apolinar Salas, who had brown skin and was barely taller than five feet. Salas had led the hardscrabble life of the undocumented for ten years. He couldn't keep a steady job without papers. He'd get one, work until the employer asked for his papers, show his fake Social Security card, wait for the employer to figure out that it was fake, get fired, find another job, and go through the entire cycle again. He wanted to do well in the U.S., he wanted to work, and having to constantly change jobs was terrible. Finally, an employer sponsored him for a green card, which completely changed his life. In 2006 he became a citizen.

At thirty-seven, Salas had been working at Cité for twelve years, having started as a dishwasher and worked his way up to "salad man." Salas was more than game. He was tired of working through lunches and breaks, even during slow periods. He had made an enemy of the chef, who had insisted one day that he wash more dishes even though the dishrack was empty and the lunch service was over. Rather than obeying, Salas told the kitchen manager, who told the chef to back off. Ever since that correction, Salas said, the chef made him do other people's work.

Cité was able to get away with these abuses because the kitchen workers were largely Mexican immigrants. Like Hernandez and Salas, they were also mostly *mixtecas* —of combined indigenous and Spanish heritage—who had been small farmers from the region of Puebla in southern Mexico. Puebla was marked by an enormous gap between the poor and the wealthy, a gap codified into popular Mexican stereotypes that cast wealthy Poblanos as white, tall, and attractive. Poor Poblanos were characterized as the *Pipope*, or *Poblano Pendejo* ("Fucking Pueblan Asshole"), short, dark-skinned, mustached, and hat-wearing—in short, not as clean and handsome as the white Pueblan.[4] Poor Pueblans have always been migrants, either to cities within Mexico or to the United States.

Mexico: Stalled Development and Emigration

It's impossible to comprehend the migration of people like Hernandez and Salas without understanding the effect of economic globalization and internal political decisions on poor Mexicans. Over time, the Mexican government has increasingly moved toward policies designed primarily to attract foreign investment. That shift was meant to stimulate Mexico's economy. It did so for wealthy Mexicans, but it also widened the gap between rich and poor, resulting in lower wages and living standards and forcing poor Mexicans to seek ways to migrate.

The neoliberal pattern played out especially in the agricultural sector. From 1940 to 1955, Mexico developed and subsidized farming. Specifically this included the "provision of guaranteed prices intended to increase the incomes of basic grains producers, and large-scale public investment in rural infrastructure."[5] During this period, agricultural production grew 5.5 percent per year. But growth declined to 3 percent per year during the twenty years that followed, with the most dramatic declines occurring in the late 1960s and 1970s—a time of political unrest, including large student protests against government corruption that peaked with the 1968 slaying of 300 student protesters by Mexican police ten days before the Olympics were scheduled to open. Interestingly, other sectors of the Mexican economy boomed during 1965–72, and migration to the U.S. slowed significantly during that time.

Eventually agricultural productivity slackened, meaning that Mexico could no longer produce all the food it needed for a growing population, and the country started importing grain just as global prices were rising. The government decided to invest in agriculture again in 1973, increasing subsidies from 10 to 20 percent of the national total. These new programs, which included measures like setting a baseline price for corn and creating rural aid programs like health clinics, boosted the economy again.[6]

In part, though, the Mexican government was funding the country by borrowing from other nations against its oil revenues. In 1976 and 1982, there were new economic crises, partly caused by the government's inability to service its foreign debt. Each crisis caused more migration, both internally and to the United States. The 1982 debt crisis led the government to apply for an International Monetary Fund (IMF) loan that would consolidate its debt from multiple countries. The IMF was founded in 1944 to act as a global finance system that could help rebuild war-torn Europe. Its membership now includes 182 countries, with the United States as the largest investor at 17.7 percent of the shares. As the largest investor, the United States also gets the largest portion of returns (the interest paid on IMF loans) and has the power to veto any decision it considers inappropriate.[7]

The IMF agreed to bail out Mexico, but only if Mexico agreed to a "structural adjustment plan," a condition that all borrowers were obliged to accept. Structural adjustment meant that Mexico's government-controlled economy would have to be privatized and deregulated to create a climate favorable to corporations, including foreign investors—the program known as "neoliberalism." By 1989 the share of government subsidies that went to agriculture had fallen by 85 percent. The guaranteed price for maize fell by 3 percent; for beans, by 20 percent. These subsidies have been called "Mexico's de facto rural unemployment and anti-poverty program."[8] There were other changes as well. Loans were no longer granted by the state but by private banks, which shut out peasant farmers because their profit margins are small and the risk of lending to them high. The government sold off utilities such as electricity and water companies to private corporations, further raising the cost of living for poor families. Between 1984 and 1989 extreme poverty among agricultural households increased by 6 percent to affect easily half of Mexico's small farmers.[9]

In 1986 Mexico joined the General Agreement on Tariffs and Trade, which required it to drop its tariffs on imported goods, essentially opening Mexican markets to foreign producers. GATT primarily affected industry and accelerated a long-term trend in favor of large export industries rather than small and medium-sized industries producing for domestic consumption. According to Professor Jonathan Fox, a leading expert on the Mexican economy, "This is essentially what free trade is, to sacrifice domestic-oriented sectors in exchange for export-oriented sectors."[10] Most sectors opened to foreign investment in 1989, starting a wave of privatizations. By 1994, 80 percent of state-owned firms, whose profits had funded public services, had been sold off. The old semi-socialist Mexican government, long controlled by the Institutional Revolutionary Party (PRI), had been troubled with significant corruption, a fact that sparked protests among Mexicans for many years. It's unclear, however, that the neoliberal governments that have been in power since the early 1990s have been either less corrupt or have helped improve conditions for the majority of Mexicans.

By the time NAFTA was being debated in 1993, Mexico was well on its way to conforming to mainstream economic globalization policies, which transfer power to corporate elites but offer very little to labor. NAFTA was designed to facilitate trade and business development within and among the U.S., Canada, and Mexico, and it reduced tax burdens for businesses that wanted to relocate, getting rid of tariffs for traded goods. NAFTA affected small maize farmers by prohibiting the Mexican government from setting a baseline price for corn. U.S. farmers can produce corn more cheaply than small Mexican farmers because they are heavily subsidized by the U.S. government.

Apolinar Salas's Puebla-based family is just the kind that was torn apart by NAFTA and other neoliberal trade agreements. They owned two hectares, or about five acres, on which they had grown corn, beans, and peanuts for at least three generations. His family kept half their crop to eat and sold the other half to wealthy families nearby. The buyer set the price, though, and the family generally got little money—enough to buy school clothes, but not enough to build a house to replace the shack they lived in and never enough to save. Salas followed one of his brothers to New York in 1986, crossing the border while it was still cheap to do so, about $800, and less dangerous than it is today.

Twenty years ago, 90 percent of the corn sold in Mexico was produced by small farmers like Salas with less than five hectares of land. Today, that 90 percent comes from the U.S., at ever increasing prices. Having lost much of their domestic market to U.S. and Canadian agribusiness, small Mexican farmers devoted more effort to home production and barter. But the government supports only production for the market, so the small *campesino* struggling for survival gets less help and the larger farmers get more.[11] The Mexican government's answer to this problem was to push sugar production, which is still subsidized. Silas's family, of course, could not eat sugar cane.

Unions and environmentalists in all three countries resisted NAFTA, wanting the treaty to include guaranteed protections to prevent a corporate-inspired race to the bottom. The Mexican government, for example, routinely and severely punishes labor unions that operate independently of the government. In response, the three countries created supplemental agreements on labor and environment in 1994, but these are widely seen as ineffective throwaways—a fact blithely admitted by Mexican finance minister Jaime Serra Puche in talks to Mexican executives.[12]

Wages actually fell in both Mexico and the U.S. after NAFTA was implemented, while corporate profits rose. In 1975, during the "bad old days" of Mexican isolationism and self-sufficiency, Mexican wages averaged about 23 percent of U.S. wages. In 1993–94, just before NAFTA, they were 15 percent of the U.S. average. In 2002 they averaged 12 percent. The basic cost of living has risen in Mexico: "In 1994 the minimum wage (currently $4.20 per day) bought 44.9 pounds of tortillas. In 2003, it bought 18.6 pounds. In 1994 it bought 24.5 liters of gas for cooking and heats. In 2003, it bought seven."[13] In the United States, worker productivity in manufacturing rose 57 percent between 1993 and 2002 while wages rose a mere 6 percent. The free trade trend continues, now moving eastward. The Sunbeam Corporation, for example, shifted its facilities from Ohio, where workers earned more than $21 an hour, to Matamoros, Mexico, where they earned $2.36 on average. In 2001, the company moved to China, where labor is valued at some 47 cents an hour.[14]

Apolinar Salas saw the effects clearly in New York City, where five of his nine siblings now live, all working in restaurants, and where he routinely runs into former friends from his hometown on the subway. He also noticed the change in Puebla, where there were now paved roads and more houses like the one his family was able to build with the money he sent back, fenced in with a clear space between them.

Color Lines Across the Industry

Hernandez, Salas, and the other Cité workers presented their case to the ROC membership in August 2003, and by September they had started putting into place the eleven-step system for making employers improve working conditions. On October 2, a group of Cité workers and ROC-NY members walked into Cité with a demand letter. The company didn't meet the one-week deadline, and ROC-NY held the first protest during a mid-week lunch rush. Salas and Hernandez picketed with bandanas covering their faces. They were right to worry. After grilling them about their participation in the protests, the chef told the workers that their October 15 paychecks would not be honored. Within eight weeks, three of the kitchen workers were fired.

But October 30 was the company's own deadline for delivering the back wages in the deal they'd made with the DOL. Sameer Ashar, the law professor who ran the immigrant legal assistance clinic at the City University of New York, had assigned his students to work on the case. They did discovery, defended depositions, filed legal complaints and charges with the National Labor Relations Board. Although the company had agreed to pay the DOL-mandated amount of $65,000 by October 30, the state statute of limitations allowed back-wage claims for six years (rather than the Labor Department's two years), and the issues of breaks, sick days, vacation, and retaliation remained to be resolved. Being able to ask a court for larger restitution, though, meant not accepting checks under the current deal with the Labor Department and the company.

The company missed its deadline for writing those checks by a week, giving Ashar enough time to actually serve a lawsuit on behalf of the workers. That day, the chef and a manager met with each worker individually. They showed Salas a check for a portion of what he was owed and ordered him to sign the release form that relieved the company from future claims. Salas, who spoke some English, didn't sign, but a number of the workers did, unclear about whether the release forms were from the company or the Department of Labor.

Later the chef tried to inspect immigration documents. "He asked my boss if my driver's license was really my license or someone else's," Salas said. "He told me that if I didn't have papers, I would be the first one fired."

As the back-of-the-house workers suffered these setbacks, Hernandez, the campaign's undisputed leader, produced an unexpected gift. After the first protest, Leonel Baizan, the restaurant's only Mexican front waiter, had approached him saying that he himself had hired a lawyer to file a discrimination lawsuit over conditions at the front of the house. Saru started calling Baizan to persuade him to attach his case to the larger one.

Ironically, Baizan also had his roots in a Puebla agricultural family, and he was a formerly undocumented immigrant who started out in Cité's kitchen. But he had immigrated as a child and had eventually gotten a green card. A friendly manager had given him a chance to move to the front of the house, and he'd taken it. Although Baizan had actually worked with both Salas and Hernandez and they came from the same region, he had virtually no relationship with them.

If Baizan did sign on, he'd be the first front-of-the-house worker to be represented by ROC-NY, which would allow it to attack the industry's rampant discrimination much more aggressively and comprehensively than it had been able to in the past. While it's relatively easy to show that overtime has not been paid, proving discrimination is far more difficult if you can't compare two workers of different colors in the same job. At the back of the house there are no white people in the lower job categories, so comparisons are impossible. U.S. discrimination law requires victims to prove that employers intentionally passed them over for someone white, or male, or young. The kind of job segregation that just *is*, that exists as a part of an industry's culture, would be almost impossible to prove and remedy through conventional channels such as courts. By adding the complaints of waiters to those of the kitchen workers, ROC-NY could draw attention to—and fight—the common industry practice of reserving the best jobs for whites, highlighting the dynamics that made it impossible for the workers in the kitchen to change their circumstances.

Baizan's mother, Sebila, was born into a family of Pueblan farmers who harvested pumpkin, corn, tomatoes, and sesame seeds. With his mother, stepfather, and younger brother, Baizan started for New York without documents when he was seven. When their *coyote* brought them to the checkpoint they paid $800 to a Border Patrol officer, who then waved them through the turnstile. Three days later they arrived at the Port Authority Bus Terminal and settled in the emerging Mexican community on Manhattan's Upper West Side in 1981. On his first day of school, Baizan's teacher told him that Lionel was his name in English, and that became his name from then on.

When Baizan went to Cité to apply for a job in 1999, he was immediately directed to the food and beverage manager, who took him to the kitchen where a dozen Latinos worked as dishwashers, runners, and prep cooks. Neither he nor Baizan asked any questions, and that was the extent of the application process.

He was introduced to the chef, who taught him where to pick up food, how to read orders, and which sauces went with the steaks. He earned roughly $3.00 per hour, the minimum wage for tipped workers, and split tips evenly with the waiters. He worked hard, often without breaks, and he took on double shifts. Sometimes he didn't get paid fully for the second shift, and he never got overtime.

The chef's behavior made a tough job unbearable. One day, Baizan was too slow to pick up a hot plate from the counter. He couldn't find a napkin to wrap it in. The chef yelled, "Where the fuck is your napkin?" Another busy night, as more than a dozen people ran around the kitchen with hot food and sharp knives, Baizan was about to take food out on a *guéridon*, a three-shelf cart with wheels, when he slipped on the slick floor. He grabbed the end of the *guéridon* instinctively, toppling it. As Baizan lay on his back unable to get up, the chef only yelled that someone should save the food. Baizan started to dream of leaving the kitchen. He would have to get promoted to back waiter, and then to front waiter. The front waiter took drink and wine orders, read the specials, and took the food order. Back waiters took dessert and coffee orders and cleaned the table. The distinctions were based on status rather than money, given the equal division of tips, but the setup gave the front waiter more influence over a diner's high-ticket choices.

Ten months into the job, one of the friendlier managers put Baizan on the floor to see how he'd fare as a waiter. The most difficult part was learning the menu codes for the computer, but soon he was occasionally acting as front waiter. The work suited him. He learned the wines and dramatically described the entrées.

For the most part, Baizan liked the customers. There were small racial incidents, but they didn't intimidate Baizan. Once a young white man came in with ten recent college grads. He greeted Baizan enthusiastically with "Hey, Pancho."

"Hi, Billy!" responded Baizan.

"My name's not Billy!"

"My name's not Pancho, either. It's Lionel and I'm your server today."

Moving up front exposed Baizan to new problems, however. Waiters competed for good schedules and section assignments, which determined how much they earned. Wednesday through Saturday nights were busy, and the best sections could accommodate parties of six or more. He expected a rotation system, but another waiter told him that he would have to pay the managers a portion of his tips to get good assignments, an illegal practice known as "tipping the house." Baizan began giving the managers approximately $100 weekly. When he didn't pay, he found himself demoted to a schedule of three days as runner and two days as back waiter.

Things got worse when the friendly manager moved on, and the new manager quickly set a pattern of giving the most physical work, moving of tables and such, to the Latinos. Those who objected were known to get reduced shifts or a firing, so Baizan stifled many of his concerns. Still, he persisted. He objected when he overheard a white waitress sarcastically offer to translate for an Ecuadoran back waiter's customers. He objected again when a manager ordered Baizan and the runners with a "Hurry up, boys!" and an admonishment not to steal anything; and yet again when a white man whom Baizan had trained was promoted ahead of him to front waiter.

He considered quitting, but wondered why he should run when he was due the same rights as white people. Thinking that he would have to do something, he started collecting floor plans, schedules, pay stubs. He recorded the money he tipped managers and the corresponding assignments. One evening, staring at his empty section, he decided it was time to find a lawyer.

The next day, Baizan searched the Internet for a lawyer specializing in discrimination cases. He randomly called an attorney, described his situation, and went in for a meeting. The lawyer wrote to the company, but never filed a discrimination claim. By then Baizan was getting calls from Saru, but his lawyer dismissed the possibility of connecting with ROC-NY, saying that he didn't work with college students. They met with the company's lawyer, whom his lawyer knew to be a reasonable man with whom they'd certainly be able to make a deal with. After that, though, Baizan found it hard to get his own attorney on the phone. Two months after getting her first call, Baizan told Saru he was ready to join up. The two of them visited other attorneys looking for someone who would take his case pro bono. Two declined before they found one who agreed to prepare charges for the Equal Employment Opportunity Commission.

Protests continued into 2004, but on June 30 Stillman set a new standard for counterattacks, going far beyond the lawyers and the occasional press release used by the others.[15] First, the company filed a defamation suit focused on the picket sign and chant that went, "It's a crime, pay your workers overtime!," a handbill given out during protests, and an e-mail Saru sent to supporters in February. In her e-mail Saru had written:

> Alan Stillman, an abusive employer, not only owes over $200,000 in back wages to 16 workers, but also denies them breaks, tells them "everyone involved in this is going to get fired!" and tells our lawyers that ROC-NY is not legitimate enough to negotiate with. These protests have dropped the restaurant's business to 60% of its original level and have pushed the owners to consider negotiations.

The company objected to every line. The suit argued that such statements implied that Stillman was a criminal, driving diners away and causing him to suffer humiliation, mental anguish, ridicule, and contempt. They noted, however, that the protests had not reduced sales by 60 percent nor forced the company to negotiate. Stillman's lawyers asked for $2,750,000 in special damages on three charges.

First Amendment attorney Kai Falkenberg picked up ROC-NY's case just days before the deadline for answering or moving against the complaint. "This is a classic SLAPP suit," said Falkenberg, referring to the "strategic lawsuit against public participation"—a tactic "that companies use to shut off protest. They're absolutely illegal in New York State." In her motion to dismiss, Falkenberg argued that the statements were part of an obvious labor protest and protected as an expression of opinion; that the company did owe back wages, according to the Department of Labor report; that the National Labor Relations Board had filed charges against the company; and that the NLRB regional director himself had written a letter to Cité stating, "This lawsuit was arguably filed in retaliation for protected concerted activity." The defamation suit was dismissed.

Saru then had the idea of getting more workers from the Park Avenue Café, Stillman's other holding, to expand the campaign's base. She put Siby on the case. Since most Mexican restaurant workers seemed to come from the region of Puebla, Siby told Hernandez, maybe they should work through Hernandez's social and family contacts to find Park Avenue Café workers. That strategy worked, and the two of them recruited two Mexicans and a Bangladeshi from the Park Avenue Café kitchen within a couple of weeks.

Saru also asked a friend of the organization who had gone to high school with Stillman's son Michael to try to arrange a meeting, and the company finally agreed in May 2004. Saru and Mamdouh met Michael Stillman and President Eugene Zuriff at a Cosi Café near Union Square. They used the meeting to deliver a new demand letter from the Park Avenue Café workers.

Zuriff offered $50,000 to make the problem go away, but said explicitly that they didn't intend to do anything about the discrimination charges. Saru and Mamdouh said they would talk to the workers about it and asked for another meeting, to which Zuriff agreed. Instead of attending another meeting, the company filed new NLRB charges alleging that ROC-NY was a union in disguise trying to organize workers illegally. Alan Stillman then wrote to their foundation supporters urging them to stop funding a group that had so clearly overstepped its purpose of "helping victims of September 11." Disappointed, Saru renewed the campaign with the first Park Avenue Café protest, which Baizan attended. Weekly protests continued.

That summer, Saru joined Mamdouh's family for part of their annual vacation to Morocco. Saru had set a goal of visiting a new country every year, and she had never been to Morocco. She accompanied the whole family to Fez, where she and Mamdouh bickered over whether to stay in an air-conditioned modern hotel with a pool (his choice, given that the temperature in Fez in July nears 100 degrees) or a traditional *riad* (her choice). He won, and she went out for a walk to clear her head. She went to an international phone center, just a small room really, to check her messages. One of them said that there was terrible news about Floriberto Hernandez, who had started the whole campaign. He was dead. She ran back to the hotel to tell Mamdouh and the two went back together to the phone booth to call the office. Office manager Rosa Fana told her that Hernandez had died alone in his apartment of a sudden onset of adult diabetes. Feeling thirsty, he drank several cans of Coke and died of dehydration within hours. Like most back-of-the-house workers,

Hernandez had no health insurance, so he had no idea that he had diabetes. Saru wrote to his sister in Mezahulcoyotl, Mexico. "Floriberto Hernandez was a great leader in our organization, a leader that organized his co-workers to fight for their rights, and the rights of all workers. As a human being he was always cheerful, charming, gentle, and positive, and we can never forget him." She wrote that she kept an enlarged photo, which was the size of a poster, on her office wall next to pictures of Gandhi and Che.

Hernandez's death was especially sad because by then Saru could see the end of the Cité campaign coming. The company had started making small changes and negotiating. Managers announced that tipping the house was illegal and would stop immediately. Baizan's abusive manager left the staff. Progress stalled for months over $37,000 in back wages, but the company agreed to a host of antidiscrimination measures, including not using immigration status as a threat.

They almost lost Baizan during that period in spite of these changes. Frustrated and scared and telling no one, he arranged a meeting with a company representative. The workers had agreed to talk to the company only in a group and only to assert ROC-NY as their representative, but Baizan hoped to speed up the process and resolve what felt like an unstable situation. He thought that if he didn't make any agreements, it would be all right.

The representative took Baizan into an office under renovation and sat in a chair across from him. Baizan talked about his experience, proud to tell his story directly. The other man sympathized, promised to make things right, and asked him to drop the discrimination charges.

Simultaneously relieved and confused, Baizan called Saru. He was considering dropping the charges, especially if he could get moved to another restaurant. "It seems like we might not even get any money for the discrimination," he said, "and it's just dragging on. It doesn't seem like it's worth it."

"If you leave now, Leonel, there are no guarantees at all that they're going to do anything differently," Saru said, talking fast from her corner desk in the crowded ROC-NY office. "We're close, we're so close to getting everything, to negotiating job security. What's to keep them from firing you after a little while to make sure you don't make any more trouble? You said you were in this for the whole thing, Leonel—please, please don't drop out now."

"I don't know, Saru. Things are so tense, I just want it to be over," he said.

"The company is playing games," she said. "They said they'd talk if we stopped the protests, and then they don't come to meetings. They're stalling, hoping that more of you guys will just drop off."

After thirty minutes of wrangling, he agreed. "OK, I'll stay in."

In December 2004, the thing that no one thought would ever happen did. The circumstances were never clear, but the executive chef was replaced by one of the sous-chefs. Just after Christmas, Saru received a call at her family's home in Southern California. The company was ready to settle. For weeks, she and the law students had been in daily contact with their lawyers, again stuck on that $37,000 and on internal posting of jobs before external advertising, so she was enormously relieved to wrap up their longest campaign. The settlement included $164,000 in back wages and damages, but more important, a number of protections for the workers. They now had an employee manual, half an hour for lunch, a time clock, five sick days per year, and paid vacation. The company agreed not to fire anyone for a year, and after that to fire only with three days' notice to ROC. Finally, management agreed to post job openings internally for one week before making them public.

Saru began the long struggle to get Hernandez's portion of the settlement, several thousand dollars, to his family in Mexico. The State Department wouldn't allow the company to release it except to Hernandez's relatives, who had no way of coming to get the money. Without documents, Hernandez hadn't risked visiting his family in the fifteen years that he had been sending money home, and they knew virtually nothing about his life in the U.S.

The Restaurant Industry Summit

The same month they won the Stillman campaign, ROC-NY's other major project was also reaching its culmination point. The research project they had been doing for three years was finally finished. They planned to release the hefty report at a Restaurant Industry Summit set for January 25, 2005. The staff had spent months organizing workers, owners, scholars, and politicians to speak and attend; the owner of the Captain's Ketch, a seafood restaurant in the Financial District, had offered its dining room for the event. The report got good early press in the *Daily News* and the *New York Times*, and the *Times* also ran a Public Lives profile of Saru. The reporter noted her impressive list of degrees and skills, her "high-pitched" squeal of a laugh, and her discomfort with being cast as the "leader" of restaurant workers.

Saru spent the day before the Industry Summit entirely on the phone. She called restaurateurs to make sure they were ready to do their parts, soothing those who felt nervous at the last minute about criticizing their own industry. She gave an interview to a small Indian paper, whose reporter asked questions that made it seem she had never eaten in an American restaurant. Saru took a call from a producer at *Queer Eye for the Straight Guy*, who wanted to give makeovers to Windows survivors who were starting the new cooperative restaurant. "You'll never believe who just called!" she told the staff, laughing. "Oh, there's my squeal," she said, laughing a little harder.

The next day, 200 people crammed themselves into the underground dining room at the Captain's Ketch. ROC-NY had turned out restaurant owners and managers, unions, City Council members, bankers, scholars, and workers. Even the president of the New York State Restaurant Association came. The event left an abiding impression of ROC-NY's professionalism. The report, *Behind the Kitchen Door*, laid out a challenge. The industry was growing. It produced large profits for many, given the fact that 24 of the top 100 highest-grossing restaurants in the United States in 2002 were located in New York City.[16] But its benefits weren't equally shared, with half of restaurant workers earning less than $10 an hour. Restaurant wages had in fact stagnated over the last ten years in comparison to wages in other business sectors.

The industry kept a great portion of its workforce, arguably the two-thirds who were immigrant workers, in the back of the house and away from opportunities, both by tolerating a great deal of labor law abuse and by discriminating against them. In interviews, employers revealed widespread ignorance of labor law and racial assumptions about who could do which job. One interviewee from the fine-dining category said, "Look, you've seen the studies—the taller, more attractive people make more money.... What I look for in the back of the house is talent, and a good work ethic.... But certainly, for the front of the house—those you see when you first come in—they have to be attractive. I just hired last year's Miss Oregon as one of our hostesses."

That's hardly explicit racism, but the overwhelming lack of color among waitstaff indicates that managers equate attractiveness with being white. For the back of the house, employers listed the elements of a "good work ethic" as "willingness to work long hours for low wages, perform tasks that others were not willing to, and work under poor working conditions." Only one made race explicit: "Kitchen is hard work. Latinos—they're good workers."[17]

Kitchen work is also low-wage, dangerous labor. Eighty percent of the 530 workers surveyed for the report earned 150 percent less than the federal poverty line for a family of four. The injury rate is high, from fire hazards such as blocked doors and nonfunctioning fire extinguishers, missing guards on cutting machines, and floors without mats to prevent slipping: "Almost half of workers surveyed had suffered work-related cuts on at least one occasion (46 percent), 38 percent had been burned on the job, and 23 percent had come into contact with toxic chemicals. Nineteen percent reported that they had slipped and injured themselves while at work. Additionally, 16 percent reported chronic pain that was caused or worsened by their job."[18] The report also demonstrated the prevalence of racial abuse in the industry: 65 percent of the workers surveyed said they had observed or experienced verbal disparagement.

The report pointed out the public and social costs of these conditions, from forcing injured people to work to the lack of health insurance. Thirty-one percent reported having done something as a result of time pressure that might have put the health and safety of the customer at risk. There were some stomach-turning examples—a man who had cut his finger deeply and was told to keep working, and another who had worked while he had the flu.

The event established ROC-NY as a sophisticated organization with the potential to reach throughout the industry. At the end, Saru announced the launch of the Restaurant Industry Roundtable, a new alliance that would include restaurant workers' organizations and employers working together to make things better.

Roseanne Martino, one of the employers interviewed for the report, was among the first to join. For twelve years, Martino had been the general manager of One if by Land, Two if by Sea, a formal restaurant in the West Village. She had a stake in stopping labor abuse in the industry because it tilted the playing field to the benefit of cheaters. Martino figured that 90 percent of employers—including some very famous restaurants—break basic labor law because it's their most effective way to cut costs.

Martino also maintained that many restaurant owners simply did not know the law. When she started at One if by Land as comptroller she was utterly overwhelmed by the huge number of minute regulations and hidden expenses. The restaurant had operated for twenty years with a manual that ignored the regulations and included statements like "No one ever gets fired. You fire yourself by not following the rules!" The rules depended a great deal on who the manager was at the time, with the owner sometimes oblivious. For years, her own accountants used to tell her that their management costs were too high—why didn't she just let the managers take a cut off the tips, since that's what everybody else did? "Because it's totally illegal!" Martino would reply.

Martino appreciated the Restaurant Industry Roundtable as a place where workers and employers could come together to solve the industry's problems. She felt that she didn't have to lie about the challenges of running a restaurant. "They really try to help you. They don't judge you and they're not a government agency that's going to slap a $1,000 fine on you that you can't afford to pay," she said. ROC had lifted up the carpet and exposed everything people had been hiding for years, and Martino didn't think they should be punished for that. About two years later, Alan Stillman closed down Cité and the industry press blamed ROC-NY for causing that and other shutdowns. Reflecting on that accusation, Martino said, "There are a lot of people who have made a great deal of money on the backs of their workers. Maybe the corporations are going down, but I'm sure the owner isn't."

The Roundtable decided to produce a comprehensive manual to educate employers about health and labor requirements, which Martino thought was critically important. After a year of extended negotiations, the Health Department agreed to give it to everyone who applied for a restaurant license. The Roundtable also began to craft legislation that would make an explicit link between the treatment of workers and the safety of customers by making repeated labor law violations a factor in renewing business licenses, which are awarded by the Health Department.

The Industry Summit's success depended on convincing other restaurant employers that they, too, had a stake in stopping labor abuse. It took the organization three years of work by many staff members and dozens of members, plus the efforts of the senior leadership of two allied organizations, to complete a comprehensive study. By telling the stories of workers and employers in the same place, they revealed the scale of the problem and its effect on the public in a fair and irrefutable way. They could then turn their attention to crafting systemwide interventions in the way business is done.

This expansive movement stood in stark contrast to the situation in the cooperative restaurant project, which erupted in further conflict a month later. While the co-op framed its movement in relation to the past, these activities were completely future-oriented. While the co-op debated limits on who would benefit, ROC in general was looking for ways to meet a wide range of self-interests, both financial and political. The organization's inclusiveness also differed from the emerging tone of the national debate on immigration policy. The systemic change that would make the greatest difference to low-wage immigrant workers, so many of whom were undocumented, was legalization. But while ROC was making more room in New York City for the immigrant voice, Congress and the national media were quickly limiting their ability to influence the policy debate. Like the co-op group, they constantly evoked September 11, using it also to define who belonged and who didn't, not in the ownership of a restaurant, but in the country itself.

Chapter 7

FRAMING THE IMMIGRATION DEBATE

The scope of public policy debates is determined by two things: how they are framed and who does the framing. Frames create a boundary around the discussion, defining the problem, locating responsibility, and influencing which technical proposals get a hearing and which are pushed to the margins. Frames rely on images, myths, and stories that signal a society's moral aspirations and standards. Frames consist of both images and ideas; using the two, framers stake out their positions. Who does the framing matters because framers can cut certain ideas and people out of the debate.

Photography provides a useful metaphor. The photographer decides what deserves to be seen, then sets the lens to a wide angle or zooms in to take the photo. Depending on how the photographer uses light, he or she can make a figure appear to be menacing or innocent or lonely. Public policy discourse works in the same way—if we take a broad view of a particular problem, the solutions we create will likely be larger and more ambitious. As the frame narrows, proposed solutions are limited as well. Some people are considered legitimate participants in the debate, while others are left out of the picture entirely.

Many people try to frame debates, but not all have the power to do so. There are multiple sources of power: money, access to lawmakers, media, voting, art, and protest are just a few.

As the immigration policy debate advanced in the years after September 11, its frames were largely determined by restrictionists and the business community. Restrictionists viewed the problem as one of criminality, while corporations viewed it as one of labor supply. Politicians fell into line behind one of these two frames, with only a few notable exceptions. Other players weighed in, including unions and immigrant rights organizations, but their power to influence the frame was limited. Immigrants themselves were largely shut out of the mainstream debate, and eventually they reacted by using protest, the only substantial power at their disposal.

The restrictionists had some significant advantages. Their ranks included people with traditional power, including well-funded think tanks and lobbyists, grassroots organizations representing U.S. citizens who could vote, and leaders in both major political parties. These organizations also had expansive access to the media, who repeated their catch phrases over the national airwaves. Their representations of the immigrant as lawbreaker and terrorist had been well established, even before September 11. They used the sacralized memory of the 9/11 attacks to reinforce the notion that a real American was a white American and to divide those Americans from the people they perceived as foreigners. Through the combination of rhetoric and policy proposals, they froze an image of the ideal American: white, Christian, born here, speaking only English, never needing a helping hand, faithfully obeying every law and regulation, and never asking for a second chance. Challenged by the fact that just about the entire country had roots in other countries around the globe, the restrictionists responded, "But our ancestors came here legally," conveniently forgetting that large numbers of their own ancestors were also once "illegal."

This frame gave restrictionists a large number of policy arenas in which they could apply their ideas. They got involved in regulating driver's licenses, militarizing the border, keeping immigrants out of public schools and colleges, preventing them from accessing public health insurance programs, and much more. Whatever specific policy debate they engaged, their solutions were all about enforcement. Immigrants had little place to speak in debates led by restrictionists—after all, only honest American citizens should be allowed to debate policy. Quickly winning a number of policies on their agenda, and having effectively isolated not just the undocumented but all immigrants, restrictionists like Mark Krikorian began to expand their policy goals to include severely limiting "mass" immigration, which really meant the immigration of poor people.

The business community used the frame of labor supply. Immigrants are workers, they argued, and the policy task facing us is one of easing their ability to work. Their primary solution was legalization of the undocumented people living in the country now, but legalization didn't necessarily mean a path to citizenship. For some people in this camp, guest worker programs that provided temporary legal status were enough. The more liberal demand here was for a program through which undocumented immigrants could pay fines, wait in lines, and eventually get a green card. Green cards are for permanent residents. Immigrants must have one for five years before they can apply for citizenship. Like the restrictionists, the business community had some real advantages—strong lobbies, relationships with politicians, and enough money to make hefty campaign contributions top the list.

The labor supply frame is less overtly dehumanizing than the criminality frame, but it has some important limitations. It implies that an immigrant's primary identity, and the only important one for the purposes of this debate, is as a worker. That identity doesn't allow immigrants to be social and political beings as well. Only immigrants who are perceived as hard workers have a right to speak in this debate—if they're too young to work, or too old, or simply unemployed, they have no standing. This frame enables labor unions to get into the debate because they represent immigrants who work, but organizations representing other immigrant populations have a hard time getting any attention.

Immigrants themselves, then, were largely shut out of the debate, especially those without documents. Huge portions of immigrant communities have not received citizenship or are too young to vote. Their representatives in national debates, advocates like Cecilia Muñoz, had some ability to speak, but only within the boundaries of criminality and corporate needs for labor. As conservatives pushed relentlessly for enforcement, Muñoz and her colleagues were forced to adopt the mantra of "comprehensive" immigration reform, that is, reform that went somewhere beyond enforcement. Eventually, a compromise Senate bill got significant attention in 2005, and even passed the Senate in 2006, but ultimately failed to become law.

To compete for influence in this difficult situation, immigrants themselves had to find their own source of power. They didn't have a lot of money, and large numbers of them couldn't vote, so they used protest to insert themselves into the frame. The scale of these protests was enormous, revealing how deeply immigrants felt the attacks, and how long they had waited for an outlet. Although there was a backlash, the marches also forced into visibility significant numbers of people who supported legalization and immigrant rights, from church leaders to newspaper editorial boards. Though they didn't shift the debate enough to win a legalization program, nor even enough to defeat many terrible proposals, they did prevent one restrictionist bill from passing. More important, the demonstrations sent the message that immigrants had a voice and they were prepared to use it.

The climate was too hostile, however, for anyone, including immigrants themselves, to take the debate to a higher level. The dominant frames of crime and work, which in turn influenced the actual policies being debated, didn't allow immigrants to claim a fuller humanity that would entitle them not just to come to the U.S. and work, but also to come and *be*. There was virtually no discussion of immigrants as actual members of U.S. society, as potential citizens. That frame would have allowed immigrants to direct the debate away from enforcement and toward a complete overhaul of the policy direction that forced so many into becoming "illegal." These solutions would have streamlined the immigration process, raised the number of green cards available, and eased family reunification. But even in 2007 all that was far beyond the boundaries of congressional debate. Neither was there any discussion of the global economic and political conditions that have driven so many immigrants to the United States. Without a frame that emphasized their full humanity, immigrants couldn't effectively counter the argument that their interests were fundamentally opposed to those of Americans.

Battles in Congress

President Bush himself had reintroduced the immigration issue in his 2004 State of the Union address.[1] Having started two wars in two years, he had spent little time on domestic policy for most of his first term, and the fact that he continually returned to immigration gave some indication of the pressure he faced from the business community to give corporations a legal way to meet their labor needs. Bush's approach, however, revealed how much the debate had changed. Before September 11, 2001, he had talked about legalizing undocumented immigrants. Two and a half years later, he proposed a guest worker program through which employers could sponsor immigrants for renewable three-year visas. The plan did not allow guest workers to apply for permanent residency, nor did it require employers to offer any more than the minimum wage, even if current wages in that job sector were much higher. Rather than providing green cards, which would have given the people already in the U.S. the rights and privileges of legal immigrants and opened a path to citizenship, this guest worker model would create a permanent underclass of people with only temporary rights to be here, which employers had to continually renew. As soon as someone lost their employer, they would again become illegal.

Cecilia Muñoz hated this proposal but took it as an opportunity to start talking about the need for a proper legalization. The context wasn't positive, however, and two things in particular made it worse. The wars in Afghanistan and Iraq had created plenty of space for defining the un-American Other. As the federal government defended its practice of ignoring international human rights standards while torturing prisoners of war, the conservative media supported that move by dehumanizing the image of Arabs and Muslims. Secondly, the 9/11 Commission's focus on the fact that six of the nineteen hijackers had overstayed visas and held driver's licenses gave restrictionists a chance to emphasize their foreignness and to cast any immigrant trying to get a driver's license as a potential terrorist. Even in this hostile environment, Muñoz began to work on some key bills that would move legalization. The most important were the DREAM Act, which would legalize undocumented youth so they could go to college, and a compromise bill that combined enforcement with legalization.

Restrictionists set the tone for the rest of the year with the first bill of 2005. At the end of January, Representative James Sensenbrenner (R-Wis.), chair of the House Judiciary Committee, introduced what became known as the Real ID Act as part of a military appropriations bill. The act would have the most profound effect on the driver's license issue, since it established national standards for state-issued licenses and ID cards. Among these changes, states would have to verify a person's legal status, set licenses to expire when tourist visas did, and modernize their technology. Real ID also changed the rules for asylum seekers and refugees, requiring them to provide documented proof of danger. Human Rights First protested that forcing asylum seekers to instruct their families at home to gather proof, such as documentation of threats, medical records, and the like, would endanger those families and ultimately force many to return to the likelihood of torture and death. Finally, the act required local police to participate in running sweeps of illegal immigrants to enforce federal immigration laws, and more than $2 billion would go to build new fences across sections of the U.S.–Mexico border. The House passed the Real ID Act in February, with only eight Republicans opposing it.

The first pro-legalization bill was also introduced in the House, providing a marked contrast to Sensenbrenner's approach. Representative Sheila Jackson Lee (D-Tex.) took a bold step in introducing the Save America Comprehensive Immigration Act of 2005. Jackson Lee, a member of the Congressional

Black Caucus and the fourth-ranking Democrat on the House Immigration Subcommittee, framed legalization "as a civil rights issue, to give a sense of fairness to individuals who had been in this country and had worked and paid taxes and wanted to come from under the shadows." The bill had "Comprehensive" in the title, but it bore no resemblance to the other compromise proposals.

Jackson Lee's ambitiously progressive proposal would have allowed the legalization of immigrants who had been in the United States for five or more years, provided they were of good moral character, enrolled in English-language classes, and completed a community service requirement. The bill focused heavily on families, making it easier to naturalize children and raising family sponsorship numbers. It generally increased the number of green cards available every year while protecting immigrants from having government entities report their status to the immigration service. Its enforcement mechanisms were largely targeted at punishing human traffickers and making sure that the Department of Justice ensured due process rights for undocumented people. It reversed parts of the 1996 Welfare Reform Act to restore immigrants' eligibility for certain public benefits. Most strikingly, it had no guest worker program—it just authorized issuance of more green cards. The Jackson Lee bill had twenty-four co-sponsors and gave heart to immigration progressives, but Muñoz knew it was too generous to go very far. It was passed from the Immigration Subcommittee to the Judiciary Committee, which, controlled by Republicans, never even debated it.

Less than a week later, just a day after the Senate also passed the Real ID Act, Senators John McCain (R-Ariz.) and Edward Kennedy (D-Mass.) introduced legislation that had occupied at least 50 percent of Muñoz's time over the last two years. The McCain-Kennedy comprehensive immigration bill became a landmark piece of legislation that incorporated three components: legalization, a guest worker plan, and enforcement. Its legalization portions differed from Jackson Lee's by making the process more rigorous. Undocumented people would get six-year visas; then, after they had paid back taxes and a fine and had proven their English skills, they could apply for permanent residency, providing the path to citizenship for which Muñoz had been waiting. Its guest worker provisions differed from Bush's because it allowed workers to apply for permanent residency after four years.

The bill had a broad array of support. Senators Sam Brownback (R-Kans.) and Joe Lieberman (I-Conn.) were at the press conference, and the U.S. Chamber of Commerce, the Service Employees International Union, the American

Immigration Lawyers Association, and the National Restaurant Association. Even Tamar Jacoby of the conservative Manhattan Institute joined the list.

The alarmist "amnesty" cries in reaction to the McCain-Kennedy bill were even more intense than those confronting President Bush because of the path to citizenship. On May 13, Mark Krikorian's column in *National Review Online* was subtitled "The McCain/Kennedy Amnesty." He ridiculed the enforcement provisions, which he said consisted of plans to make plans. "It's like John Kerry going duck hunting," he wrote. "He's wearing the right outfit, but he's obviously insincere."[2] Krikorian also didn't approve of the plan to have the Labor Department, rather than ICE, administer the Social Security verification work for employers; he argued that they should simply expand the program that ICE had developed over ten years. He gave a nod to the bipartisan support, but pointed to signs in the other direction—the rise of the Minutemen, who had just gotten an endorsement from California Governor Arnold Schwarzenegger, and the passage of the Real ID Act. These things, he wrote, "are all signs that the McCain-Kennedy amnesty bill may well be the last gasp of the anti-borders crowd."[3]

The word *amnesty* comes from the Latin *amnestia*, meaning oblivion or not remembering. In English law it came to mean "a general overlooking or pardon of past offenses by a ruling authority," especially to be applied when a reconciliation was needed. Possibly the world's most famous cases are those of South Africa, when the post-apartheid Mandela government established the Truth and Reconciliation Commission, promising freedom from prosecution to people who had committed murder, torture, and other crimes during the previous era, as long as they confessed.

As always, Muñoz formulated her response to the amnesty frame by calling her demand legalization instead. This time she could list all the provisions that made it not an amnesty but rather a way of making things right. Undocumented people had to pay a fine and back taxes. In press interviews, Muñoz referred to the many other transgressions that we allow people to remedy, like breaking the speed limit or not paying taxes. She reminded audiences that the entire country colludes in the transgression; anyone who eats in a restaurant or stays in a hotel depends on undocumented workers, whether we acknowledge them or not. The system was indeed broken, she agreed, and legalization was the best way to fix it.

The Senate never voted on the McCain-Kennedy bill in 2005 because there wasn't enough support to get it out of committee. However, it would provide the core ideas for future comprehensive immigration bills, although these would have far more enforcement and less generous legalization. By December 2005, however, Muñoz faced another threat. For weeks, she had known that Sensenbrenner was planning to introduce an enforcement-only immigration bill that she expected would be draconian. Normally, a Congress member introduces a bill, gathers co-sponsors, and collects reactions through hearings and study. That period gives the rest of Congress and advocates a chance to comment, including proposing amendments. The bill is then "marked up" with any changes the sponsor agrees with, then sent to the House floor. All this usually takes weeks or even months, but Sensenbrenner kept his bill tightly under wraps, preventing anyone in Muñoz's circle from seeing a draft. He introduced it on December 9, it was marked up the next day, and pushed through to a floor vote within a week.

HR 4437, or the Sensenbrenner bill, as it came to be known, proposed a number of enforcement measures, including stepped-up employer sanctions and $2 billion for a border fence. But it was one of its smaller provisions that particularly preoccupied Muñoz. Sensenbrenner proposed changing the law to make it a felony to be in the country without authorization. Currently, crossing the border is a misdemeanor, and remaining in the country is a civil violation, a matter of immigration bureaucracy. Going even further, Sensenbrenner included a clause making it a felony to "harbor" undocumented people.

The day after the bill was introduced, Muñoz's colleague Michelle Waslin stopped at her office. She was particularly alarmed by the felony clause, since it opened the door to further criminalizing not just of immigrants, but any organization that provided services to undocumented people. The two had decided to focus attention on this criminalization clause, but other immigration advocates questioned whether the bill really intended to do what its language implied.

The difference between current law and the bill was slight. If played out to a not-so-extreme conclusion, however, the bill would implicate all private social service agencies providing any kind of support without checking papers, including the Catholic Church and ROC-NY. There was not only the possibility that the authorities would draw conclusions lawmakers didn't intend, but that, once alerted, those same lawmakers would in fact find it a good idea. Waslin and Muñoz called around to confirm their understanding and decided to move ahead with the alarm. Muñoz told the *Atlanta Journal-Constitution* that the bill broadened the definition of smuggling and harboring illegal aliens so much that groups caring for dehydrated border crossers in the desert could be arrested. "It potentially criminalizes acts of kindness," she said, warning the GOP of the risk to itself in unusually frank language. "Republicans pull those kinds of stunts at their own peril," she said. "Those are in-your-face, ugly proposals that my community won't soon forget."[4] Muñoz didn't typically use polarizing language, but she needed to arouse some fear of Latino voters among members of Congress.

The next few days were particularly dramatic. On December 9 Sensenbrenner called for a floor vote. Despite the importance of the vote, Muñoz couldn't be on Capitol Hill. Her childhood friend was performing in the "Christmas Revels," an annual folk music show, which the family never missed. The performer's family was staying at her house, and Muñoz's husband was away, as was her cousin, who might have taken the girls. Muñoz had to go.

In the car on the way to the show, she got a call from two members of the Congressional Hispanic Caucus. They told her that rumors of the Democratic Party caving in to Sensenbrenner were true. All week the advocates had been calling the Democratic Party leadership to get them to "whip" the bill. On high-priority bills, party leaders call Democrats to urge a yes or no and to ascertain their intentions. The party refused to treat this bill as such a priority, so Muñoz and her colleagues had decided to whip the bill themselves. She herself had called the office of Rahm Emanuel (D-Ill.), who controlled the party's investment in close races and who had pledged to oppose the bill; a staffer assured her that Emanuel was going to vote no. As they called other congressional aides asking how their bosses were going to vote, they started hearing that members wanted to vote no but that Emmanuel had been telling the members of Frontline—the ten Democrats facing the toughest races—to vote *yes*. He wanted to avoid giving Republican challengers a chance to call Democrats "soft on illegal immigration."

Throughout the evening, Muñoz was on her Blackberry—the only time in five years she had broken her vow not to use it during family events. As she hunched over it furiously tapping out e-mails to colleagues at the Capitol during intermission, a neighbor-friend shook her head and sent Muñoz a chastising look. At 7:30, congressional staffers reported watching Rep. John Salazar (D-Colo.) agonizing over his vote, standing with Emanuel on one side and two Hispanic Caucus members on the other. By 9:00 p.m., the bill had passed, 239 to 182. Not one of the Frontline members had voted no, although Emanuel had.

Even Mark Krikorian, who praised the bill and was an enforcement-only man, thought Sensenbrenner had overreached, albeit unintentionally, by making the first illegal entry a felony. "Politically, it seemed like overkill to a lot of people," he commented. Nevertheless, the Sensenbrenner bill passed the House on December 12 in a highly polarized atmosphere. The Congressional Hispanic Caucus accused House Democratic leaders of forcing Frontline members to vote yes. Muñoz added her voice, this time applying the electoral pressure on Democrats as she had done on Republicans. "We were disappointed in leadership on both sides of the aisle. Republicans brought up a bill that was extraordinary in its ugliness ... but frankly there is also some real disappointment at Democratic leadership, particularly those urging Frontline members to support this bill," she said. "There was no evidence to suggest that this was the correct political move.... We intend to hold both sides accountable."[5] Editorials around the country condemned the bill as mean-spirited and ineffective.

"We Are America"

As restrictionists gained the upper hand in Congress, immigrants had to find another source of power both to prevent the Sensenbrenner bill from passing and to revive the legalization discussion.

While D.C. advocates like Muñoz were attempting to hold down Congress and the national press, their sister network of grassroots immigrant rights groups, organized into a formation called the Fair Immigration Reform Movement (FIRM), planned a series of marches around the country. They adopted the slogan "We Are America," which became the name of the mainstream coalition to oppose Sensenbrenner and demand comprehensive reform. They called marches around the country, starting with Washington, D.C.

On March 8, Muñoz arrived in a cab at the Capitol to a roar the size of 40,000 people rather than the 5,000 to 20,000 they had aimed for. She knew that Sensenbrenner's staff could hear the huge march. She thought he must be shocked at the reaction his little clause had generated. Over the next two weeks, immigrants took to the streets against HR 4437, in crowds ranging from a few hundred in downtown Cleveland to an astounding 750,000 in Los Angeles. Some tens of thousands conducted a work stoppage in Georgia. Police and organizer estimates diverged (by as much as 400,000 people in Chicago), but the reaction was intense by any count.

On March 26, Muñoz went up against Sensenbrenner himself on a Sunday morning news show. She often turned down appearances on such shows to preserve some semblance of a normal family life, but this was too good an opportunity. She sat alone in a small, cold studio room on a leather chair with a spotlight and camera trained on her. As was her custom, she went into a silent meditation for five minutes, knowing that she would have to listen carefully since she could not see the host or her opponent's body language. As soon as the introductions were over, Sensenbrenner began invoking rhetoric that played to fears of hordes of foreigners taking over the United States.

"One of the reasons we have 11 million illegal aliens in this country is because we haven't enforced the immigration law for a very long time. And if we don't do anything about it, demographics say that we will have 30 million illegal aliens in this country in ten years. They will flood our schools, they will flood our hospitals and overtax our social services."

"Chairman Sensenbrenner's bill," Muñoz shot back, "doubles what we did ten years ago when we passed an enforcement-only bill, and if enforcement by itself did the job, we wouldn't be having this debate right now. There are 11 million people living and working in the United States. This bill ultimately does nothing about that. We really need to deal with that reality if we're going to have a law that's effective and that works."

Muñoz challenged Sensenbrenner's frame with her own. She presented an image of immigrants as community members and as workers to counter Sensenbrenner's images of criminal aliens. Shifting the image allowed her to raise the question of larger immigration reform. Her primary goal was to use Sensenbrenner's politically overreaching idea to argue that legalization would be a good thing and to raise the question of broader immigration reform. "There's no amnesty on the table in this debate. What's wrong with the chairman's bill is that he criminalizes all 11 million people who are here, it criminalizes those who offer help and charity to those people. That's the wrong approach." Muñoz predicted that the implementation of this law would guarantee a growing undocumented population, as most enforcement measures had throughout U.S. history.

Sensenbrenner denied responsibility for creating a divisive atmosphere, blaming the debate's rising heat instead on the protests. "It's not the bill that has created the climate," he said. "It's the fact that we have not enforced our immigration laws, and we have 11 million illegal aliens in this country.... I'm sorry that we have all of these demonstrations. They're the ones that are toning up the rhetoric."

Criticisms like Sensenbrenner's, though, had no effect on the quickly and spontaneously growing local mobilizations, which were riding high on a new organizing model. In late March, Cardinal Mahoney of Los Angeles declared that he would direct church employees not to comply with the new law if it passed. On March 27, dubbed "Black Monday," 125,000 students across the country walked out of middle schools and high schools, marched to city halls, and blocked freeway traffic. They organized each other through text messaging and social networking Websites, inventing an entirely new activist mode of operation. Within days, similar student walkouts took place everywhere. Several hundred in Aurora, Illinois. Three thousand in Las Vegas. Hundreds of young people were charged with truancy.

Muñoz's friends called her from all over the country marveling at the phenomenon. Marches continued for another two months. On April 10 alone, they involved at least 1 million people in 102 cities nationwide: 100,000 in Phoenix and New York; 75,000 in Fort Myers, Florida; 25,000 in San Jose, California; 10,000 in Indianapolis and Lexington, Kentucky; 1,000 in Pensacola, Florida. Muñoz kept her daughters out of school for their local march, as did thousands of other parents. The press was filled with images of children wearing signs saying, "My mother is not a criminal." More marches followed on May 1.

The backlash was immediate and intense. Both conservatives and liberals echoed the message that the marches were needlessly polarizing. The anecdotal presence of Mexican and other national flags fed the accusations that Mexicans were trying to destroy the border. There were counterprotests organized by the Federation for American Immigration Reform and the Minutemen. In San Diego, 200 people built a six-foot-high, quarter-mile-long section of barbed wire fencing along the border. Minutemen founder Jim Gilchrist showed up at an anti-legalization rally in Colorado and vowed to add 500,000 new members to the group. Filling in for Bill O'Reilly, Tony Snow, who later became the White House press secretary, called the pro-immigration marchers those "who want to engage in racial and national separatism." That charge was ironic, considering the multiracial sweep of many of the marches. Although the marchers were predominantly Latino, they were joined by Irish, Polish, Russian, Chinese, Cambodian, Bangladeshi, Senegalese, Ivoirian, and West Indian immigrants, especially in Seattle, Chicago, and New York. It was Americans, not immigrants, who were so focused on creating division and encouraging separation.

Mark Krikorian called the marches the best possible gift to the immigration control movement. Americans' robust "national ego," he said, would never tolerate outsiders telling them what to do. In a *National Review Online* column that demonstrated his fondness for obscure vocabulary he wrote, "What we're seeing in the streets is a naked assertion of power by outsiders against the American nation. They demand that we comply with their wishes and submit our immigration policies for their approval, and implicitly threaten violence if their demands are not met ... ubiquitous Mexican flags, burning and other forms of contempt for the American flag, and widespread displays of blatant racial chauvinism and irredentism [the desire to return lands to their original owners]." He called for Americans not to give in to *dhimmitude* ("wherein a decadent host civilization capitulates to the chauvinist assertions of outsiders") as Europe had: "... the issue is whether we have the civilizational confidence to push back and tell the illegal aliens and their fellow travelers that making immigration policy is the exclusive province of the American people, and that foreigners, legal or illegal, are not part of the American people until we say they are." He compared the protesters unfavorably to the Civil Rights and antiwar marches of the 1960s, which he saw as patriotic in nature, or at least conducted by American citizens.

Earlier waves of immigrants had, of course, also made big demands on the United States during the labor struggles of the early twentieth centuries. Krikorian would say that those immigrants were legal, but in fact many were not, especially those who came after 1920. Regardless, those immigrants had no more status among Americans than today's immigrants do. They were considered undoubtedly, even dangerously, foreign, yet their organizing led to some of the most enduring features of U.S. labor law, from the eight-hour workday to the minimum wage.

The backlash had an additional social element. Critics implied that protests had transformed immigrants themselves. They used to behave like proper guests grateful for the generosity of their hosts, but now they were showing a sense of entitlement to rights and benefits that weren't theirs to claim— namely the right to complain. The *Bradenton Herald* in Florida quoted a white man who worked as an interpreter at the local hospital and who had surveyed his co-workers for their reactions. "The feeling was that we serve them here without reservation, and give them the utmost care they deserve as humans," he said. "They get free care and we don't pursue them. Most are extremely thankful. But get them on the protest line and things have changed."[6] People who were either criminals or just here to work had no right to expect full inclusion.

The marches finally gave those who supported immigrant rights a prompt to speak up—and there was plenty of support. A number of editorialists supported the marches. The Knight-Ridder editorial board wrote on May 2, "The sight of all those people in the streets, all those empty desks and shuttered shops, proved the foolishness of addressing illegal immigration by deportation and prosecutions." The editors recognized the "moxie" of those coming to work for pathetic wages and congratulated their courage, urging Congress to act.[7]

Beyond these practical results, however, the marches were unquestionably important both to immigrants and to their movement. They represented a long-overdue pushback against the vilification and violence that drives so many underground, and they gave immigrant communities their largest national popular platform in half a century. Many protests grew organically, cropping up without prompting and outside the control of any particular organization or coalition. The movement grew because it provided immigrants with a release valve for the anxiety and anger that naturally follows repeated public humiliation. The cover of collective action allowed immigrants to reveal themselves and ask for a system that would not force them to sneak around.

The marches represented a new organizing model for a mass scale, just as ROC-NY was working to build one in New York's restaurant industry. The most effective organizing models arise without having to be forced. They're grounded in the social networks that tie a particular community together, in the cultural and political habits of that community, and in the community's existing leadership. The mobilization tactics behind the marches weren't connected to any one organization. They both emerged spontaneously as the mobilization grew and helped generate that growth in the first place. An effective organizing model was key to reframing the immigration debate because it created space for new framers, in part by revealing just how large their sheer numbers were.

The marches built key infrastructure for future action. Some hundreds, perhaps thousands, of local leaders emerged, including a great number of U.S. citizens in their teens and twenties who used new cheap and free technology to encourage each other's participation. The ethnic media, which reaches millions of readers and viewers daily, activated social and family networks. The movement also generated new alliances. Although a few black leaders organized counterprotests, many called for solidarity. Black churches from Los Angeles to Georgia provided logistical and moral support. Unions turned out their members in massive numbers. While politicians clearly feared speaking out for legalization in an anti-immigrant climate, there was no question that both major parties took note of the significant constituency in favor of immigrant rights.

In the end, a version of the McCain-Kennedy comprehensive bill passed the Senate in 2006 but not the House, stalling immigration reform for another year—but the Sensenbrenner bill failed to become law as well.

Changing the Frame

Language plays an important role in all policy debates, and the immigration debate was no different. The imagery invoked by particular words is in many cases more important than facts. Linguists and social psychologists tell us that the brains of human beings are hard-wired to attach meaning to images, that the combination of images and ideas comprise a frame, and frames put together comprise a view of how the world works.

Most people hold a dominant frame, but other frames compete for space in the brain. For example, individualism and collectivity are frames with images attached. Images of self-made millionaires pulling themselves up by their own bootstraps reinforce the notion that people are solely responsible for their own fate, while those of families or communities working together evoke the notion that we are all responsible for each other. The individualism frame can then be used to propose less government intervention, and the collective frame to argue for more. Framing images don't have to be true, but they do have to be familiar. Facts by themselves are inadequate to disrupt a dominant frame: research shows that people dismiss facts that don't reinforce their leading frame. The only way to counter a prevailing frame is through imagery, storytelling, and mythology. Facts matter, but mostly to reinforce a frame once it is activated.

It is, of course, possible to manipulate facts to reinforce particular frames. The restrictionist movement was perfectly willing to ignore facts that contradicted its stance while reinforcing negative stereotypes—and, when all else failed, to resort to dehumanizing rhetoric. Krikorian's organization, for example, regularly cites low levels of English-language learning among today's immigrants, particularly among Mexicans. Krikorian focuses exclusively on first-generation immigrants, despite consistent evidence that today's immigrants learn English at exactly the same rate as previous generations of immigrants. The second and third generations of these families also behave exactly like those earlier waves of immigrants. The second is fully bilingual, and the third speaks only English. ROC-NY member Apolinar Salas, for example, took ESL classes for three years; his small daughter spoke only Spanish at home for her first three years. But she learned English almost instantaneously in preschool.

When restrictionists accused immigrants of using public resources without paying taxes, they ignored the significant amounts that even undocumented people pay. They tried to blame the country's health crisis on immigrants, despite evidence that they actually use less public health care than citizens. According to a 2005 study by Harvard and Columbia Universities, immigrants, including the undocumented, use fewer health care resources than native-born citizens. Immigrants accounted for 10.4 percent of the U.S. population, but only 7.9 percent of total health spending, and only 8 percent of government health spending. Their per capita expenditure is less than half that of nonimmigrants. Thirty percent of immigrants used no healthcare at all in the course of a year. The Oregon Public Policy Center estimated that undocumented immigrants in their state contribute between $66 million and $77 million annually in property, state income, and excise taxes.

In danger of having their positions undermined by such facts, restrictionists relied on the trusty tool of dehumanizing imagery. In July 2006, Steve King (R-Iowa) presented to Congress his proposal for a "super fence" along the border. "We could electrify it," he said, "not enough to kill somebody, but enough to make them think twice. We do that with livestock all the time." If the problem eased, he suggested, we could open it up again and "let the livestock run through." Don Goldwater, Arizona's leading Republican gubernatorial candidate of 2006, wanted to arrest border crossers, imprison them in tents patrolled by the National Guard, and make them build the coveted fence.

Even after many years of working on immigration policy, Muñoz was shocked at the new, vitriolic tone used by restrictionists. She had never before heard members of Congress compare immigrants to animals. It wasn't her habit to respond to the racialized frames that the other side used, but she was increasingly forced to grapple with them. Her opponents began to attack her organization directly with accusations of being a racially separatist organization, and she could see that while she had been fighting a battle of facts and policies, the other side had been fighting one of images. It was impossible to insert rationality into a debate that was so bound by angry, fearful reactions to immigrants who were equated with criminals and terrorists.

These trends hit Muñoz in increasingly explicit ways. As NCLR resisted the CLEAR Act (requiring police departments to enforce immigration law) throughout 2006, the act's author, Rep. Charlie Norwood (R-Ga.) sent out a press release on congressional letterhead denouncing NCLR as "a pro-illegal immigration lobbying organization that supports racist groups calling for the secession of the western United States as a Hispanic-only homeland." The press release called for NCLR to end its opposition to the CLEAR Act and continued, "If Americans don't wake up now, they'll wake up one day soon to find their nation has been stolen by La Raza and pals. Call your House member today to vote YES on HR 6089—*or throw them out of office November 7.*"[8] (Emphasis added.) Norwood ignored NCLR's repeated offers to meet and clarify the meaning of their name and mission.

To Muñoz, these accusations were nothing short of laughable. NCLR represented the most mainstream Latino community in the United States. It would be difficult to find another more dedicated to being able to work both sides of the aisle and less prone to taking radical positions. NCLR demanded an apology and urged Norwood to reimburse the U.S. Treasury for using public resources for his rampage, pointing out that his electoral message violated congressional ethics rules. Their point-by-point rebuttal explained their use of La Raza (the people, or the community, from "La Raza Cósmica," coined by a Mexican writer in the early twentieth century to reflect the fact that Latinos were a mixture of all the world's peoples), and reminded readers that their affiliates served thousands of low-income white and Black people as well as Latinos. As for returning the United States to Mexico, they said, "such a claim is so far outside of the mainstream of the Latino community that we find it incredible that our critics raise it as an issue." Norwood had also accused them of supporting the slogan "Por La Raza Todo, Fuera La Raza Nada" (for the people all, for others nothing), which had never been the motto of any Latino organization.[9]

Norwood said he'd apologize only if NCLR met seven incredible conditions, which included repudiating any claims to American territory and agreeing to have a third party supervise their programs to ensure equal access. NCLR did not attempt to meet these "conditions," of course, and Norwood died a few months later, but Muñoz encountered the "extremist" accusation continually from then on. By ignoring the facts and invoking a deeply held image of people of color wanting to take their land back by force, Norwood had delegitimized an organization that served poor white communities as well as others. Muñoz's work got harder and harder.

Immigration Policy and Racism

Although the 2006 election was marked by constant immigrant-bashing, it resulted in a major congressional shift toward the Democrats. For the first time since 1994 they controlled both the House and the Senate. President Bush acknowledged that his party had taken a "thumpin'," even as he vowed not to leave Iraq. The election deposed James Sensenbrenner from his position as committee chair, raising hopes among immigration activists.

Despite the new Democratic majority, the McCain-Kennedy comprehensive immigration bill had become more conservative. By the spring of 2007, the bill included legalization, but with quite stringent requirements including thousands of dollars in fines and a touchback provision, which meant that undocumented people would have to leave the United States and apply from elsewhere for legal entry. For many immigrants, for example, as well as for large numbers of asylum seekers, touchback requirements would have presented an insurmountable barrier to legalization. The bill's guest worker program gave workers few rights in relation to their employers, no control over their own visas, and no path to citizenship. On the enforcement side of the comprehensive equation, it further criminalized illegal entry, funded more fence-building along the southern border, limited family reunification immigration to spouses and minor children, and generally made it more difficult for people to enter and remain in the country—all without creating any of the needed reforms in the larger immigration system.

Whether or not this version would move to the House of Representatives came down to a cloture vote near the end of July.[10] An earlier cloture vote in May had failed to pass, and the longer debate went on the worse the bill got. The day of the final cloture vote, Muñoz was in the Senate's reception room, where civil rights leaders have maintained a tradition of last-minute lobbying and keeping watch to hold senators accountable. Muñoz arrived at the reception room while a group of fifty day laborers organized by Casa Maryland were learning to speak their message in English: "Don't let reform die today." Listening to them practice, Muñoz burst into tears. Another sixty immigrants were outside on the lawn.

While she waited, Muñoz had a number of conversations with senators going in to cast their votes. They stopped Senator Orrin Hatch, who said categorically, "I am not voting with you." Several Democratic senators walked by, making a concerted effort to avoid the group. One walked in, saw Muñoz, and turned his head to face the wall.

She had the most extraordinary conversation with a Republican senator with whom she had worked closely on other bills. He stopped to talk with the group, introducing himself to each worker individually. He said that he intended to vote with them, but if he saw the vote going the other way, he would change his own. As the voting went on, the yes voters began to fall in a domino effect as the majority voted against cloture. The senator came back into the reception room, although he could easily have left by another door. He had indeed changed his vote. "I recognize that this is a profile in cowardice," he said. "I want to get there with you, but our country's not ready yet."

The cloture vote failed, killing immigration reform for yet another year. It was unlikely in 2008, Muñoz knew, as Congress prepared for a national election in which a pro-legalization position would make politicians easy targets for the close-the-borders crowd. The day laborers took the news stoically. One, a priest, led them in a brief prayer. They then gathered themselves up and left, telling each other that they would keep looking for a way to move forward.

Later that day, Muñoz spoke to a colleague who had been facilitating a health training in Atlanta. As soon as they received news of the failed call for cloture, people quietly got up and started leaving.

"Where are you all going?" Muñoz's colleague asked.

To some other state, they replied. Georgia's law requiring all public service workers, from police officers to teachers, to check papers was scheduled to take effect the next day. Since they had no hope of reprieve from the federal government, they had to leave Atlanta. Immediately.

Muñoz felt abandoned and frightened by the level of hate being directed toward her community. Where was the progressive movement on this issue? The Opportunity Agenda had analyzed the blogosphere, which is overwhelmingly liberal, to find its contents stacked three to one against immigrants. She began to feel that NCLR and the national immigration groups had made a mistake in their own framing of the debate. They thought they were having a conversation about various policy options, something they excelled at. The country, though, was having a conversation about race. Muñoz knew this all along, of course, but had made a political calculation. Until recently, explicit racial talk hadn't reached the Senate floor, and most of the people she'd been trying to reach were in the middle. As a rule, it didn't seem very smart to accuse people of racism when she wanted their support.

Muñoz had tried to get a legalization passed under the wire so that at least 12 million people could be protected before they dealt with the question of racism. But in leaving racial issues alone, Muñoz now realized, they had failed to push back against a rhetoric that was only spreading. Making further progress seemed to require addressing the xenophobia directly to try to separate most Americans from what was still a small, though rapidly growing, number of advocates willing to spew falsehoods and stereotypes.

Cecilia Muñoz wasn't the only person at NCLR to come to the conclusion that they had to speak out against discrimination, but it took some time to get the whole organization to agree to a new strategy. Many of her colleagues were uncomfortable with accusing their opponents of being racist—they thought it would simply mean throwing the word around indiscriminately at individuals. "Some of this isn't about policy," she responded. "This is about us. We have to hit that squarely. Immigration policy is just the veneer under which people are attacking us." Muñoz convinced them that, at the very least, the times called for a shift in tone, and a sharp warning that enough was enough.

NCLR unveiled this message at its July 2007 convention in Miami. In her welcoming address, President Janet Murguia said, "When the Senate voted to deny a path to citizenship for the twelve million, it also voted to cave in to bigotry. When the Senate voted to reject hope, it voted to embrace fear .... We thought we were having a debate on immigration policy, but it's really a debate about who decides what it means to be an American." The community couldn't rely on anyone to protect them or stand up for them, she said. They would have to do it themselves at the ballot box.[11] The following night, Murguia repeated the bigotry charge on Lou Dobbs's CNN show. Dobbs, who had devoted himself to rooting out illegal immigration, but who usually treated Murguia quite gently in comparison to other pro-immigration guests, stopped inviting her back for a time. Muñoz herself gave a quote to the *Washington Times* saying that immigration reform was giving way to a "wave of hate," which quickly became the topic of conservative talk radio nationwide.[12] The amount of hate mail to their office rose enough in volume and harshness (an e-mail to Murguia read, "Can you explain to me why I shouldn't put a bullet in your head?") that NCLR alerted the FBI and instituted new security measures at its D.C. office.

Extending the Attack to Legal Immigrants

The restrictionists, however, realized that their experiments in framing were allowing them to expand the policy discussion to include reducing legal as well as unauthorized immigration. They had established the frame well enough that they could move on to more ambitious policy proposals. Mark Krikorian took a leading role. Legal and illegal immigration were inextricably entwined, he argued. All the arguments against illegal immigration—economic, fiscal, cultural, and security—added up to only one, said Krikorian. The only way to keep out illegal immigrants was to reduce the number of foreigners in total.

In a column entitled "Legal Good/Illegal Bad? Let's Call the Whole Thing Off," he argued that legal immigration created the framework and infrastructure enabling illegal immigration. "Legal immigration creates the networks that allow illegal immigration to take place," he wrote, "and the screwy mechanics of the legal immigration system raise expectations abroad such that people see themselves as entitled to come to America, whether they have permission yet or not."[13] Today's information-based economy, Krikorian believed, cannot accommodate hundreds of thousands of "peasants," and modern travel and communications technology kept immigrants too tied to their communities of origin, preventing the transfer of loyalty to the United States.

According to Krikorian, the days of mass immigration had come to an end. He advocated letting in only professionals as immigrants, about 250,000 annually (a reduction of approximately 75 percent from the current numbers), along with about 50,000 of the "world's most desperate people" as asylum seekers. Ten years ago, Krikorian's argument would have been considered extreme. Even now, most restrictionists say they are against only illegal immigration. "The people who say that are trying to make themselves feel better," said Krikorian. And so, the momentum is not just toward enforcement, but rather toward actual reduction of immigration.

In hard policy terms, the restrictionists had won this round of the fight for a better, more humane immigration policy. The most frequently used counterframe advanced the image of immigrants as workers rather than terrorists, but this picture didn't allow immigrants to be seen as fully human with political and social gifts as well as economic ones. The debate largely presented immigrant and American interests as conflicting. Only if their activism matures and grows can immigrants have any hope of broadening the debate to address the root causes of unauthorized immigration and to fight for a more open system.

Americans now face a choice about how we will treat immigration, but we're unprepared to make that choice rationally. There's no evidence that creating a permanent class of noncitizens, people who are essentially treated as though they don't exist in our workplaces, schools, and governments because they have no rights, helps struggling Americans. The crimmigration frame has no more than a placebo effect—it makes Americans feel more secure while stripping them of the things that could actually make them so. The effect is blinding, obscuring both the negative consequences of punishing immigrants and the alternatives that could truly improve life for all.

A number of the laws meant to control immigrants have deep implications for all U.S. citizens. After Colorado passed tougher anti-immigrant laws in 2005, for example, its farmworkers ran and crops rotted in the fields.[14] A year later, facing a major shortage of agricultural labor, the state's Department of Corrections proposed having prisoners pick melons, onions, and peppers at 60 cents an hour—a move that would have further driven down wages for the working class, immigrant or not. The Real ID Act, to take another example, may require people to prove their legality with birth certificates and documents that verify their Social Security numbers—and many people don't have birth certificates, including Katrina survivors and the elderly. If they have no IDs, the state will, officially, be required to cut off their public benefits, deny them driver's licenses, and prevent their entry to public buildings.

Opponents of the Real ID Act point out that the new standard IDs will in fact enable identity theft at unprecedented rates. In addition to displaying your name, birth date, sex, ID Number, and digital photograph, the Department of Homeland Security could require fingerprints and/or an optical scan. The cards must also contain "common machine-readable technology" such as a bar code and physical security features. This means that a great deal of personal information, far more than currently exists on a license, would be available to any talented computer hacker who had stolen a wallet. Finally, as immigrants, both undocumented and legal, flee unfriendly towns, there has been little discussion about how to replace their economic contributions. "Real Americans" get their towns back, but with a smaller tax base and fewer workers and consumers.

Immigrant labor inevitably brings down wages in some sectors, but its overall economic contribution is positive. While immigration does drive down wages in low-wage sectors by about 5 percent, it also brings "many secondary effects that offset the increased supply. Most immediately, when immigrants earn money, they demand goods and services. This population increases the demand for labor, which in turn creates more jobs and pushes wages back up."[15] In fact, numerous cities, such as Utica, N.Y., and Baltimore, Maryland, have revived themselves in response to loss of industrial jobs and the outmigration of young people by recruiting and welcoming immigrants. Restrictionists have made virtually every issue into a referendum on "illegal" immigration, and in doing so they have managed to block the expansion of key social services that would help lower- and middle-income Americans, such as the Children's Health Insurance Program, with the money spent on immigration enforcement being diverted from many other pressing needs.

Also missing from the debate is any discussion of what drives immigration in the first place, and the role that the United States plays in both encouraging neoliberal economic policies that increase the gap between rich and poor and in militarily displacing people from their homes. The United States controls the International Monetary Fund, which requires countries to privatize public services and deregulate their economies to look more like that of the U.S. The most tragic example of recent military irresponsibility is, of course, in Iraq. Since the war, 2 million Iraqis have fled their country, and another 2 million wander internally. The United States has admitted fewer than 800 of these refugees, while Sweden has accepted ten times that number.

Many people have begun to call for a more just immigration system. In April 2006, nearly 100 groups, including the AFL-CIO and a number of national church organizations, released a National Declaration for Fair and Just Immigration Reform. The elements of a progressive immigration policy, they wrote, start with a genuine and simple legalization route for undocumented immigrants, preclude more guest worker programs, prohibit wasting resources on further militarizing the border, guarantee due process rights, strengthen and enforce labor protections for all workers, and ultimately expand legal immigration. These are some of the principles on which Congresswoman Sheila Jackson Lee based her immigration proposal. Getting them a real hearing in the debate wasn't possible as long as Americans accepted the notion that our national identity developed in a vacuum hundreds of years ago, never to be challenged or changed. Global migration continues as it always has, but modernity has indeed reshaped it. What is outdated is not the role of "mass migration" but rather the idea that nations are and should be isolated from each other economically, politically, and culturally.

Chapter 8

GROWING A MOVEMENT

While restrictionists were shutting immigrants out of American communities, Saru and Mamdouh were expanding the ROC-NY community to include native-born Americans. The organization's identity was growing: what had been primarily an immigrant workers center was on its way to becoming a place for all restaurant workers. The opportunity to grow came in two forms. Their latest campaign had involved 250 workers from a prominent restaurant chain; unlike the others, this one was initiated by white front-of-the-house workers, who comprised the majority of campaign participants. Second, by the middle of 2007 Saru and Mamdouh were preparing for a major transition in their own lives. They were leaving ROC-NY to a new team of leaders so that they themselves could build a national association of restaurant workers. Both the campaign and the expansion were fitting developments in the organization's strategy.

ROC-NY's largest campaign fulfilled the organization's goal of engaging workers at all levels of the restaurant hierarchy. Early campaigns focused on immigrants of color stuck in dangerous, poorly paid back-of-the-house jobs; the Cité campaign had given them a chance to reach out to the few waiters of color who had managed to get to the front of the house. In October 2005, when a group of white waiters at one of the city's most prominent chains approached them for help, there was no question that ROC would provide it, on the condition that the white waiters would reach out to the back-of-the-house immigrant workers. Until that campaign, front- and back-of-the-house workers thought they had nothing in common. After the campaign, it became clear that abuse in one part of a restaurant indicates that there is abuse throughout. The campaign proved to be their toughest fight to date, nearly three years of hard work. It would also produce their biggest victory.

Exploitation of workers wasn't rampant in just New York City, of course, but in restaurants throughout the country. That reality led Saru and Mamdouh to the decision to start a national association of restaurant workers. They were driven in part by frequent calls from activists in other cities who had read about their work and wanted advice—but they got so many calls because industry conditions were created at the national level. Federal laws, including those that made so many people immigrate without documents, gutted the enforcement power of the Department of Labor and created a lower minimum wage for tipped workers than for everybody else, reinforcing the industry's power structure and enhancing the ability of employers to exploit workers. To make real change, they needed an organization operating at a bigger level. So it was that when Saru proposed taking their work national Mamdouh readily agreed. In the summer of 2007 they organized the first national convention of restaurant workers and prepared to start new projects on the Gulf Coast and in Michigan and Chicago.

Although being an organizer was the hardest work Mamdouh had ever done, and going national would make it even harder, he didn't hesitate to agree. He had started out simply going along with Saru's leadership, taking a wait-and-see attitude about whether he would stay. He had refused her repeated requests that he become the co-director of ROC-NY in name as well as in fact. They had fought with each other endlessly and often with great heat. But it was clear to everyone around them that they were a team. Their life experiences and their personalities were complementary.

Most of all, though, by doing the work they had deepened their commitment, both to each other and to the movement as a whole. The two had charted a course for the organization that made it increasingly influential in the city's restaurant industry. They had won hundreds of thousands of dollars for dozens of workers, along with numerous improvements in working conditions. They had taken up discrimination issues and attacked the racial hierarchy so common to high-end restaurants. Their two-year effort to craft and pass the Responsible Restaurant Act, which would allow the Department of Health to withhold license renewals from restaurants that had a pattern of labor violations, had finally been introduced in the New York City Council. Colors, the cooperative restaurant, had opened and was doing reasonably well. They had enjoyed overwhelmingly good press, locally for their campaigns, and nationally for the restaurant.

All this made it inevitable that front-of-the-house workers would eventually find them.

In the middle of 2005, Columbia University journalism student Jennifer Mascia called Saru in search of a campaign story. Saru told her they had no active campaigns at the moment—she thought they were wrapping up a discrimination campaign against Chef Daniel Boulud, a culinary celebrity and the owner of Restaurant Daniel in midtown Manhattan. Mascia would have to look elsewhere for her assignment.

"While I have you on the phone, can I ask you about something else?" Mascia asked. Mascia, coincidentally, was also a server at the Redeye Grill, a beautiful restaurant with huge windows on the corner of 57th Street and 7th Avenue. "We tip out our managers. Do you have any idea if this is legal?" The owner of Mascia's workplace was Sheldon "Shelly" Fireman, known as the Mayor of 57th Street because of the five expensive restaurants he owned clustered around Lincoln Center and Carnegie Hall. "Tipping the house" was the same problem that ROC-NY had fought at Cité. It's unlawful for managers to be part of a tip pool unless they have significant serving responsibilities. Saru told Mascia that the practice was absolutely illegal, and that she should come in with some other workers to see if ROC could help them.

Mascia put the problem on hold for two months. However, in July 2005, an incident at work brought it up again for her. One busy night, one of the managers had to put a lobster fork at one of her tables because she couldn't find a busser to do it. The manager gave her a hard time about that, and in response she asked, "Isn't that why we tip you out?" The simple comment led to a fight that almost resulted in Mascia's suspension. Remembering Saru's comment and wondering why all the managers were so upset, Mascia went to ROC-NY the next day. She didn't know that one of her co-workers had also written anonymously to the Labor Department, complaining that the company was requiring workers to buy their own uniforms at $100 cost. Mascia's co-workers were also suspicious about their working conditions, but they weren't talking to each other.

Mamdouh spoke to Mascia and another Redeye worker. Treating them as he would any potential member, he explained their system. They would have to join the organization, pay dues of $5, and bring other people from the restaurant if ROC were to pick up their campaign. When he reported on the conversation at the next staff meeting, Saru was, of course, excited about taking on another industry leader, so they proceeded. As the campaign got started, however, Mamdouh was surprised to encounter resistance among the staff to organizing white workers.

Mascia got her co-workers involved, and thirteen Redeye workers met at ROC-NY on a Sunday in late October 2005. Near the end of the first Redeye strategy meeting, after they had agreed to get as many servers as possible to sign a demand letter, Saru told them that they would have to try to get back-of-the-house workers involved. Mascia was taken aback. The group looked around at each other warily. One said, "What? There's nothing going on at the back of the house." Saru insisted, and the group agreed to try. After the meeting, though, they talked about it privately.

"They're all illegal. How are we going to get them on our side?"

Nevertheless, they agreed, and Mascia made her presentation to the ROC membership at the end of October to a warm and enthusiastic response. A ROC organizer was assigned to help them recruit other workers.

Mascia never knew that the ROC staff was embroiled in an intense debate about whether to expand to white front-of-the-house workers. In a regular Tuesday staff meeting, the organizer assigned to the Redeye Grill, frustrated that so many of the members she was recruiting were white, raised questions about whether organizing white workers fit into ROC's mission. The staff quickly split down the middle, spending the entire two-hour meeting debating the issue. The staff on the skeptical side felt that it would be impossible to get immigrant workers to join a campaign that white workers had started. Many of those white servers were the very people who treated immigrants badly. Someone worried that immigrant workers would be intimidated by the whites. There was anxiety that white people would take over the organization. They were an immigrant workers center, and there weren't many other organizations like them. This part of the staff didn't have much faith that the power immigrant workers had built would last if more privileged people were to come in.

But at least half the staff, including Saru, Mamdouh, and Siby, were absolutely against turning away white workers. Saru thought the presence of white workers would end the isolation that workers of color felt. "I think it would give them courage to know the front was organizing too," she said. The organization's campaigns had to both build their base and have an impact on the industry. They were committed to undoing the industry's racial hierarchy, but they had to take more than a worker's racial identity into consideration. For Siby and Mamdouh, the organization's rules couldn't be changed just because a new group of workers had come in. That would be too much like the way the system itself forged exceptions for various groups of people, changing the rules as it pleased. The Redeye workers had gone through ROC's process and agreed to reach out to the back-of-the-house workers. They were ill-equipped to do that, to be sure, but that was a problem to be solved, not a reason to turn them away. "We cannot close our doors to anybody," said Mamdouh.

The staff resolved the issue by taking a straw poll. Four were favorably inclined and two were not. "We need to help them reach out to the back of the house for this to work," Saru said, before assigning a second organizer to the campaign.

They were on their way into their biggest and toughest campaign ever. Fireman fought back harder than anyone else had, trying to discredit ROC-NY with the National Labor Relations Board, through the press, and through other restaurant owners. But the campaign took on an organic momentum, much like the one that had led to huge immigration marches across the country. It was fueled by the fact that workers in all of his restaurants knew each other and got news of the campaign through the papers. The campaign grew and grew, attracting not just restaurant workers but other allies as well.

The Redeye workers presented their demand letter in November 2005. It was signed by fifty-five workers, including fifteen bussers and a dozen people from the back of the house. They listed $3 million worth of complaints ranging from misappropriated tips and minimum and overtime wage violations to sexual harassment and racial discrimination in promotions. The campaign was too large to handle for ROC-NY's main legal ally, the Immigrant Rights Clinic at the City University of New York Law School, and its director Sameer Ashar insisted that they look for additional legal support. ROC recruited a large corporate law firm. The company immediately responded by filing National Labor Relations Board charges alleging that ROC-NY was a union in disguise, illegally trying to win collective bargaining agreements. The NLRB eventually ruled that it had no jurisdiction in the case, since ROC was not a labor union.

In January 2006, the lawyers filed a federal lawsuit against the company. In response, the company immediately began firing workers perceived to have signed on. Thirteen workers were sacked before the lawyers won a preliminary injunction against retaliatory firings. Fireman filed both state and federal suits against ROC-NY and Saru for defamation and "tortious interference" with business contracts. He claimed that, since ROC-NY had opened Colors, it was a competitive restaurant company. He asserted that they were protesting at his restaurants to steal business from his midtown clientele to the West Village. The claims were dismissed. How could ROC be both a union, as the company had claimed to the NLRB, and be a restaurant company at the same time? That victory helped, but it didn't do anything about the retaliatory firings, and the Redeye employees were disheartened at the retribution taken against their colleagues.

Press from the lawsuit filing attracted workers at Fireman's other restaurants. Shelly Fireman had started his empire in 1972 with Café Fiorello, a glass-fronted upscale Italian bistro on Broadway at 72nd Street. Since then, he had opened four more elite restaurants: Trattoria Dell' Arte, Brooklyn Diner USA, Shelly's New York, and Brooklyn Diner East, in addition to his Redeye Grill. The first additional workers to come in were former staff from Shelly's.

Recruiting former workers caused another problem for ROC internally. The rules required members to be workers who were still in the restaurants. The goal, after all, was to change the industry, not just to get a few benefits for people who had left it, but some of the former Shelly's workers were approaching the two-year statute of limitations on their claims—there was no time to recruit workers inside before deciding whether or not to take up the issue. ROC decided that having current workers within the Fireman Group, if not within Shelly's, would have to be enough. Mamdouh quoted an Arab proverb, "Sometimes the wind takes the boat in a different direction than the sailor originally wanted." With the number of workers growing, Saru had to get a second law firm to provide legal help; Linda Neilan and Justin Swartz from the workers' rights firm Outten & Golden filed the class action suit on behalf of the Shelly's workers.

The Fireman campaign spilled over to disrupt their progress with Daniel Boulud, owner of the posh Restaurant Daniel on the Upper East Side. The Restaurant Daniel campaign had come to ROC through the Equal Employment Opportunity Commission (EEOC), the government agency that handles discrimination complaints. A Daniel busser had gone to the EEOC claiming that his repeated requests for promotion had been rejected while white applicants that he himself had trained were given server positions. He found out about ROC and eventually brought nine other Daniel workers. Boulud had responded immediately to their demand letter, but the agreement had been stalled by his demand for complete confidentiality, to which ROC-NY could not agree. By March 2006, however, several months into the Fireman campaign, Saru had negotiated a compromise that the company and the organization would issue a joint press release, and things were again back on track.

The very day the parties were meant to sign the agreement, Bouloud backed out, saying that another restaurateur with whom ROC was fighting had told him to stop negotiations. ROC commenced demonstrations in front of Restaurant Daniel, a full eight months after delivery of the demand letter. Bouloud then made the mistake of suing ROC for defamation, a common tactic but one that brought him all the press he had earlier been trying to avoid. His resistance also gave ROC a public platform to raise the discrimination issues that they continued to believe were at the heart of the restaurant industry's abuse of workers. That summer ROC took signs protesting discrimination to Bouloud's cookbook release and kitchen demonstration at Macy's. This was the first time that two of ROC's targets had attempted to collude against the organization. It would prove to be an inadequate intervention for both.

In April, workers from Café Fiorello came on board, bringing in tipping, sexual harassment, and race discrimination issues. Eventually, they numbered sixty workers, most still employed by the restaurant, and would turn out to be the most dedicated of all the workers. Sekou Luke, a server who had emigrated from Jamaica to the United States as a child, said that there seemed to be a quota for black and other servers of color, no more than two or three total. He was the only black man working in the front of the house in any of Fireman's restaurants. Luke, a thoughtful, energetic thirty-year-old, recalled a conversation with a manager in which he'd tried to get an interview for a friend, also black. The manager told him that Shelly was only looking to hire Italian-looking males at that time. Luke was so disturbed by the incident he thought about it for several days. He discussed it with his parents and one co-worker. The comment put several other incidents into context, like the fact that each time Fireman himself came to the restaurant, Luke was sent downstairs to answer phones.

The Fiorello group became the most diverse, active, and inspired set to enter ROC-NY. In spite of the company's attempt to retaliate against them with specious disciplinary measures, they protested, developed a Website for the whole campaign, and organized bar meetings to recruit other workers. The campaign grew to more than 140 workers and the Café Fiorello workers were added to the Shelly's class action in July 2006. Meanwhile, students at the Union Theological Institute heard about the campaign and began holding weekly prayer vigils in front of the restaurants, appealing to the moral conscience of diners.

In response, the company generated the most negative press ROC-NY had ever had, much of it vilifying Saru. Columnists, lobbyists, and former public officials all weighed in to warn New Yorkers and the industry that ROC was trying to change their way of life. They relied heavily on images of Saru as a dangerous radical and of ROC-NY as a threat to all-American capitalism, manipulating facts to fit their frame. The first attack was an op-ed by Tom Elliott in the *New York Post* accusing ROC-NY of shaking down innocent employers and trying to infiltrate the New York State Restaurant Association.[1]

His piece was rife with inaccuracies that would get repeated in other articles. Elliott dug up the grievances of the former cooperative members, claiming that Colors employees "had invested money in what they believed was a cooperative enterprise." In truth, none of the former members were ever actually employed at Colors, and none had invested a dime. Elliott also repeated Fireman's accusation that they were an extension of the union, that their aim of helping Windows workers "drew in $500,000 in start-up cash from UNITE HERE Local 100 which represents restaurant workers," which was also untrue. The two points that were accurate, though, were that two of ROC's targets were no longer in business. Noché had been closed, and Cité had been put up for sale after their campaigns. He left out the fact that a third had also closed—the owner of the Park Avenue Country Club had been convicted of tax fraud involving millions of dollars. More such coverage followed, and the company created five-foot-tall replicas of these articles and put them up in front of its restaurants during protests.

Saru took these attacks in stride, although it was a sharp contrast to the press she had received earlier. The ROC team thought it very sad that the state of the labor movement was such that calling a group a union was meant to be the highest insult. They could only dream that HERE actually had significant money to contribute. Customers sometimes misunderstood the presence of huge reprints of the negative articles, asking Saru how she had gotten the employer to advertise their campaign. "It's good these conservatives are paying attention to us now," Mamdouh said in a staff meeting. "It means they're scared of our little organization."

But the workers were a little more disheartened. Fireman had been steadily firing Redeye workers involved with the campaign. A busser was fired for hugging a co-worker on the picket line before going in for his shift, and six other front-of-the-house workers were next. The company rooted out its undocumented workers in the back of the house and fired six of them. In June 2006 Saru asked Mamdouh to come to the regular Sunday meeting to speak to the workers. Mamdouh broke his rule against leaving Queens on the weekends. He could see that most of these white workers had little experience of standing up for their rights, having rarely had to do it. He told them the story of the Thanksgiving sit-down at Windows.

"We were all making a lot of money," he said, "so we had a lot to lose. But we knew that it was the right thing to do and we made it happen."

Re-inspired, the Redeye workers wrote a letter and twenty-five of them walked into Fireman's office to demand a halt to the firings, especially of the six undocumented workers currently on the block. They didn't succeed, but by then Saru had convinced the lawyers to file for a preliminary injunction. Fireman workers from all the restaurants packed the courtroom to standing room only on the hearing date and sat for hours, whispering to each other nervously, all prepared to testify against the retaliations, although only three were called. Those three withstood aggressive questioning by the Fireman legal team, who produced no witnesses on the other side. The judge gave them a temporary restraining order, which was eventually made a preliminary injunction affecting the entire company.

Unwittingly, the company then gave ROC a chance to connect the Fireman campaign to its primary policy campaign—passing a new regulation at the city level that would make labor violations a factor in Health Department decisions to renew restaurant business licenses. Knowing that employers who violated labor law looked for additional unscrupulous measures to cut costs, the coalition of owners and workers that ROC built had crafted the Responsible Restaurant Act. The act would allow, but would not require, the city's Department of Health to deny renewal licenses to restaurants that had repeated and egregious labor violations. The Fireman Group showed that there was direct connection between the safety of diners and the treatment of workers. After firing undocumented bathroom cleaners involved in the campaign, managers tried to make bussers, who handle food, also clean the bathrooms. This wasn't the company's only health problem. A professor at New York University had his students map the restaurants with the largest number of health violations so that ROC-NY could compare it to the labor violations list. In a "you can't make this stuff up" moment, Saru and Mamdouh were astonished to learn that two of the top eleven restaurants with health violations were the Redeye Grill and Shelly's.

The company continued to resist, but the campaign continued to grow. A *New York Times* article in June 2006 fueled more expansion. Trattoria Dell' Arte workers joined the class action suit that August, followed by those from the Brooklyn Diner in the fall. By the end of 2006, 250 workers had signed on to the lawsuit, and some 30 formed a committed leadership team. The workers had filed lawsuits as well as numerous EEOC charges and sustained a two-year citywide campaign. The company offered to begin mediation soon after that, and for a time the workers stopped protesting. By March 2007, however, they would start again as the company stalled, refusing to address the discrimination charges or put a monetary figure on the table. The company, though, had started to make some concessions in some, though not all, of the restaurants. They ended the practice of tipping the house at Brooklyn Diner and Shelly's, stopped making workers pay for their own uniforms, and instituted "show up" pay, which guaranteed workers three hours' wages when their shifts were cancelled on short notice. More than another year went by.

The end, however, was inevitable. By the spring of 2008, ROC-NY and the Fireman Group were moving toward an agreement, the largest in the organization's history. The workers would win a nearly $4 million settlement and a whole host of additional changes, for both the front and the back of the house.

Unity Front and Back

For native-born workers in the restaurants, the Fireman campaign was the first time they had organized around conditions in the industry. Most had grown up working class, and many could trace their own families' immigration histories. They were being abused by their employer, as were the back-of-the-house workers. Sometimes the issues were exactly the same. In spite of these commonalities, though, the two sets of workers were completely disconnected from each other.

Mascia was the most likely person to make the connection, but the structure of the restaurant industry prevented her from seeing it. She knew her family had a tough immigration history, she'd grown up with racially tolerant parents, and she had friends among back-of-the-house workers. Her mother's family had escaped the pogroms of eastern Europe at the end of the nineteenth century. Mascia had grown up hearing about how her great-grandmother had to hide in a closet with her family at the age of six, her own uncle holding a knife to her throat and prepared to use it in order to save the rest of the family if she started to cry. Both sets of grandparents had been born in the United States, but returned to live in the Ukraine and Italy as teenagers in the 1910s and 1920s before returning to the United States to marry and raise families.

Mascia had grown up in Orange County, California. Even in the 1980s, Orange County had a large population of undocumented Mexican immigrants, who formed the bulk of her father's landscaping employees. Mascia's mother worked hard to maintain good relationships with the Latinos, speaking to them as equals and often leaving her daughter under their watch. When the Proposition 187 debate broke in 1994, Mascia's mother, upset about the way Latinos were vilified, said, "Why don't they just put yellow stars on everybody?"

Mascia actually had friends among the Redeye Grill bussers and runners. A Bangladeshi busser with whom she discussed the news of the world was the first person to suggest that she apply to journalism school. Yet she had no idea about the level of mistreatment they suffered until ROC-NY helped her recognize it. Bussers, for example, are part of the tip pool. If managers were taking some of the tips, bussers as well as servers lost money. But this had never occurred to Jennifer Mascia when she wrote her first letter to her co-workers. She didn't send that letter to anybody working in the back of the house.

Mascia would always remember the day she realized what she had been unable to see. One Sunday she sat on a bench near the restaurant between her double shifts, listening to a kitchen worker calmly tell ROC staff that their paychecks were docked money if they called in sick, and that the company regularly shaved their hours to avoid paying overtime.

Mascia said nothing and went back inside for her second shift. She entered the restaurant through its side door as the staff was eating what is known as the family meal in the back dining room. The first person she encountered was another waiter who had also joined the campaign. He asked her how she was; she looked up at him and said, "You wouldn't believe what I just heard." As she told him the kitchen worker's story, she was shocked to find her eyes misting and her voice choking, triggering tears from her co-worker as well. As their eyes connected, the two waiters shared a silent understanding that the issue of working conditions in the restaurant was far bigger than them, that the back-of-the-house workers faced survival issues going far beyond losing $5,000 in income each year. People were watching, though, so they stifled their reactions and went back to work.

Mascia began to see the irony. The waiters had documents and were allowed to have a voice; the back-of-the-house workers had their rights stripped by their immigration status. "The white workers thought the back of the house would drag them down," said Mascia. "But when they started coming to meetings more than waiters, people got it." Given the chance to speak, the people at the bottom did so loudest and longest.

Jeff Baskin, forty-six, was a waiter at Trattoria Dell' Arte. Baskin was born in Canarsie, Brooklyn, and moved in 1971 with his family to Holbrook, Long Island, at the time the last exit on the Long Island Expressway and referred to by New Yorkers as "the country." Baskin, whose light brown eyes carry an irreverent gleam, worked pretty much his entire life, starting with two paper routes when he was thirteen. At fifteen he cleaned the floor at the plastic bag factory where his mother worked before leaving for his second job scooping ice cream. He was the first person in his family to go to college. Unable to rely on financial help from his parents, Baskin took out loans and worked his way through college, bussing tables, delivering pizza, and tending bar.

Baskin called himself an American Jew, in that particular order because the American comes first, but he also wanted an identity through which he could express his support for Israel, where he had never been. His ancestors, like Mascia's, had also escaped the pogroms of Ukraine, and he often compared his family's history to the musical *Fiddler on the Roof*: "It was either America or getting beaten by drunk Cossacks," he said. His ancestors, Baskin thought, were not so different from the dishwashers at the restaurants where he had worked. The technicalities might have been different, but the concept was the same, and he admired the courage it took to come to a new country without knowing the language, without knowing what the future would hold, in order to make a better life for future generations. Although his family didn't like to discuss it, he had the distinct sense that during the Depression his grandfather had done whatever he had to do to ensure the family's survival.

An open immigration system, he thought, was correct and right. It was what had created America in the first place. One of the things Baskin loved most about working Christmases in New York, for example, was that the workforce and the customers that day were always Muslims and Jews. "Not one person of Muslim faith ever looked at me and thought, *Jew*," he said, "and I never looked at anyone and thought, *Muslim*. They saw me as a co-worker first, and I saw them as co-workers first." He could understand that other Jews were concerned about immigration after September 11 because they felt particularly threatened by the entry of hostile Arabs. But to him, the government had to be able to prove that someone was a member of a terrorist organization in order to ban them. Osama bin Laden had thousands of relatives, he pointed out. Should we be allowed to keep them all out just because their names were bin Laden?

In spite of their own global family histories and working-class backgrounds, none of the white workers ever paid much attention to the national immigration debate beyond thinking that Lou Dobbs needed to shut up. These American workers had held too narrow a view of their problems, and they didn't really think immigration policy affected them. An organization that seemed to have nothing to do with white people—whose staff and members were overwhelmingly people of color, overwhelmingly not citizens, overwhelmingly "illegal"—had turned out to be the one place where the white workers could find a way to stand up for themselves. ROC had built itself by fighting the racial hierarchy in the restaurant industry, but it recognized that the source of that hierarchy wasn't the white workers, it was the larger system that tolerated bad conditions for some, which inevitably meant there were bad conditions for everybody. Now it was time for the organization to turn its attention to those overarching structures.

"ROC U!": ROC Goes National

When Saru proposed going national, Mamdouh was ready. ROC-NY was in a good place. Colors, the cooperative restaurant, had stayed open more than two years, the period during which 60 percent of all new restaurants usually fail. It had problems, including the lawsuit that former co-op members finally filed against ROC-NY in 2007, but also a new and promising strategy. ROC-NY had added a huge new piece of research, a testing project in which it would send in comparable white workers and workers of color to apply for jobs to document the differential treatment each received. The staff had grown to seven full-time people and numerous interns, and ROC had a growing budget. Most important, new leaders were available to take over the organization. At the beginning of 2008, ROC-NY board appointed new co-directors who had the same complementary skills that Saru and Mamdouh had. Rekha Eanni was a lawyer/organizer like Saru. Sekou Siby had been a restaurant worker like Mamdouh.

Mamdouh and Saru still dealt with their stress through chronic and intense bickering, which they came to accept as part of their relationship. The two disagreed about everything, and not discreetly. They argued about whether every protest was necessary, about how much time off the staff should get, about whether the meetings should start on time, about why Saru couldn't learn how to use the combination PDA and cell phone that Mamdouh had bought. The ROC staff, interns, and volunteers watched them battle it out at nearly every staff meeting, forcing Siby to tell them to stop. Some days,

Mamdouh wanted nothing more than for the workaholic Saru to leave him alone. He was grateful when she found a boyfriend, because then Mamdouh was guaranteed an occasional full weekend off. Saru wanted Mamdouh to take more responsibility for the organization's discipline. He still threatened to quit every time they fought. Mamdouh's wife, Fatima, shocked at the testy way they spoke to each other, would say, "Isn't she your boss?"

"No!" they would reply simultaneously.

But this way of dealing with their conflicts, while hard to watch, was part of what made them a great team. They weren't afraid to fight, with each other or with restaurant employers. They didn't believe in hiding conflict, but in dealing with it directly and immediately. Nor were they afraid of making up, just as they did with employers who ultimately did the right thing. They were different people and each very stubborn—both the differences and their stubbornness gave them the staying power they needed to stick with the work when times were hardest. Their ability to fight but continue to work reinforced their closeness.

They hatched the idea of going national during a three-week retreat in the summer of 2006, at the height of the Fireman campaign, where they wrote a comprehensive history of their work together. There were two important reasons for expanding. First, there was tremendous demand—workers from all over the country had been calling them almost since the beginning, seeking advice about how to get control of their own abusive industries. People needed help everywhere because of the second reason: national policies affected local restaurants, but restaurant workers themselves had little ability to shape these policies. Restaurant owners had the National Restaurant Association. The Hotel Employees and Restaurant Employees, Mamdouh's former union, had a significant presence on Capitol Hill, but it wasn't enough, especially for the huge majority of restaurant workers who were not unionized. Most restaurant workers had nothing that could compete with their opponents or support their allies at the national level. They had to be able to deal with federal policy, especially immigration policy and economic policy, to really change conditions in the industry.

Saru and Mamdouh, working with an expansion committee of members, planned the general scope of the new organization. They wanted to build ROCs in five or six cities, helping to raise money and supervise the staff. These new organizations would conduct campaigns against individual employers and push new local policy changes, while simultaneously banding together with others to pursue national legislation. Hopefully, they could start coordinated campaigns, hitting national restaurant chains in multiple cities. Throughout 2007 Saru and Mamdouh traveled the country meeting with potential partners. Many of these potential partners were fellow members of the Interfaith Coalition on Worker Justice. There was also a similar organization in San Francisco, where Young Workers United (YWU) organized in nonunion workplaces much as ROC-NY did. YWU included retail as well as restaurant workers, and they were excited about being part of a national effort.

Saru and Mamdouh chose the Gulf Coast, from where local activists had approached them, and Michigan as the first expansion sites. These two places gave them a chance to focus not just on white and immigrant workers, but also on black Americans, continuing the trajectory they had started with the Fireman campaign. New Orleans had traditionally been a big restaurant town, and the city's French Quarter had survived Hurricane Katrina fairly well and was among the first parts of the city to be rebuilt. Black workers, evacuated during the storm and blocked from returning to their homes, had been displaced by immigrant contract workers brought in by companies such as Halliburton, which also managed a number of security contracts in Iraq. ROC could address the exploitation of immigrant workers with little status while simultaneously taking up the critical issues of low-wage American workers, in this case black Americans.

In August 2007, the expansion committee hosted the first national convention of restaurant workers in Chicago. Workers and organizers hit the city that weekend to plan and launch their new organization. A workers' center from Detroit sent a multiracial group of immigrants and citizens. Young Workers United came from San Francisco and brought a number of restaurant activists, most under the age of twenty-five. The Chicago crew both hosted and participated.

Together they drew a picture of the industry nationally. Each group analyzed their city's industry, covering the demographics of the workforce and describing the industry's mini-empires, the Shelly Firemans and Alan Stillmans that they had to deal with. In New Orleans, both wage theft and racial discrimination, widely prevalent even before Katrina, had now become rampant. In San Francisco, Young Workers United was determined to help the Chinese Progressive Association build a real base in Chinatown. "Here's how globalization works in the restaurant industry," said Sonya Mehta, an Indian American woman with a talent for facilitation. "When a major garment manufacturer moved their operations overseas, all those garment workers lost their jobs and flooded the restaurant industry. They're desperate, so they'll work under much worse conditions than the current workers." In Detroit, the team had to think through how to revive the city while organizing in restaurants. Detroit, once the center of the auto industry and union jobs, was now among the top ten cities losing their population, and with it their tax and consumer base.

After the regional presentations, the group began to define the new organization's goals. They dreamt about the possibilities, for the time being without a reality check to balance their ambition. In San Francisco, every restaurant worker would know Young Workers United and bad bosses would fear its name. San Franciscans needed to build worker solidarity, especially in the very isolated Chinatown. The Chinese Progressive Association had to find a way to get its members to see their self-interest in a broader movement: "Chinese people are such a critical mass, sometimes [they] don't think they need other people."

The New York crew wanted to get three ROC members elected to the City Council, and a job training and referral system that was respected by all.

The Chicago team started with "We are going to build our own cooperative restaurant." Hearing this, Siby and Mamdouh exchanged knowing glances.

"Everybody wants a co-op," said Siby.

"Exactly," Mamdouh replied. "But do they understand what a co-op means?" Likely, he thought, they understood no more than he had. If they did, he thought it wouldn't be such an attractive proposition.

The Michigan group went last, pretending that it was 2012. "Seems like just yesterday it was 2007." Everyone laughed. They projected having 2,000 active members, framing a regional strategy, and desegregating the restaurant industry, saying about the last, "You can do it too!" The top ten restaurants in their city would pay higher wages than the rest, and other employers would look to them as examples.

One of the Detroit participants reflected on the project of building an organization that could absorb white, black, and immigrant workers. Quamara Bilqis Muhammad, a twenty-five-year-old African American Muslim who goes by the moniker "Peaches," was born in New Mexico and raised all over Michigan. Muhammad, who has experienced discrimination in the industry because she wears *hijab*, acknowledged the tensions between U.S.-born workers and immigrants. She noted that immigrants appear to have an intense family and work ethic, willing to live together in cramped spaces and work impossible hours for terrible wages, making it very easy for employers to pass up black and white American workers. She believed that building a

ROC in Detroit would require a good deal of mutual education and some change in behavior, both among native-born and immigrant workers. Native-born workers have to stop blaming immigrants for the industry's conditions, while immigrant workers have to learn to demand more. "We need to bond together with immigrants," she said. "At first it might be hard, but once they see the benefits, good sense is good sense. If you know you have to pay an immigrant worker the same as a white or black worker, you're not going to make them work eighteen-hour days and run them into the ground." Muhammad saw great potential in that bonding; the changes they could establish together might be enough to keep her living in the otherwise economically depressed state of Michigan. "The cool thing about the food industry," she said, "is that as long as there are people in America eating, there will be a need for restaurants."

Eventually, it came time for the group to talk about the implications of building something bigger out of all these local efforts. They had to choose a national policy focus and select a name. They debated various options for federal legislative campaigns. People were already fighting for federal immigration reform and a public health insurance system. Big labor was pushing the Employee Free Choice Act, which would make it easier for people to unionize, and it wanted support from the workers centers. Could their new organization reform the Department of Labor so that it would actually protect workers? Should they throw down on the federal minimum wage? Problems emerged with all these ideas. Immigration reform was not fated to pass anytime soon; none of these organizations had been involved in the health care fight; the Employee Free Choice Act appeared to be going nowhere. YWU pushed for paid family leave.

Discouraged by all these obstacles, someone asked why they should bother with national policy at all, prompting a dozen quick responses. If they wanted to affect workers on a grand scale, they had to do it. For issues like the minimum wage or immigration reform, it was the only way. In the first case, federal law set the floor: if the national minimum wage was too low, the ones states adopted would also be low. In the latter case, only Congress had the constitutional power to make immigration law. Most compellingly, restaurant workers currently had no ability to counter the powerful industry voice nationally. The National Restaurant Association had 300,000 members. "In every city, people are afraid of them," said Mamdouh. They were the only source of national information about the industry.

With their motivation for addressing national policy reinforced, the group agreed to take up three issues: paid sick leave, minimum wage reform, and immigration policy.

The strategy that Saru and Mamdouh had laid out five years before, just six months after September 11, had brought them inexorably to this point. They had chosen to frame restaurant workers not just as workers, but also as immigrants and potential citizens. They had decided not to provide services, but to build a political organization in which the immigrant worker's voice was central, in dramatic contrast to the national immigration debate. They then worked out from that center to engage everyone else involved in the industry, ultimately including native-born front-of-the-house workers, employers, and customers. They didn't just critique the industry as it was, but created new models to show how it could be.

ROC-NY's work had produced two important lessons for the rest of the industry, and for other industries. First, fighting racism was the key to building an inclusive movement and industry. Focusing on race—not exclusively, but explicitly—allowed immigrants of color to reveal their full potential. Once that happened, they could create an organizational atmosphere in which everyone else could do the same. Second, an intrepid organization could get a lot done locally, but local conditions were ultimately determined by national and global policies. Local change would always be limited without interventions at those levels. The only hope for local groups lay in connecting themselves to something bigger.

The final task at the national convention was to choose a name for the new organization. Saru suggested something that showed scale, something that had the word national in it. Mamdouh noted that they had initially wanted to use the word *organizing* in New York before someone had talked them out of it. Maybe this was a chance to return to that idea. The decision, though, was up to the group. They tried out several possibilities.

Then someone said "ROC United." The group, exhausted as it was after three days of nonstop meetings, sounded a collective Yes. The word "united" was perfect. It captured both scale and the concept of organizing. A proper vote was taken, and ROC United became their new name.

The meeting closed with the ROC chant and a group photo. The mood was giddy, as if people were running on nothing but adrenalin. In addition to doing the chant in Spanish, Bengali, Arabic, and English, they added Malay and Polish. For the photo, fifty people jostled their way into place. The Michigan couple that had brought their three-year-old daughter took a prominent spot in the front. The tallest men, like Siby, stood in the back. The photographer lined up the shot. Siby and Mamdouh found a spontaneous way to make people smile, much better than saying "cheese."

"ROC U!" Siby yelled.

"ROC U too!" Mamdouh yelled back.

The ensuing laughter held a tinge of relief. Meeting for twelve hours a day and three days in a row, this group had taken a huge step forward. They had expressed their hopes and outlined at least a dozen serious obstacles. Many more problems would emerge before they won a single thing, but now they had many more people in many more places with whom to share the struggles and learn the lessons. They would guide each other to victory.

Chapter 9

DREAMING GLOBALLY

In the summer of 2007 Mamdouh took his family for a three-week vacation to Morocco. Many things had changed there since he'd emigrated twenty years before. A new king, Mohammed VI, had been crowned in 1999, and he had ended the "period of fire and steel," established a more liberal political atmosphere, and passed some progressive laws. He had pardoned thousands of political prisoners, adopted a new law expanding women's rights, and announced that protecting human rights and ending poverty were priorities.

Many of the conditions that had pushed Mamdouh out still existed, however. Human rights groups continued to document government abuses in the form of arrests, beatings, and prison sentences. Mohammed VI continued a neoliberal economic program, privatizing large sectors of the economy in order to attract foreign investors. Emigration had become a major influence on Morocco's economy, since Moroccans abroad sent large amounts home in remittances. School attendance was up, but unemployment rates remained extremely high, especially among Morocco's young people. Moroccans were still leaving, with nearly 3 million, about 10 percent of the population, living outside the country. Most, like other branches of Mamdouh's own family, went to European Union (EU) countries, which have a far shorter history as immigration destinations than does the United States.

Europe was frequently seen as having liberal policies because it had built a regional union with essentially open borders. While EU statutes have some promising elements with potential for replication, the European model is based on the same three blind spots present in the United States. It doesn't account for an incomplete globalization; it reflects the belief that cultures can and should remain static; and it sees immigrants and native-born residents as adversaries. As such, Europe's models are still deeply flawed and won't get us close enough to the fair system we need.

Europe's own vaunted unity is today predicated on keeping out the Other—in this case, Africans, Turks, and, to some degree, eastern Europeans. Europe in fact struggles with immigration in much the same way the United States does—indeed, the way in which the entire world does. Its laws contradict each other. On the one hand, countries like Italy create integration programs to ease people's lives and to prevent human rights abuses. On the other hand, the immigration process is restrictive—people are allowed in, but in smaller numbers than labor markets demand. They fill labor shortages, but their status remains uncertain; for most, legal status is at best temporary and is tied to having an employer. Borders are patrolled with increasing violence, and large numbers of migrants drown trying to cross the sea every year. Unauthorized immigrants are treated as criminals and their punishments grow increasingly harsh. The contradictory stance—punitive on the one hand and welcoming on the other—leaves both Europeans and immigrants in limbo, stuck between what they used to be and what they could become.

Morocco itself is now not only a source of emigrant workers but has also become a gateway for sub-Saharan Africans, who cross the desert on foot to get to Morocco's northern shores, where they embark on small inflatable rafts to reach southern Europe. The king has meanwhile invited Moroccans who have emigrated to return to Morocco, but few of them do so and those who do were mostly members of the wealthy elite when they left. Their return has brought in some investment and jobs, but rather than transforming the country they reinforce the old hierarchical social structures dividing rich and poor, royal and commoner.

Mamdouh found this out for himself. He was in the general habit of taking the family to Morocco for summer vacations. He had thought he would be quite happy to move back there permanently, but his family didn't want to—not Fatima, nor the kids. Mamdouh stopped by his old neighborhoods. The shanty neighborhood where his father's store had been was now a graveyard for dozens of abandoned, broken-down buses, the sooty wall that used to be white still separating it from the highway. He visited the old house at Moulay Rachid, the family's home after leaving their shanty neighborhood. It was a brick structure situated on a narrow cobblestone alley. When the family lived there it had been two stories, but two others had been added over the last ten years. He entered through a narrow doorway: two rooms were on the first floor together with a small bathroom. That arrangement was repeated on three more floors, but all the living space together can't have amounted to more than 260 square meters. They kept one floor in which his parents lived with his sister-in-law, Mohammed's wife, Rachida. They rented the six other rooms to ten, sometimes twelve women who worked in the garment factories on Casablanca's north side. Sitting down for a glass of mint tea with his sister-in-law and two of the women, Mamdouh learned that they were from the countryside and had come to Casablanca to find their fortunes. Although they earned little (about US$200 per month), they were not going back. His sister-in-law showed him her pay stub. She'd been cheated of some of her hours, which would affect her pension; when she had complained to her boss he had blown her off, saying he would change it if she could prove she had worked more hours. The boss was, of course, in charge of the timekeeping.

After a few days in Casablanca, Mamdouh decided to take Fatima and the kids for a short visit to Rabat, an hour north along the coast. One of his Moroccan friends in New York had offered to let them stay at his house very near the beach, in a modern complex with a pool. By now, Iman was a tall, gangly girl of twelve, with very dark eyes thickly fringed with long curly lashes like Mamdouh's. Zaki was ten, a joker who managed to keep up a steady stream of conversation, even without anyone to talk to. And the baby, Mohammed, was already two and looking exactly like Mamdouh himself—round cheeks, big eyes, and curly hair. They brought a lot of other people along—Mamdouh's niece Bushra, his nephews Hamza and Kamal, a friend's ten-year-old daughter, and Fatima's aunt from Sidi Kacem. At night the family split up between the house's two bedrooms and downstairs sitting room, where they slept lined up head to foot on the built-in sofas along the wall.

In Rabat, Mamdouh's visit with friends highlighted the differences that still existed between social classes in Morocco. The only people who returned to stay were those who had had money to begin with. One day, the whole family went to visit his friend Ali.[1] Ali's father owned a prosperous clothing store in Rabat's souk. While his brother had stayed home to help run the businesses, Ali himself, a well-fed-looking man with a broad friendly face, had defied his father's wishes and gone to New York on a tourist visa in the late 1980s. He had met Mamdouh through the Moroccan network, and whenever Mamdouh changed jobs, he took Ali with him. Married now, with a young daughter, Ali had returned to Rabat. But like so many middle-class Moroccans who return from abroad, he was having a difficult time. His wife didn't really want to live in Rabat. She'd been raised in France and preferred to live there. He was having a hard time adjusting to the vagaries of Moroccan life—the traffic, the bribery, the lack of respect for lines. Ali lived in his parents' house where he'd grown up, but he had also bought into a new condominium development near the beach, intending to rent the apartment for extra money.

As the two families shared mint tea and almond cookies, Ali said he was surprised to have run into an Algerian the day before, someone he and Mamdouh had also known in New York. The Algerian had a garment business, and Ali hoped to do some work with him, so he had promised to take him and his wife to the Casbah that afternoon.

The next day, Ali realized that the police had followed him and the Algerian family during their outing to the Casbah. Morocco was suspicious of Algerians because Algeria supported the Polisario Front in Western Sahara, a rebel movement that claimed to represent the region's indigenous people against Morocco's military presence in the area. The police had visited the house, questioning Ali's mother about the Algerian. "Tell your son to stay away from him," they told her. That was the career Mamdouh had been offered and turned down while he was at university.

On another night, Fatima and Mamdouh were invited to dinner at the home of different friend, a man who had lived in France for twenty years. He and Mamdouh had met in New York, introduced by mutual friends. He, too, was from a wealthy family, far wealthier than Ali's. Mamdouh drove to a neighborhood of enormous houses. He wore jeans and a simple shirt, while Fatima wore a white silk *hijab* edged with an eyelet pattern that he had taken to be pressed the day before. In her usual modest fashion, she had on black slacks and a long-sleeved white blouse.

He and Fatima walked across a marble-tiled entryway outside the front door. His hosts answered the door graciously. The man was slim, his wife even slimmer. He wore jeans, she wore a Juicy Couture sweatsuit. He looked Moroccan. She was also Moroccan but looked European. Her nose was small, and her lips were puffy. The house itself was huge, easily large enough to hold 200 people on the ground floor alone. They sat down to dinner in front of a stone fireplace, Fatima and Mamdouh on one loveseat, the host couple across the glass-topped coffee table on another. Two maids served their dinner, bringing enough food for a dozen people. The first course was salad, tomatoes, cucumbers, shrimp, and eggs arranged to resemble a flower. The second course was fish stuffed with cellophane noodles and shrimp. The third course was a

Moroccan classic and Fatima's favorite—chicken with olives and preserved lemon, served with soft Moroccan bread. Last, flan. The wife ate very little. A round crystal ashtray sat next to her. After smoking a cigarette, she called the maid, who replaced the ashtray with an exact, but clean, replica.

They talked mostly about cultural topics, moving comfortably back and forth between Moroccan Arabic and French. His friend's wife was a serious Francophile who found Americans inelegant and uncouth. Eventually, though, the conversation turned to Morocco's current situation. The workers in the woman's factory were impossible to deal with—lazy, slow, and needing constant supervision. Mamdouh started talking about how abused restaurant workers were in New York as though she had said, "My workers are so poor and they need so much help." Mamdouh should be sure to take his guests only to the nicest parts of Morocco—why leave a bad impression? But that wouldn't be fair, Mamdouh replied. His guests would think that there was no poverty in Morocco, one of the poorest countries in the world. This couple represented a significant element in Morocco's development program—getting emigrants to repatriate. It seemed a pretty inadequate economic program: relying on wealthy migrants to come back and spur change for the poor. This couple, at least, didn't seem to have much interest in that part of the plan.

When dinner ended three hours later, Fatima and Mamdouh kept quiet until they got in the car, extremely aware that their ancestors could have been the servants of this couple's ancestors. If they hadn't emigrated and made some money, they'd never have been invited into the rigid world of Moroccan elites.

"Oh, my God."

"You know I don't like all that, with the servants and the formality. It's too much," Fatima said. "It seems so unfriendly."

"It's only this kind of people who come back here to live."

"I thought we'd never get out of there."

"I need an ice cream." They stopped at a roadside stall near a fair. After all that rich food, Mamdouh just felt like he needed something normal. He ate an ice cream bar, with its waxy chocolate and grainy vanilla, and felt better.

A Neoliberal Monarch

When King Mohammed VI was crowned in 1999 he took great pains to distinguish himself from his father, but his own governance has produced mixed results. Both the Moroccan and the foreign press dubbed him the "king of the poor," since he focused his early speeches on social programs for the poor, on creating equal rights for women, and, perhaps most important, on reversing his father's human rights record. Moroccans are making progress in some areas, but the the government has so far been unable to stimulate full-scale social change.

Mohammed VI continued the same kind of neoliberal economic program his father had pursued. Over the years, Morocco has joined the World Trade Organization, signed free trade agreements with the European Union and the United States, created six commercial courts, and simplified its customs procedures, all to make the country more attractive to foreign investors. As formerly state-owned enterprises were privatized, foreign investment rose dramatically, reaching $1.2 billion in 1997, four times the 1996 figure. Although the state has sold off large holdings like Maroc Telecom, the royal family has become a primary investor in this newly privatized economy; indeed, the king controls more than 30 percent of the capitalization of the companies on the Casablanca Stock Market. His companies hold virtual monopolies of such important products as milk, sugar, and edible oils.

Mohammed VI has also started social programs for the poor, including establishing public benefits to get the rural areas through a terrible two-year drought. Yet the poverty indicators have been slow to change, and unemployment remains extremely high. Morocco has one of the highest illiteracy rates in the world—nearly half its population has never been taught to read. Eighty percent of rural villages have no access to paved roads, running water, or electricity; 93 percent have no basic health care facilities. World Bank and Moroccan economists both noted a growing poverty rate at the end of the 1990s, an increase from 13.1 percent in 1990–93 to 19 percent in 1998.[2] Labor exploitation remains common and severe. A 2006 report by Morocco's labor minister noted that the law was applied in only 15 percent of companies.

Ultimately, Morocco's economic program has widened the gap between elites and the middle class. Although neoliberal reforms have created new classes of work, including financial services and information management, there hasn't been enough economic growth to guarantee employment for the emerging middle classes, who are increasingly leaving the country to make a living. Under the structural adjustment programs of the early 1980s, Morocco shrank one of the best sources of income for ordinary Moroccans: the public sector. For years, the government has warned the country's young people that they would have to look to the private sector for work. But the private sector doesn't provide enough jobs, and the jobs it does provide are doled out according to social connections and strict hierarchies.

The new middle class was competing with the old elites for the same jobs. Urban unemployment rates among educated twenty-five-to-thirty-four-year-olds have risen dramatically with market reform, reaching as much as 30 percent of the active urban labor force by 2000, including 100,000 university graduates. With unemployment so high, most young Moroccans have seen no option but to leave the country. While it is understandable that they would do so, this is neither a real development program nor an inclusive political program. Most of these young people have no idea that the migration they have fantasized about will leave them stateless, encouraged to leave Morocco but unable to become full citizens in another land.

Unemployment is actually higher among the educated. In 2000, 46.3 percent of people aged twenty-five to thirty-four with baccalaureate (sixth-year) or higher-level degrees were unemployed (41.1 percent of males, and 54.4 percent of females). The rate among the same age group without sixth-year degrees was 17.8 percent. *The Economist* has reported that increasing numbers of these educated young people are crowding into inflatable rafts to cross the Straits of Gibraltar and find agricultural work in Spain. Sociologist Shana Cohen found that the vast majority of young people she interviewed in Casablanca were looking for ways to get out of the country. "The fantasy of migration into an open terrain must end with narrowly written migration and visa laws," she wrote.[3] At least, that is true in current immigration systems.

The king's ambitions for changing the status of women also encountered complications. Following an alarming report on the condition of women, Mohammed VI proposed sweeping reform, a massive state-financed plan to improve education and reproductive health, increase political representation and employment, and revise the family code (including outlawing polygamy). Religious fundamentalists rejected the plan wholesale, turning out 200,000 people for demonstrations, the largest crowds since independence, in Casablanca. The king quickly withdrew the plan, replacing it with a milder version in 2004.[4]

In human rights, the king made his most dramatic changes, but here, too, the record moved in fits and starts. He granted some independence to the courts. He started with allowing more press freedom; he also pardoned thousands of political prisoners and invited prominent exiles to return. He introduced a program of human rights education in the schools, allowing the Moroccan Association for Human Rights to conduct it. But according to Amin Abdelhamid, the former president of the Association for Human Rights, the judiciary is still closely tied to the executive branch, which consists of the king and the prime minister. After terrorist attacks in Casablanca in 2003, the police arrested more than 2,000 people. More than 1,000 of them were found guilty after one of the most botched judicial procedures ever witnessed in Morocco. The outrage was such that less than a year later the king felt obliged to pardon a large number of the convicted. The Equity and Reconciliation Commission was interviewing the victims of past abuses, while the Moroccan police, as documented in reports by Amnesty International and Human Rights Watch, were torturing suspected Islamist terrorists in a new secret detention center located a few miles from the king's palace in Rabat.[5]

Corruption among the country's elites continues unabated. A current anticorruption campaign has revealed widespread financial fraud and embezzlement in banking, social security, agricultural credits, public housing, state contracts, public companies, municipal councils, and international aid projects, such as one program to provide school lunches for needy children.

"There is a parliament, a judicial system," notes Abdelhamid, who is fighting for a new constitution that would, among other things, mandate the separation of church and state. "But there is a parallel system that governs. Nice king or not-nice king, he is still a king."

Italy's *Clandestini*

After ten days in Rabat, Mamdouh took the family back to Casablanca to reunite with the Italian branches. His sister Saida had driven for three days with her husband Maati, two of her three children, Lakbira's daughter Nedia, and the family dog, a tiny terrier named Charlie. When Mamdouh and Fatima pulled up to the house, they found that Saida had already arrived. Fatima hugged each person while holding Mohammed in her arms. Saida, who shared Mamdouh's curly hair but had their father's angular features, pinched Mohammed's plump cheeks. Mamdouh and Maati shook hands and patted each other's backs. Lakbira's two daughters—Bushra, who had also been at the beach, and Nedia, who had gone to Italy two years earlier—squeezed each other tightly. Lakbira and Nedia sat very close to each other on the couch. Mamdouh's father, Bouchaib, stood to the side and watched happily. The smaller kids endured all the hugging, getting outside as quickly as possible to chase each other and the dog endlessly around the perimeter of the house. They got hold of a digital camera and went crazy taking pictures and checking themselves out on the little screen. Eventually all settled down for tea and cookies. Mamdouh's nephew Hamza, his brother Mohammed's middle child, served the tea, holding the teapot high above each glass according to custom. Halfway into tea, Mamdouh's mother Aicha came upstairs, throwing her arms akimbo and wearing a quizzical expression, as if to say, "What, no one's interested in me unless I bring the food?"

That night, the family didn't eat until 1:30 a.m. They put together all the coffee tables in between the two sitting rooms and piled around it eating the five different kinds of pasta that Nedia had brought. Even with some twenty people eating, there was enough pasta left over for a full meal. The kids continued to play until the middle of the night, singing songs and making up games, much as Mamdouh's parents had done with their own cousins in their rural villages.

Two weeks later, Mamdouh went back to New York and Saida returned to Italy. Saida's brood, though, had gotten a little bigger. She was taking Bushra, twenty-seven, and Hamza, eighteen, back with her, having arranged work contracts for them. Bushra would join her sister Nedia as a *badante*, or domestic worker for the elderly; Hamza would work in construction.

Saida and Maati were well established in Ruffano, a town of 12,000 people in the largely agricultural region of Puglia, located in the heel of Italy's boot, a mere fifteen-minute drive from the Adriatic. Maati was a robust, handsome man who smoked heavily. He went to France first, visiting his brother in Nice and his sister in Paris in the late 1980s. Maati had attended school only through fifth grade, becoming a professional soccer player as a young adult. He played for a few months in France, but he couldn't get a proper visa and therefore had to move on.

The European Union is frequently cited by immigrant rights advocates as a model of regional integration between poor and wealthy countries. The Schengen Agreement, which allows the citizens of any member country to travel freely within the zone, appears to be an ideal version of an open borders policy. On the surface, both assertions are true. To build the EU, the wealthier countries provided "social cohesion" funds to the poorer ones, knowing that true integration would be impossible if some countries had inadequate schools, health care, and physical infrastructure. The Schengen Agreement allows people to move around Europe largely without document checks, much as Americans do around the fifty U.S. states.

The other side of the Schengen Agreement, however, is strict restriction of immigration from outside of Europe, particularly immigration from Africa. The applications of Italy, Spain, and Greece to participate in the agreement, for example, were challenged on the basis of their long coastlines and vulnerability to the entry of undocumented immigrants. Europe is open to immigration by other European citizens, while attempting to stop what some politicians have called the "tercermundialization," or third-worldization, of the continent by former colonial subjects.

Most immigrants started out going to France, the United Kingdom, and other northern countries, but after northern Europe restricted immigration substantially in the 1970s, they began entering through southern Europe, starting what is known as the Mediterranean model of immigration. Southern Europe for its part has shown great ambivalence toward its immigrants. After centuries of being countries of emigration, Spain and Italy are now destination countries, a shift that they are struggling to deal with.

As of 2006 there were 2.4 million known immigrants in Italy, and according to Caritas-Europa, nearly half, or 1 million, are undocumented. The conflict over immigrants' status has played out in such a way that the country has adopted opposing stances. In 1986, Italy passed its first law legalizing unauthorized people and reinforcing equal rights for immigrants. These laws were largely oriented toward creating a supply of temporary labor; immigrants were meant to come, work, and eventually return. Although few were initially allowed permanent legal residency or citizenship, over the years new laws have opened space for people to gain legal status, and the state has established programs to welcome and acclimate new immigrants to Italian culture. In 1998, Italy passed a relatively liberal comprehensive immigration law that granted substantial rights to immigrants. Even these measures, however, reflected a conflict over immigration: the integration centers Italy created in a progressive moment are called the Centers for Temporary Stay and Assistance (Centri di Permanenza Temporanea, or CPTs).

By the late 1990s, however, the Italian Right had made immigration a focus of debate (as have right-wing parties throughout Europe). Using anti-immigrant rhetoric, the National Front argued for criminalizing immigrants and for conducting mass detention and deportation. The National Front repeatedly popularized the term *clandestini*, criminalizing first the undocumented but eventually virtually all immigrants. Prime Minister Silvio Berlusconi, a conservative, aligned himself with the National Front throughout his election campaign and then supported the passage of the Bossi-Fini Act in 2001. The National Front and other Italian political organizations have continued to use high-profile incidents involving immigrants to great effect—for example, reacting to the 2002 landing of a boatload of Iraqi Kurdish immigrants in Sicily by declaring a national emergency that greatly expanded police powers to prevent immigration, including destroying smugglers' boats en route.

The Bossi-Fini Act tied legality to employment, so that any immigrant who became unemployed also became illegal. In describing the laws one cabinet minister said, "We do not want immigrants, except for the minimum number necessary for the requirements of our economy, for the minimum amount of time possible, and in times of absolute precariousness, so that it will be easy to free ourselves of them when we are ready."[6] The conservative laws "institutionalized irregularity" for immigrants so that they never have a stable situation. You are legal for a moment, but then become illegal after losing a job, or if you are unable to prove that you have been working for the required six years to apply for residency because you were working in the underground economy. Italy has a particularly large underground economy, dominated by small firms and constituting 28 percent of the national economy (larger than in any other advanced capitalist country). More than half of the underground economy is located in the southern regions of the country, where there is also widespread unemployment and poverty.

Scholar Kitty Calavita writes that this contingency status threatens legal as well as illegal immigrants: "Legal and economic marginality are mutually constituted—with the fragility of legal status contributing to immigrants' disempowerment vis-à-vis employers, and their concentration in the underground economy jeopardizing their ability to legalize. And they both derive from the same source: the contingency of immigrants welcome as marginalized Others."[7] These others have been steadily criminalized and racialized—that is, treated as people of color even when there is no difference in skin color, as in the case of Albanians and the Roma.

Unable to stay legally in France, Maati went to Italy. He stopped in Reggio Calabria and got temporary work authorization in 1990. But the north was full of homeless North African immigrants selling drugs and committing petty crimes to survive, and Maati decided to keep going until he found a safe place. He found Ruffano through Saida. A friend of the Mamdouh family had gone to Italy without documents, but he wanted to go home and see his son. Saida asked Maati to take the man his passport. The friend didn't want to risk traveling even inside Italy without documents, so he asked Maati to make the long trek down to Ruffano in Puglia, which Maati discovered to be far friendlier to foreigners than any place he had been in France or northern Italy.

He felt immediately at home in Ruffano, similar to the feeling Mamdouh first had when he landed in Florida. Maati started playing soccer and eventually found a job (and sponsorship for immigration) delivering diesel fuel to gas stations around Puglia. By the time he had been there three years, he had

returned to Morocco temporarily to marry Saida. When their first child was
a year old, Maati requested and got sponsorship through his company for
the family.

Saida had arrived in 1994 not speaking a word of Italian. She started going to school to learn the language and in 2000 she responded to an ad in
the newspaper seeking people who wanted to become interpreters for immigrants. She was accepted into a government-sponsored program and was
then certified as an official interpreter. She covered the entire eastern side of
Puglia, while a Tunisian woman covered the western side, interpreting for
immigrants in the schools, the hospitals, and the courts.

In Italy, *clandestini* are so reviled in the press and in political life that Saida
spoke the term in a virtual whisper. Every year, she interpreted for at least
twenty people who had braved the rough crossing from Africa to Europe,
throwing their passports into the sea. Because of the Schengen Agreement
and the Italian constitution, Europe cannot deport people if the authorities
cannot prove their point of origin, so many migrants destroy their documents. Before stricter enforcement forced them to go in boats by sea rather
than overland, immigrants often burned their papers, creating a new phrase in
Morocco of "burning" to go somewhere. Today, they drown their papers.

One man told Saida that he had crossed with twenty-two people in an
inflatable raft from Libya. The smugglers took all the valuables off the passengers, including rings, wallets, watches, and cash, and told them to throw their
papers into the sea. The raft took off, but when two of the migrants started
fighting, the smuggler who was piloting threw the two of them into the sea as
well. The authorities watch the shore for such migrants, who are then placed
in a detention center for sixty days before they are released with orders to
leave the country. This man, like most, didn't, making his way to Ruffano,
where Saida found him a construction job. In fact, she rarely had trouble finding work for such people. All it took was a little asking around. This isn't sur-
prising, considering that the Italian government caps the immigration quota
at 600,000, even though employers request twice that number.

Most immigrant detention centers are quite humane, but a few have terrible records of abuse and bad conditions. Journalist Fabrizio Gatti investigated
their conditions by adopting an Arab identity, jumping from a cliff into the
Mediterranean Sea, and waiting for the authorities to "rescue" him. He was
taken to the detention center in Lampedusa, sent to sleep on a mattress that
was home to 200 flies, sharing one toilet, with no door, toilet paper, or electricity, with fifty-two other men. That night, a new group of immigrants ar-

rived. Without enough beds, some had to sleep on the poisonous floor, which was covered with sludge that Gatti realized later was from the overflowing toilets. When Gatti asked for food for the new arrivals, who were starving, an officer tossed in a can of soda. One immigrant cried out, "We are clandestine, but we are not animals." Such stories are disturbingly common.[8]

By contrast, Saida and Maati were lucky enough to escape such experiences, and they've settled in well. Saida became active in one of Italy's three major labor unions, rising to the post of secretary of the immigrant section. It was extremely difficult for immigrants to become Italian citizens, but Maati managed it and Saida was on her way. The process required ten years of work history in Italy, uninterrupted by even a vacation to one's home country. The family lives in a two-story, three-bedroom, two-bathroom house near the town center, decorated with family photos and Persian rugs. Italian is the cross-generational language of the household, although the children all speak Arabic as well, and their eldest daughter Najoua is quickly learning English in middle school. Saida thinks of Morocco as her country, she said, but she wouldn't go back there to live. They would never be able to keep their lifestyle, modest as it is, in Morocco without a great deal of money. Italy was better for their children. "Like there is the American dream," said Najoua, "we also have the Italian dream."

Over the last five years, Saida had gotten work contracts for three nephews, two nieces, and a nephew-in-law. For two years, her niece Nedia had worked as a *badante*, essentially a domestic worker who mostly took care of the elderly, as do most immigrant women, working virtually around the clock to perform the care that used to be managed by the infirms' families. In large part they are compensating for a shrinking Italian birth rate, which is leaving large numbers of elderly people without care. Nedia was working for an eighty-five-year-old woman who had been married to a wealthy man. She worked nights, starting at 7:30 p.m. with dinner, administering medicine at 10:00, getting up six times during the night to take her charge to the bathroom, more medicine at 7 a.m., then coffee, a bath, and some massage. The woman cried when Nedia left for her vacation in Morocco. This was a light job. Before that, she cared for an eighty-two-year-old full-time day and night, getting a two-hour break each day. When Bushra came, the two sisters found a family they could work for together.

Hamza had gone to Italy prepared to do any kind of work God sent him, as long as it wasn't selling drugs. He was apprenticed to a carpenter and living down the street from Maati and Saida in Ruffano, sharing an apartment with two other immigrant men. He was at his aunt's house for dinner almost every night, and the steady diet of cheese and pasta filled out his bony frame in just six months. He was enjoying his new life, but he now wanted to go to America. Maati made fun of him. "For months, all he could talk about was Italy, Italy, Italy, begging us to bring him to Italy. Now it's all the time, America." Hamza didn't realize how easy things were for him, Maati thought.

Europe's Crimmigration Problem

In their tiny community of Ruffano, where everyone knew everyone else, Italians didn't cross the street fearful of approaching immigrants, but in the rest of Italy, immigrants were increasingly being cast as criminals. A poll asking Italians to rank immigrants of various nationalities on a scale from good to bad revealed Arabs and Muslims scoring the worst, on par with the newly hated Roma. Then came Russians, North Americans, Jews, Subsaharan Africans and Asians, Eastern Europeans, Latin Americans, and other EU members.

The country's immigration laws in themselves created a whole new class of crimes that only immigrants could commit. Because they can get only temporary residence status, which has to be renewed, and because there are long delays in the process, the law makes legal status so precarious that immigrants have to work constantly to regularize themselves on a perpetually temporary basis.

In theory, an employer is supposed to request an immigrant by name, the immigrant then has to apply at the Italian consulate in his or her home country, and only after authorization does the immigrant then make the journey to Italy.

According to Dario Melossi, a criminologist at the University of Bologna, everyone knows that the idealized version of this process is a fiction. Only a few people actually come in this way, working through family connections as Saida's nieces and nephews had done. The vast majority enter illegally, begin working in the underground economy, find an employer to sponsor them, sometimes paying a bribe to the sponsor, and then apply for legal status. Now people can apply online, but in earlier days they had to stand in line at a police station. Hundreds of immigrants would stand for for long as two days in those lines while according to the official application process they were supposed to be thousands of miles away. A permit might be valid for one or two years, but it can take up to five months to get one, so as soon as an immigrant gets a permit, he or she must start the process all over again for the next permit.

During that period, Melossi said, "The important thing is not to make the wrong encounter." He's heard stories of unauthorized Romanians and Albanians who managed to find sponsors going on buses back to their countries to apply properly at the consulates, only to be stopped and marked as illegal, which means they can't reenter legally, even if they have sponsors, for at least five years. This habit of doling out legal status incrementally, writes Kitty Calavita, make for "immigrants' inevitable stints of illegality . . . the mirror image of their contingent status and begrudging welcome as the uninvited guest whose job it is to clean up."[9] This would, of course, also be the effect of tying legalization to guest worker programs, as President Bush had proposed for the United States.

As in the U.S., Italy's use of crimmigration is heavily racialized. Conflating immigrants and criminals has made immigrants vulnerable to racial profiling and police brutality. As in the United States, although there is no evidence that immigrants commit crimes more frequently than Italians, the Italian press has fully adopted the image of the criminal immigrant. In 2002, Berlusconi announced a series of roundups of petty criminals and immigrants named "Operation High Impact." Likening his speech to George W. Bush's "Axis of Evil" State of the Union address, Calavita noted that Berlusconi symbolically criminalized immigrants as "an army of evil—that lays in wait for the citizens, who will be protected by the army of good."[10]

Dario Melossi surveyed legal residents in Emilia Romagna, asking who had been stopped by the police in the last year. More Italians than immigrants initially answered yes, but when the survey then asked who had been stopped on foot rather than while driving, the numbers were much higher for Middle Eastern and African immigrants. Immigrant men had been stopped ten times as often as Italian men. Spatial segregation makes it very easy to target immigrants. The Bossi-Fini laws made it illegal to rent to unauthorized immigrants, and so they are forced into segregated and substandard housing, which in turn makes them easily identifiable as foreigners. Only 30 percent of immigrants in Italy live in "normal" housing, that is, a fixed address that meets safety and health regulations. Entire families frequently live in shantytowns and on the street, making them easy targets for police sweeps.

Italy's prisons are full of immigrants, who are routinely denied the ability to make an effective defense. In 1998, they were 49.2 percent of those admitted to prison (about 90 percent of these are undocumented). In northern Italian prisons, immigrants comprise 70 to 80 percent of inmates, although they are at most 13 percent of the overall population in the North.

The overall picture, as Saida and Maati have learned, isn't all this bad. When Italians and immigrants know each other, they get along quite well. Italians remember the terrible treatment their own ancestors received at the hands of Americans and other Europeans when they themselves were emigrants. Many cities and towns have tried various integration schemes. The CPTs offer language classes and employment assistance. The social movement organization ARCI (Associazione Ricreativa Culturale Italiana) provides those and other services, including housing assistance and tutoring for immigrant schoolchildren. Some municipalities, including Ruffano, where Saida lives, have some form of local voting rights for immigrants. In 2006 Romano Prodi's Center-Left government finally gave citizenship to all children born in Italy—previously citizenship had been entirely hereditary, so that a third-generation Italian American living in New York had citizenship rights that were denied to the children born in Italy of immigrant parents.

Italy's efforts to criminalize immigrants, however, make true integration impossible. The current situation gives employers and the state a great deal of flexibility while limiting free movement of immigrants. None of the punitive measures, which Calavita calls "symbolic laws," cuts the flow of migrants; they just leave immigrants unable to protect their rights. As of 2007, 8,800 people had reportedly died trying to get to Europe, a figure that immigrant rights groups believe is far below the actual number.[11] If immigrants were truly integrated into Italian society, says Calavita, they would begin to act like Italians, losing the very character that creates their economic value in the first place. Calavita quotes scholar Maurizio Ambrosini: "From a strictly economic point of view, the best immigrant is . . . one who has just arrived, is . . . willing to work hard, [and is] undemanding in terms of both health and other services."[12] As we have seen, however, the Italian fantasy that immigrant guest workers will come for a while, earn some money under these conditions, and eventually go home has no grounding in fact. As terrible as conditions in Italy can be, they at least provide some semblance of survival and mobility.

This conflict between the desires of immigrants and the countries that receive them is as pervasive in Europe as it is in the United States. In the northern countries that began bringing in guest workers starting in the 1950s on, the conflict has produced generations of disenfranchised ethnic minorities, and those communities are increasingly rising up, in dramatic and dangerous ways. For many years, North Africans in France have complained about racial profiling, police brutality, and workplace discrimination. France's own right wing, led by Jean-Marie Le Pen, targeted immigrants with vitriolic language.[13]

In 2005 France experienced three full weeks of riots led by residents of Paris's ghettoes. The riots were sparked by the deaths of two French/North African teenagers who ran into an electrical substation to escape a police identity check. Some 274 cities and towns across France were affected, more than 10,000 cars torched, and 300 buildings firebombed.[14]

Evoking a deep association between the ghettoes and gangs, the French government reacted with sweeping arrests of immigrants and ethnic minorities, as well as with more restrictive immigration laws. Analysts pointed out that a much wider range of issues were driving the unrest, including political neglect of the poor and the breakdown of relations between police officers and young people of color in the inner city.[15]

Later that year, Prime Minister Dominique de Villepin announced the restriction of the "re-unification of immigration families," including making it much harder for immigrants to gain legal status by marrying a French citizen. He vowed to make it more difficult for students who did not belong to the European Union to enter the country. More than ninety such students were deported.[16] The ambivalence continues. In 2008, President Nicolas Sarkozy announced plans to rehabilitate ghetto housing and create 45,000 new jobs in those areas. Months earlier, however, he had announced his intention to require DNA tests for immigration applicants, as eleven other European countries already have. The tests would prove whether a family's child was really its own. Opponents pointed out that DNA testing would set a double standard, one for the French and one for immigrants. The French see the parent–child relationship not just one of blood, but also as one of choice. If one recognizes a child as belonging, then that defines the family.

By restricting immigrants' rights, France is following widespread EU practice: maintaining its own identity on the basis of keeping out non-Europeans. As sociologist Dario Melossi notes, "There are open borders but not for those who really need it, people coming from situations that are mostly less developed than in Europe." Ironically, Melossi argues that Third World migrants are the ones who are best equipped to meet the identity challenges posed by the formation of the European Union. They are free-moving, not "saddled with any specific national loyalty," and "unencumbered by the heavy load of tradition and heritage" that has made it so difficult to bring together all of Europe under one integrated body.[17]

That, however, is hardly how immigrants are seen today. Instead, Europe is looking for ever more stringent measures that would keep them out, or, perhaps more accurately, immobilize them once they are in.

Morocco, in the meantime, is simultaneously encouraging its young people to go abroad and bring the money back while policing sub-Saharan Africans trying to get to Europe with increasing harshness. Morocco's northern border includes the areas of Ceuta and Melilla, which are occupied by Spain. Once Africans reach Ceuta, it becomes difficult for Spain to deport them because of EU standards, so Ceuta's five-mile perimeter is protected by two six-meter-high razor-wire fences and watched by Moroccan troops.[18] Every year, thousands of sub-Saharan Africans attempt to cross these fences. According to the *New York Times*, 5 were killed and nearly 100 injured when Moroccan police shot into a crowd—two were shot, one bled to death, and one was trampled in the panic. A few months later, another eleven people died attempting to cross in September and October of 2005. The Spanish government responded by doubling the height of the fences.

Globalization for People

When Mamdouh went to visit his brother Mohammed's grave near the end of his vacation, he was heartbroken to see emaciated African immigrants, who had no doubt crossed hundreds of miles of desert on foot, begging for alms in the parking lot. The scene stood out to him as proof that migration was a global phenomenon, that human beings were determined to leave poor countries—even Morocco, which was itself destitute, had attracted people from even poorer countries because they had no choice but to move. Morocco had entered the age of globalization, but in the same incomplete way that Mexico had. While corporations and elites were free to move their capital around, workers had too little bargaining power in relation to both the government and private businesses. In fact, keeping workers in an unequal position enables the very mobility that elites enjoy.

Although Mamdouh was happy with his life and didn't regret having left Morocco, he could see that emigration by itself was no substitute for a good economic development program accompanied by real democracy. King Mohammed VI had made some significant changes, but the government had stopped short of fully enfranchising all of Morocco's people. That would require Moroccan elites to give something up: power, money, and control of the country's workforce.

Poor countries, however, cannot hope to make those kinds of changes by themselves. The wealthy countries that were receiving poor migrants had created immigration rules designed to take migrants' labor and then send them back when they were no longer wanted. Europe, like the United States, washes its hands of the conditions that force immigrants to come, refusing to recognize that those were the very conditions that drove migration, and that immigrants in turn helped to create economic stability and growth. Wealthy countries have thus swung wildly back and forth between punishing immigrants and trying to integrate them. This pattern has mostly resulted in greater flexibility for employers, who are able to keep their labor costs down, and political victories for restrictionists, who can pretend they are preserving national security and identity.

Even in "enlightened" Europe, immigrants in this age of near globalization are forced to sacrifice their humanity, no longer belonging to their old homelands and not yet belonging to their new ones. The principles on which the European Union was founded—that we live in one world, and are all responsible for each other—could be extended to embrace the globe. Immigration policy could be one part of a full globalization, rather than just an enabler for the world's elites. As the Morocco Human Rights Association asserts in its motto: Globalization has to be for everything, human beings as well as goods.

Chapter 10

EVERYBODY MEANS
EVERYBODY

To Mamdouh, immigrants were no different from anyone else. Migration was a core human urge. As long as people have occupied the earth, they have traveled to escape enslavement and repression, poverty and hunger. They have moved from the country to the city or from one nation to another and back again. They usually aren't the laziest or least enterprising people in their home countries, but otherwise they were no different from any of the Americans he had met—no better and no worse. Some were religious, others not. Some were parents, others single. Some were kind, others mean-spirited. Most were willing to do whatever they had to do, within the bounds of reason and morality, to earn a living and create a better life. Immigrants were thus more than just a pair of arms available for picking and hauling and cleaning. As a worker, and as an organizer, he could see that immigrants had made some people in some places really wealthy, and that neither immigrants nor ordinary Americans got their fair share of that wealth.

All of Mamdouh's experience revealed the ways in which the current debate over immigration policy has ignored the critical realities affecting his life.

First, globalization is incomplete. Extending the neoliberal economic model all over the world has given corporations additional power and flexibility by shrinking the role of government (and its ability to enforce labor law), by deregulating corporate behavior, and by lowering taxes and tariffs. Immigration policy has enhanced corporations' advantage over labor by immobilizing workers. Legal immigration is reserved for only two-thirds of the people who want to move to the U.S., and so hundreds of thousands of people every year are forced to migrate without papers if they want something better than a life of poverty in their original homes.

Much of the economic insecurity Americans legitimately feel stems from this economic model. Public schools are underfunded and health insurance is too expensive because our own government continually cuts taxes for the wealthy and refuses to make health care a public responsibility. The accumulation of wealth and power by corporate elites is simply considered more important than the public good. Rather than seeking to change neoliberal policies, however, Americans have focused on rooting out undocumented immigrants.

Second, immigration restrictionists justify such policies by evoking America's right to preserve its cultural identity. Suffering from the losses that neoliberalism has caused in their own economic lives, and reacting to the intense collective trauma of September 11, some Americans have tried to regain their sense of security by freezing the image of a real American. Restrictionists have communicated this image by using language that dehumanizes foreigners, going so far as to compare them to animals. They initiated anti-terrorism sweeps of Muslims, South Asians, and Arabs, none of which has produced a single terrorism-related arrest. They transformed the image of Mexicans into that of illegals and then equated terrorism with the so-called illegal. Thus, immigration policy has become increasingly merged with criminal justice into an approach called crimmigration. While expanding the economic, social, and national security arguments against immigrants, the most adamant restrictionists have begun to attack all immigration, not just the unauthorized kind.

Finally, crimmigration positions immigrants and U.S. residents as having opposing interests—when we should be joining forces to create effective new policies that will benefit all of us. Punishing immigrants has a negative effect on the country, breaking down our social fabric and encouraging racism. This approach minimizes the enormous economic contributions immigrants make in the form of work, taxes, and consumption; the political contributions of their organizing; and the cultural contributions of their cuisines, languages, and family models. In contrast, by turning our attention to the ways in which the interests of immigrants and the interests of American citizens reinforce each other, we can improve life for everybody.

Evidence suggests that when residents and immigrants actually speak to one another directly, it doesn't take long for them to find plenty of common interests. Many, perhaps even most, U.S. residents are able to see these true connections once they are able to make contact.

Americans thus face a fundamental choice about who we are and what we want. On the one hand, we can follow the route laid out by the restrictionists. We can put all our faith in the notion of an unchanging American identity. We can live in a haze of nostalgia and shut out the Other to protect our own definition of that identity. When we encounter hard times, we can decide that it's every man for himself, choosing who we will help based on the color of their skin or their native language. Those who take this path must prepare to spend the rest of their lives defining the cost of membership, rooting out the Other, and trying to keep those outsiders from sharing what we have. It isn't far-fetched to imagine that eventually these forms of exclusion will be, indeed already are, applied on the basis of something other than race and nationality—poverty, occupation, gender, age, and so on.

Fortunately, there is an alternative path. We can move forward on two fronts to equalize power between workers and corporations and to reshape the conditions that drive people to migrate in the first place. First, we need a new immigration system that expands legal immigration and protects the rights of immigrant workers. That will produce immediate benefits, not just for undocumented immigrants, but also for American workers who will no longer have to compete with a large supply of exploitable labor. This immigration policy needs to be situated in the context of a larger national economic policy that protects workers against abuse and discrimination, creates large numbers of public sector jobs, provides a decent social safety net, and develops accessible and affordable training and education opportunities for everyone. Not everyone will benefit from such a system—it can only be funded through taxes, so the wealthy will have to give something up.

Taking the alternative path will also require us to remove the stigma of illegality from those who are here now so that we can incorporate them into American society and move on to crafting the kinds of globalization policies that improve life for regular people all over the world. Legalization of those who are currently undocumented is the minimum change needed, and we should press for it immediately. The rhetoric of illegality might be technically correct, but we clearly apply it in discriminatory ways—it is rarely used to describe an Irish undocumented person, for example. In this way, it is incompatible with the fundamental American value of fairness. It also dehumanizes people and blocks our ability to seek real solutions. When people break other laws, we don't attach the stigma of illegality to their entire beings. If we hope to unify American communities, we must provide a way for those who have broken immigration laws to redeem themselves. "Reconciliation is better managed by an amnesty, and passing over that which is passed," wrote philosopher and statesman Francis Bacon in one of the first uses of the word. In this case, it is not necessary to provide a full amnesty with no price whatsoever; a reasonable way for people to make things right, including fines and lines, would go a long way.

At the same time, we need to find ways to share wealth and equalize political rights around the world. Until we have such global equity, people will continue to migrate from countries with poor public health or education systems to countries with better ones. They will leave countries with very low wages and no unions for the places that have them. And they will try to escape repressive political systems to reach countries that recognize human rights. There is no shortage of creative ideas about how to build transnational public welfare systems and global labor rights. The European Union has enacted some of them, and we are seeing promising proposals from economists and political thinkers around the world.

It is important to move on these two fronts—equalizing power and equalizing global opportunity—simultaneously. Immigrants and Americans who are suffering now need immediate relief—they cannot wait for a new globalization to take shape. If we don't move to complete the globalization project, however, we will still be mired in the same self-defeating debate twenty years from now. As we argue over enforcement versus amnesty, entire communities will be vilified and we will continue to waste money and energy on enforcement mechanisms that do not work, although they do result in great danger to migrants. Both unauthorized and authorized migration will slow down for a time, and then climb right back up again. The harsher possibility—cutting back legal immigration to the levels of the 1920s—will only foster more undocumented immigration, just as it did then.

Continuing in our current mode will cost us a great deal, both socially and economically. Maintaining a crimmigration policy will have tremendous consequences for the social fabric of the United States, doing terrible damage to what has been Americans' enduring self-image as a welcoming, family-oriented people. Even if it were logistically possible to drive out the 12 million undocumented immigrants who are here now, and to prevent anyone else from entering in the future, both the social and economic cost of doing so would be far greater than proponents of this strategy are willing to acknowledge. Some people might find that cost worth paying if it would allow us to protect Americans from terrorism—but there's no evidence that it would.

This debate doesn't take place at just the federal level. From 2003 to 2007, several states and more than forty towns and cities adopted policies to drive away undocumented immigrants by creating an increasingly harsh social and legal climate, claiming that they had to do so in order to secure the country's borders because Congress would not act. At last count, a hundred more were debating similar proposals.

States have focused heavily on barring undocumented people from receiving public benefits and driver's licenses. Colorado, Georgia, and four other states have passed laws to prevent undocumented immigrants from receiving public services. Federal laws already contain such prohibitions, but some states have added local benefits to the list, including adult literacy classes and assisted-living subsidies for the elderly. North Carolina debated not letting undocumented students enroll in community colleges at all, while Arizona and Oklahoma considered not issuing birth certificates to children born to undocumented immigrants. The number of states that make it possible for undocumented people to get driver's licenses has also been steadily shrinking. As of 2007, only seven states still did.

Local ordinances typically penalize landlords who rent to undocumented people and employers who hire them. They often require local police departments or social service workers to check for documents whenever they suspect a person is undocumented, a clear invitation to racial profiling. In some cases, they directly criminalize immigrants. The mayor of Hartford, Connecticut, ordered the arrest of people suspected of being undocumented under trespassing laws. Numerous other cities have banned day laborers from standing on street corners or in parking lots waiting for work. Some town councils have targeted not only undocumented, but all immigrants with English-only ordinances, claiming to preserve an American way of life.

The proponents of punitive local ordinances object loudly when accused of being anti-immigrant or racist, but there's no other honest word for their rhetoric and the targeted nature of their solutions. Alex Kotlowitz reported on one such example for the *New York Times*. In the town of Carpentersville, Illinois, a slate of council members was elected after sending out flyers that included statements like "Are you tired of waiting to pay for your groceries while Illegal Aliens pay with food stamps and then go outside and get in a $40,000 car?"[1]

Once elected, the council's first act was to propose an English-only ordinance. Repeating all the specious charges—they don't speak English, they commit terrible crimes—these leaders presented Mexicans as fundamentally different from themselves, who were the children of earlier waves of immigrants who "made this country great." The rhetoric was immediately racialized. Adam Ruiz, a second-generation Mexican American, encountered a man at that town council meeting who told him, "This is a white man's meeting."[2]

Immigrants—both legal and undocumented—began to leave, as they have in numerous other places. Real estate agents on the town's east side told Kotlowitz that the number of homes for sale had doubled from the previous year: "Some people say they want to leave town, either because they or a family member is illegal or simply because they feel unwelcome." One woman was switching from public to Catholic school, fearful that the divisiveness generated by the proposal would put her children at risk. Another man was selling a rental property he had owned. In other cities, white nativists celebrate the shrinkage of their Latino populations. Entire business districts have closed down. When immigrants leave, however, they take with them their small businesses, the money they pay in sales and property taxes, and their labor. Federal school funding is predicated on the number of students; when someone moves her children to a private school, her public school loses money.

Our enforcement mechanisms institutionalize racism. The number of undocumented immigrants arrested in workplace raids increased more than sevenfold from 500 to 3,600 between 2002 and 2006. Although many such raids ostensibly address crimes that have nothing to do with immigration, their effectiveness is questionable. In Greeley, Colorado, for example, federal agents who conducted raids on the Swift meatpacking plant announced that they were concerned about identity theft, but less than 25 percent of those arrested had false Social Security cards.

The discriminatory nature of these raids is often invisible to the general public. "They took the workers out in cuffs," a Colorado activist told *Guardian* correspondent Gary Younge in Greeley. "Why didn't they take the bosses? Why don't they raid the expensive ski resorts of Aspen or Vail? Why don't they raid Las Vegas? Those places would fall apart without undocumented workers, but then rich people would complain."[3] Hotels and restaurants, which we know hire large numbers of undocumented people, are rarely raided.

At the same time, the climate we create by driving immigrants underground makes them vulnerable to crime and prevents them from cooperating with law enforcement. Cecilia Muñoz receives regular reports about immigrants caught in false roadblocks and forced to pay in order to be left alone. In Southern California, police arrested a couple dressed in the uniforms of county sheriff's deputies who had stopped a Latino boy, ordered him to submit to a search, and took all his money.[4] Two police officers happened to witness the incident, which led them to chase the couple's car. This couple had shaken down more than twenty other immigrants in this way, none of whom had reported the theft. The *Washington Post* reports that some cities were refusing to follow the Real ID Act's mandate to enforce immigration policy because it prevents the undocumented, and therefore their documented family members, from reporting crimes. An undocumented Guatemalan said that he had been robbed several times in Texas, but, because that state requires local police to enforce immigration law, he had never called the police there. When he got mugged in Hightstown, New Jersey, however, he called them right away when he was mugged.[5]

Immigration has nothing to do with national security, yet the two are constantly tied in the popular media. One of Mamdouh's colleagues told him a story that clearly illustrated the irrationality of this position. LeeAnn Hall, the director of the Northwest Federation of Community Organizations, was traveling through northern Idaho visiting members of the Idaho Community Action Network. In 2006, Hall went to meet with her members in the town of Weippe, located very near the Canadian border. The town had been slowly dying—only 383 people lived there, but the community was tightly knit and compassionate. Hall's goal was to get her members there to join the fight for immigration reform, including legalization.

She arrived to find the townspeople full of the day's big news: after months of searching, federal officials had caught the white supremacist who had been shooting up the local lumber mill for weeks. People told her all about their sightings—he'd worn a red cap, ridden a bike, gotten his food from dumpster diving, and was thought to have snuck into someone's house to take a shower and steal coffee. It was widely believed that the terrorist had been living on the white supremacist "Almost Heaven" compound where Colonel Bo Gritz teaches paramilitary and survivalist skills. As she sat down with her members for lunch, Hall, who is white and comfortingly down to earth, raised the topic of immigration reform. She asked the group for their thoughts on immigration with a "come on, you can tell me." After a bit of avoidance, someone finally said that what concerned him was terrorism.

"You've had a terrorist here all summer," said Hall. "Is he an immigrant?"

"No."

"Are there many immigrants around here?" There were a number on the

other side of the forest picking tomatoes for a local contractor who was un-
derpaying them.

"Are you afraid of them?"

She got a somewhat sheepish "no" in response.

The idea that armed white supremacists living nearby were less frightening
than Mexican families crossing a deadly desert to work in beet fields, dairies,
and meatpacking plants was absurd, but it was also something this community had stopped questioning. When Hall suggested jokingly that they had
been listening to a bit too much of Lou Dobbs, her members laughed, then
moved on to discussing the tough spot in which these immigrants must find
themselves.

Ultimately, reinforcing the idea that only a white American is a real American generates fear and social isolation, which harms our national identity
more than we can yet imagine. Immigrant families hide out in fear, with enormous psychological damage to their children. An Urban Institute study of
three brutal raids found that 900 deportees left behind some 500 children,
most of them under the age of five. Preschool teachers said that three-year-
olds were arriving with all their belongings packed into their baby backpacks,
in case their families had to run.[6] Faced with the ever-increasing notion that
only white people can claim an American identity, second-generation youth
often react by withholding their loyalty. T. Abu El Haj conducted a study of
Palestinian American teenagers in the Boston public schools, who reported
that the many instances of being treated as terrorists made them feel more
Palestinian than American, even though they had been born here and had
never been to the Middle East. One ninth-grader reported being sent to the
principal's office when her teacher thought she had said "terrorist" rather than
"tourist."[7]

Despite these obstacles, immigrant communities, especially members of
the second generation, do their best to be a part of the larger communities
in which they find themselves. Studies show that thousands wait patiently
to get into English as a Second Language classes; it is the fastest-growing
portion of adult education. The National Association of Latino Elected Officials surveyed 184 ESL programs in twenty-two cities and sixteen states,
finding that more than half had waiting lists, some as long as three years.[8]
Some programs were placing immigrants in the wrong ESL level until a slot
in the proper level opened, and there was a particular backlog in intermediate
and advanced classes. Immigrants are also waiting to become citizens, in spite
of a 300 percent fee hike instituted in 2007; more than 1 million are on the

backlog list at the immigration administration, which still uses a paper system. In Minnesota, 280 Muslim girls have joined Girl Scout troops; "When you say you are a Girl Scout, they say, 'Oh, my daughter is a Girl Scout, too,' and then they don't think of you as a person from another planet," said one. "They are more comfortable about sitting next to me on the train."[9]

Annette John-Hall, an African American columnist for the *Philadelphia Inquirer*, reflected on the ways in which the English-only crowd had silenced the workers at her local nail shop, destroying the "air of conviviality that created a place of comfort for everybody." She reported on an incident in her local convenience store, where a group of young Latino men had entered. As the other customers cast hostile looks (as though they were "the second coming of Osama bin Laden") the men said nothing to each other or anyone else, bought their coffee, and left as quickly as possible. Is this really what Americans want to be?[10]

Most people in the U.S., like Hall's members in northern Idaho, don't support racism. Their limited options for improving their own lives, however, seem to leave little choice. As established American communities face fiscal crises and the increased unemployment and underemployment that comes with recessions, as their health suffers from a lack of care and housing costs rise exponentially, it is understandable that they seek solutions to these problems. For low-wage workers, the vast majority of them African, Latino, and Native Americans, the 5 percent drop in wages caused by the exploitation of immigrant workers, particularly the undocumented, represents money and opportunity they can't afford to give up. The questions, of course, are who is responsible and what is the solution? Immigrants are a far easier target than the corporations and government officials who have decided to ease the movement of capital while restricting the movement of workers. Their decisions include domestic policies that limit government spending on public services such as health care and schools. Yet even a small rise in taxes on those earning over $250,000 would create enormous resources, as would ending the war in Iraq.

Bringing the Bottom Up

This book has used the lens of the restaurant industry to both show how corporate globalization works and to provide principles that guide us to alternatives. Restaurants are filled with workers who have been pushed out of their own countries by corporate globalization and IMF/World Bank structural adjustment programs. Although it is counterintuitive, the trajectory of Mamdouh's work reveals that the key to improving an industry or a community is to embrace rather than to further marginalize the people who occupy the bottom of the hierarchy. In its current forms, the industry mirrors neoliberalism in giving business flexibility while trapping workers; innovative restaurant owners, though, show us how local economies can provide good wages and rising opportunities for everyone.

A great deal of money flows through the industry, but its financial benefits are not equally shared. Although productivity is rising, with the industry growing as a whole, workers' wages have stagnated. Because there is little enforcement of labor laws, many, perhaps even most, employers cheat. Corporations that want to try new things are able to get the capital to do so. Workers, on the other hand, don't have the same ability to create alternatives. Employers discriminate against workers of color by creating a racial hierarchy that reserves the industry's best jobs for white people—and this hierarchy is key to preserving the image of America as a white country, especially among elites. Diners expect such a hierarchy in high-end restaurants, and they never question it. Everyone who relates to restaurants participates, if unwittingly, in the setup, unaware of the social and economic costs of accepting the system as it is.

Nevertheless, in spite of globalization, most economies are still really local. As a key source of economic growth, restaurants also hold promise for producing good jobs that cannot be outsourced. As such, they could show us how to build new economic structures, anchored in communities with good wages and opportunities to create a career ladder. The industry is growing. According to the National Restaurant Association, it is the largest private sector employer in the country.[11] In New York City, the Department of Labor reported that restaurants were one of the highest contributors to overall job growth between 2002 and 2004.[12] That growth is even higher in other states. In Arizona, restaurant jobs are predicted to increase by 25 percent between 2004 and 2014, by 25 percent in Georgia, by 23 percent in Nevada, and by 15 percent in California. Large restaurant chains account for much of the growth, and these are not tiny mom-and-pop businesses, but large, well-capitalized corporations that can easily afford to follow labor law. When they don't, small employers have the hardest time competing.

It doesn't have to be this way. Some restaurants follow labor law, guarantee workers the right to organize, make sure workers have health insurance, provide training and promotion systems, and buy their raw materials nearby, which helps generate secondary jobs. They do all these things *and* still turn a decent profit. They accept limits on their flexibility as employers and operate to meet the highest self-interest of all involved, rather than the narrowest goal of low prices and massive profits. Moreover, restaurants provide an important place for cultural exchange, providing one of the most accessible ways for U.S. residents to be with and get to know their country and their world. By changing the racial hierarchy within restaurants, we can also build a more egalitarian culture outside of restaurants.

If all restaurants followed this pattern, some might argue that they would be more expensive than they appear to be now, and others will argue that diners will be driven away. Rather than refusing to enforce labor law, however, there are other things cities can do to make it possible for smaller businesses to survive without abusing their workers—providing a tax break on rent, for example. Cities, states, and countries grant tax breaks to multinational corporations all the time. In addition, a public health insurance program or the regulation of insurance premiums would lower costs for employers. These ideas may seem costly, but we would save money in other areas—for example, in providing emergency care to injured or sick workers who are uninsured. Right now, the public doesn't see the accounting for these costs; they're invisible. The only expense the average person sees is a price on a menu, which hides the meal's true cost.

Immigration policies, then, have to protect worker organizing and mandate conditions better than our current minimum labor standards, both for those who stay at home and for those who migrate. Representative Sheila Jackson Lee understood this when she crafted an immigration bill that expanded the number of green cards, included no guest worker program, created a path to citizenship for undocumented immigrants who are here now, and guaranteed the right to organize. Subsequent immigration reform proposals have included new training programs for unemployed and underemployed American workers, who are disproportionately black, rural, and young.

Jackson Lee's proposal got no hearing in Congress, and the training programs for Americans got little media attention, but it's worth reminding ourselves that there are public officials who are thinking in these original ways. They need the support of every person who is looking for a real solution.

There are plenty of additional ideas built on these principles. If the business community insists on a guest worker program, Cecilia Muñoz has advocated one that allows the immigrant to own the visa and gives him or her the option of staying and applying for a green card. Jennifer Gordon, the author of *Suburban Sweatshops* and the founder of the Workplace Project, proposes union-based immigration, in which workers would sign up with truly transnational unions. While neither of these options would provide as much freedom of movement for labor as corporations currently have, they do begin to equalize the relationship between immigrant workers and their employers. The very least we can do is legalization. That will happen: it is inevitable because both practicality and corporate politics demand it. But we have to fight for a generous legalization within this larger context, or its benefits will quickly be limited.

Mark Krikorian argues that the country's economy is so different from the last century's that these proposals are insane. Earlier waves of immigrants entered a heavily industrial economy at the height of innovation and growth, he says. Economies based on services, such as that of the U.S. today, don't offer the same kinds of growth. Krikorian does not acknowledge, however, that those industrial jobs were also terrible until unionizing immigrant and native-born workers transformed them through a combination of workplace and political pressure. He posits that service jobs cannot pay more than poverty wages, an assumption that Mamdouh's own experience as a waiter belied. Elites have to stand up, Krikorian insists, to protect American workers and their national identity.

Presumably, though, these are the very same elites who have led the economic globalization that has abandoned people worldwide, including working people right here in the United States. Corporate globalization has created both the push that has someone like Mamdouh looking to emigrate and the pull that attracted him to the United States. Restricting immigration in this climate will not create the better working conditions that American workers are seeking. Only a true overhaul of the global economy, starting with easing the movement of workers across borders, has the potential to address those problems.

We have the sorry example of NAFTA to prove that our current trade agreements are profoundly self-defeating. The political leaders of Canada, the United States, and Mexico, regardless of political party affiliation, colluded to create a situation that would enable the destruction of the Mexican economy, and, in spite of their promises to the contrary, drive millions of Mexican workers to migrate within their own country and to the U.S. in order to survive, while simultaneously enabling the loss of over 750,000 jobs in the United States. "George H.W. Bush's job numbers were bogus," writes economist Jeff Faux in the *Global Class War*. "They were arrived at by adding up the jobs gained by exports without subtracting the larger number of jobs lost to imports. This is like balancing your checkbook by adding in the deposits without subtracting the checks you wrote."[13] NAFTA thus played a major role in expanding inequality among Americans.

Far from begging the United States for NAFTA, Mexican farmers, teachers, and other workers, who now make up the vast majority of undocumented immigrants coming here over the last decade, protested mightily. Their February 1, 1994, demonstration in Mexico City was the largest rural protest against the government since the 1930s.[14] After similar protests by labor unions and environmentalists, the three governments assured their citizens that they had built in protections while telling each other not to worry because these supplemental agreements were toothless enough to placate the discontented while ensuring that capital could operate freely. Within five years of passing, "Eastman Kodak had shed 1,145 jobs by shifting production to Mexico," writes Faux. "General Electric had moved at least 5,524 jobs. Allied-Signal, whose CEO had spearheaded the USA-NAFTA lobby, sent 1,633 jobs to Mexico. Johnson & Johnson abandoned 410 U.S jobs to Mexico, and Kimberly Clark moved 1,327 jobs there."[15]

Much of what passes for globalization in today's public discourse is actually neoliberalism, or corporate deregulation writ large. Agreements like NAFTA repeat patterns of corporate movement that created similar hardships for working people in the nineteenth and twentieth centuries, only this time across the entire world. Proponents of neoliberal economics have berated Americans and others for being small-minded when they resist such corporate freedom.

Thomas Friedman, for example, in his *The World Is Flat*, calls this version of globalization beneficial, theorizing that Americans simply don't like it because it levels the playing field for Indian entrepreneurs to compete with American business. Even in a "fair" version of this kind of globalization, according to Friedman, low-wage workers in wealthy countries will suffer. Because wages would average out between those of rich countries and those of poor countries, the already low wages of American workers at the bottom of the economy must necessarily drop. Friedman, without irony, writes that these workers must develop their skills to compete in a global high-tech economy, preparing themselves to move up the employment chain, becoming more specialized, anchored, and adaptable so that corporations cannot afford to outsource them and their work. "Untouchables, in my lexicon, are people whose jobs cannot be outsourced," he writes.[16]

Yet even Friedman recognizes that some workers, through no fault of their own, will lose their jobs to relocation. He advocates stronger safety nets to protect such workers, with larger subsidies for health insurance, unemployment, and underemployment. He does not, however, advocate welfare programs, which he believes encourage people not to work, but contradictorily, wants the government to provide wage insurance for workers who lose their jobs. Friedman doesn't say what is to happen if the worker can't find another salary among these welfare programs that encourage work. Given the recent history of shrinking U.S. welfare benefits and our inability to pass a workable public health program, it is unclear how long Americans would have to wait for this safety net to appear. Socially conscious corporations are on the rise, but such corporations currently form only a small percentage of all employers, as we have seen in the New York City restaurant industry. To hope that most employers will provide a livable wage—far higher than the minimum in any of the NAFTA countries—without either a legal mandate or worker pressure constitutes wishful thinking that still leaves employers holding all the power. As an argument for American workers to join the global assembly line, it is wholly inadequate.

Placing our faith in corporations to act as good citizens assumes that the wage value assigned to different kinds of work reflects some kind of natural order. The restaurant industry, for example, cannot be outsourced. It isn't even really a service industry, according to Professor Jonathan Deutsch, assistant professor of tourism and hospitality at Kingsborough Community College of the City University of New York. Rather, it is a form of light manufacturing, since restaurant workers both create the product and deliver it to the customer. Yet restaurant jobs are deeply undervalued. There is no natural reason that a team of restaurant workers—waiters, bussers, runners, dishwashers, and prep cooks—cannot earn a living wage, with enough money for savings, home ownership, and college educations. The only reason they generally don't is that the vast majority of employers will not pay such wages, and government will not force them to. Immigrant workers compete easily with other workers in part because of immigration policy, but much more because American employers will not follow the rules of a truly free market. If a job doesn't attract workers, Adam Smith said, raise the wage.

To tell U.S. workers, then, that they should stand in solidarity with Third World workers so that Mexican wages can rise and Americans can get higher unemployment benefits hardly advances the supposedly all-American value of elevating honest hard work above all else. Real globalization must therefore include free movement of workers worldwide while giving them full access to the tools of social and political, as well as economic, integration. In a system that respects the full humanity of workers, they would have their families, they would be able to vote, they would have access to housing and health care, and they would have the option to stay, return to their place of origin, or move on to another country. They would certainly need to have access to labor unions or other organizing models that we know are the most effective means by which workers can improve their conditions.

Immigration is value-neutral on its own merits. Some people want to move and will; others don't want to but find they must; and others still will never move no matter how hard things become. While we need not assume that everyone should stay in their home countries, or that all should leave, we can recognize that creating ease of movement will allow people to maintain human ties that may ultimately lead them back to their original homes. Millions of migrants throughout United States history have done this kind of repatriation. Forced repatriation, however, simply builds resentment and, usually, in the case of people who have not been able to travel easily back and forth because of their immigration status, a highly negative return experience.

The holistic answer is to create a different kind of globalization. Here, too, there are many ideas and experiments from which we can learn. We can start by creating regional agreements, not just to benefit corporations and increase trade, but also to handle governance and public welfare. The key is to ease the movement of workers while equalizing social and political conditions.

The European Union offers parts of a good model, and the European experience suggests some problems to avoid as well. It would be important to have a single monetary system so that money bought the same amount of housing, food, and transportation from country to country, and so that each country's currency was stable. The European Union also started with wealthy countries sharing social cohesion funds with poorer countries. The poorer countries used those funds to build their infrastructure and improve their public health and education systems, promising in return to control corruption and waste. Finally, the European Union has designed a regional government—all European citizens are thus able to influence the EU's choices through democratic engagement. Some economists, in fact, believe that corporations should remain where they are while workers move around, citing European examples in which German companies remain in Germany, while workers from high-population countries move to low-population countries. Knowing their workers can go elsewhere at any time keeps Europe's wages high, which in turn fuels local economies as high-wage earners buy food and housing. Europe's xenophobia aside, this system has produced benefits for European workers and consumers alike—and corporations haven't been doing too badly, either.

The biggest problem with the European Union, of course, and one that future globalization would need to resolve, is that it still marks a boundary to keep out the world's poorest people. Policy that expands legal immigration would be one way to avoid forcing people to migrate without authorization, but there are other ways beyond easing migration to improve conditions in the developing world. The British economist Robin Blackburn, for example, suggests creating a global pension fund—open to the destitute elderly of both wealthy and poor countries—that would be funded by a modest tax on global trade.[17]

We could start by creating a North American Union between Canada, the United States, and Mexico, and including the Caribbean countries as quickly as possible. Economist Jeff Faux, the founder of the Economic Policy Institute, has developed a substantial proposal for such a union. Like the EU, our regional union would allow social cohesion funds to flow from the wealthier countries to the poorest ones; we would have a transnational health and welfare system; we would adopt a regional Bill of Rights that protected people from economic, social, and political abuse; and, lastly, a system of transnational citizenship would allow people from any member country to hold both their own and the other governments accountable.

Such a system would have enormous benefits for Americans as well as for immigrants. The workers' Bill of Rights would guarantee a livable minimum wage. Although that wage would be set by each country (to guarantee a basic dignified standard of living, which none of the minimum wages currently do), the Bill of Rights would allow citizens anywhere to hold employers and government accountable for its enforcement. Social cohesion funds may sound like U.S. charity to Mexico, but they are necessary for modernizing and equalizing the Mexican economy. In Europe, the wealthy countries knew that without such funds, people would be driven out of the poorer countries seeking better lives elsewhere, creating artificial labor surpluses that would drive down wages in the wealthy countries. In exchange for social cohesion funds, Mexico would agree to prevent corruption and democratize the use of human development resources. Rather than having its people move to the United States to earn enough money to send their children to college, Mexico itself would invest social cohesion funds to provide higher education to all of its people.

A trinational health, education, and commerce system is the most likely to guarantee access to human development for all. Through such a system, the United States and Canada could address the fiscal pressures that come from burgeoning populations that require decent education, housing, and health care. We don't have to accept the premise that such things are scarce because of the "natural" state of the free market. Handling these responsibilities regionally would help us prevent the race to the bottom of corporations looking for the most favorable tax policies and the race to the top by workers looking for the best and most human services.

These ideas undoubtedly seem unattainable in today's polarized political climate. Even the mention of giving legal status to undocumented people arouses accusations of ignoring criminal behavior. The concept of expanding immigration rather than shrinking it, and the idea of tying our countries closer together rather than driving them apart, will provoke restrictionists and inevitably prompt talk of North American Union conspiracies and the future conquest of the United States. Yet these are the ideas that hold the greatest promise, not just for immigrants, but for those existing Americans whom restrictionists claim to care so much about.

What is outdated is not migration, but rather the way in which we conceive of the nation-state. The idea that such states make decisions independently of all other countries, conferring the benefits of citizenship only as they please, has existed for only a few hundred years. As corporations bypass the nation-state, and as human beings respond by pressing for equal power to do the same, a new system must and will emerge. If these ideas are politically marginal today, it is up to us to bring them into the mainstream. A great number of people have been sitting silently in the middle of the debate, thinking that these issues don't affect them. If the media and public officials offer us something other than false solutions, it will be because we demand better options, ones that really address the problems that confront us.

Moving in these directions will be easier if we recognize that American culture, and Americans themselves, are ever changing, having already gone through several major transformations. In this way, we are not unique—cultural change is a fact of human nature. Because it takes place over several generations, the process is invisible to those who are not inclined to look. Some of the best aspects of the American identity, in fact, are innovation, adaptability, curiosity, and informality. These elements of our collective character drive Americans to travel all over the world seeking new experiences. They also lead us to build communities that have the ability to expand. American culture in particular has been heavily influenced by the entry and integration of poor immigrants, who tend to come and stay, rather than wealthy immigrants, who repatriate at a higher rate. The quintessentially American hamburger and American English both evolved through the contributions of generations of immigrants, indigenous people, and descendants of African slaves. Americans who choose to adopt this view of their identity—that it is ever changing, that we are shaped not just by what is happening around us, but also by our own reaction to those events—will face the uncertainty of an evolving self. We will also, however, be able to preserve what is best in American life while leaving behind some of its most limited, and limiting, aspects.

Embracing the Complications of Being/Becoming American

Where we enter this world is an accident of birth; where we are when we leave it is equally unpredictable. We like to think that we've made decisions, chosen the United States over Morocco or Mexico, or chosen to go rather than stay, but forces beyond our control push and pull us into extreme situations. They both constrain our choices and provide our opportunities. Mamdouh may not have thought that he would ever be an American, but he became one indeed. He paid taxes. He ate spaghetti and meatballs. He took his kids to the park. He bought a home. He voted, and he spoke English, quite precisely in fact.

In his decision to become politically active, to engage in the enterprise of improving his community—a community that gradually grew from other Moroccans to include first other immigrants and then native-born people—Mamdouh followed a path carved by millions of other immigrants, internal migrants, and their children throughout U.S. history. Those Americans fought bitter struggles to ensure a decent standard of living so that workers would have rights in relation to capital. Without these predecessors, we would have no expectation of social mobility, of the eight-hour workday, of protection from discrimination or of the enfranchisement of all citizens.

Mamdouh's story teaches us that being an American is complicated, marked by feelings of great love and at times by equally strong expressions of criticism. Changing the system is one of the fundamental ways in which Americans express their American-ness. These earlier generations were attacked, deported, imprisoned, and, yes, illegalized because these are the tools with which elites control their surroundings. Yet, even among those who have been most frequently abandoned there remains a strong feeling that the United States, with all its brilliant and flawed facets, is home. It is not, however, and should not be, an unchanging fortress that locks its gates to those who now appear to be strangers.

We are all accidental Americans in some way. Sometimes the accidents that established our presence were happy ones—an unexpected chance to come to the United States, or the good fortune of being born into privilege. For others, the accidents were tragic and violent. To make policy, then, as though there were such a thing as a natural American is a futile exercise that will give us at best a false sense of control. By embracing a humane immigration policy and a new form of globalization, we can guarantee that the people who end up in a certain place really want to be in that place, that they're willing to make themselves part of its social, civic, and political fabric, both conforming to and improving it as necessary. Being a citizen in a fully connected world, then, could stop being an accident and actually become a choice, one born not of desperation, but only of desire.

NOTES

Introduction Coming to Citizenship in a Near-Global Age

1 J. DeParle, "Migrant Money Flow: A $300 Billion Current," *New York Times*, November 18, 2006; Dilip Ratha and Zhimei Xu, *Migration and Remittances Factbook 2008* (Washington, D.C.: World Bank, 2008). Available at www.worldbank.org/prospects/migrationandremittances.

2 Jeffrey S. Passel, "The Size and Characteristics of the Unauthorized Migrant Population in the U.S. Estimates Based on the March 2005 Current Population Survey" (Washington, D.C.: Pew Hispanic Center, 2006).

3 Migration Policy Institute Staff, "The U.S.–Mexico Border" (Washington, D.C.: Migration Policy Institute, June 1, 2006). Available at www.migrationinformation.org/Feature/display.cfm?id=407, citing U.S. Customs and Border Protection Public Affairs Office data.

4 Jeff Faux, *The Global Class War: How America's Bipartisan Elite Lost Our Future—and What It Will Take to Win It Back* (Hoboken, N.J.: Wiley, 2006).

Chapter 1 Leaving Home

1 Jim Paul, "Riots in Morocco," *MERIP Reports* 99 (September 1981), pp. 30–31. See http://links.jstor.org/sici?sici=0047-7265(198109)99%3C30%3ARIM%3E2.0.CO%3B2-G; John Walton and David Seddon, *Free Markets and Food Riots: The Politics of Global Adjustment* (Cambridge, Mass.: Blackwell, 1994).

2 Edward Cody, "Disastrous Drought Increasing Tension in Volatile Morocco," *Washington Post*, November 12, 1981.

3 "IMF Austerity Measures Cause Food Riot in Morocco," *Multinational Monitor* 2, no. 8 (August 1981). Accessed at http://multinationalmonitor.org/hyper/issues/1981/08/imf.html.

4 C. R. Pennell, *Morocco since 1830: A History* (London: Hurst, 2001), p. 370.

5 John Mariani, *America Eats Out* (New York: Morrow, 1991).

6 Peter Rachleff, L. S. Chumley, Jim Seymour, and Jack Sheridan, *Starving Amidst Too Much: & Other IWW Writings on the Food Industry* (Chicago: Charles H. Kerr, 2005).

7   Roger Waldinger, *Still the Promised City? African-Americans and New Immigrants in Postindustrial New York* (Cambridge, Mass.: Harvard University Press, 1999).

8   Howard G. Goldberg, "Windows of the World: The Wine Community's True North," *Wine News Magazine* (October/November 2001). Available at www.thewinenews.com/octnov01/comment.html.

Chapter 2   Us and Them After 9/11

1   Barbara Misztal, "The Sacralization of Memory," *European Journal of Social Theory* 7, no. 1 (2004), pp. 67–84.

2   "If we distinguish a continuum of the memory openness ranging from closed or frozen memories to open-ended and often shared across group lines memories, it can be said that the first type of memory can subordinate just treatment of individuals (members and nonmembers) to the identity and interest of the group … (Misztal, "Sacralization," p. 78).

3   The Fiscal Policy Institute estimated that the 9/11 attacks cost New York City 105,000 jobs and $9.3 billion in lost wages, largely in Lower Manhattan, from businesses dying or relocating outside the city. The job loss was concentrated in low-wage industries. The restaurant industry lost some 13,000 jobs, and some 60 percent of all the jobs lost were among workers who earned less than $11 an hour. People who didn't lose their jobs found themselves with sharply reduced hours and wages. Over half the layoffs were concentrated in five typically low-wage industries: restaurants, retail, air travel, hotels, and building services. By the end of 2001, the travel industry nationwide had lost 237,000 jobs (David Dyssegaard Kallick, Matthew Mitchell, and James Parrott, "Revitalize New York by Putting People to Work," Labor Community Advocacy Network and the Fiscal Policy Institute, March 13, 2003. Accessed at www.fiscalpolicy.org/research_NYC.html).

4   Ann Coulter, "This Is War: We Should Invade Their Countries," September 13, 2001. *National Review Online.* Accessed at www.nationalreview.com/coulter/coulter.shtml.

5   Jennifer Van Hook, Frank D. Bean, and Jeffrey Passel. "Unauthorized Migrants Living in the United States: A Mid-Decade Portrait." Migration Information Source (MIS), Migration Policy Institute (MPI). 1 September 2005. Available at www.migrationinformation.org/feature/print.cfm?ID=329.

6   Francine J. Lipman, "Taxing Undocumented Immigrants: Separate, Unequal and Without Representation," *Tax Lawyer* (Spring 2006). Available at SSRN: http://ssrn.com/abstract=881584.

7   Saba Waheed, Wendy Bach, Laine Romero-Alston, Ray Brescia, and Andrew Kashyap, "Ripple Effect: The Crisis in NYC's Low-Income Communities after September 11th" (New York: Urban Justice Center, September 2002).

8   David Barstow and Diana B. Henriques, "A Nation Challenged: The Families; Gifts to Rescuers Divide Survivors," *New York Times,* December 2, 2001.

9   Daniel Wise, "In 14 Test Cases, Sept. 11 Fund Master Gives 'Fair Compensation' to Families," *New York Times,* October 1, 2002.

10 Frank Keating, "Dishwasher or Stockbroker, a Life's a Life," *Washington Post,* January 20, 2002, p. B7.

11 Nicole Wallace, "Online Giving Soars as Donors Turn to the Internet Following Attacks." *Chronicle of Philanthropy,* October 4, 2001. Available at www.philanthropy.com/free/articles/v13/i24/24002201.htm.

12 Mireya Navarro, "For Illegal Workers' Kin, No Paper Trail and Less 9/11 Aid," *New York Times,* May 6, 2002.

13 Steven Greenhouse, "A Husband Lost, and a Daughter Out of Reach," *New York Times*, December 2, 2001.

14 This name and some others have been changed to protect confidentiality.

Chapter 3   Crimmigration

1 "Rethinking Mexican Immigration," *New York Times*, July 23, 2001, p. 16.

2 In 1853, an article in the New York *Evening Bulletin* reported on living conditions in a local "hovel": "The walls were discolored by smoke and filth, the glass was broken from the windows, chinks in the frame work let in the cold air, and every thing was as wretchedly uncomfortable as it is possible to conceive. Yet in every one of these squalid apartments, including the cellar and the loft, men and women—blacks and white by dozens—were *huddled together promiscuously*, squatting or lying upon the bare floors, and keeping themselves from freezing by covering their bodies with filthy rags as chance threw in their way" (emphasis mine): Noel Ignatiev, *How the Irish Became White* (New York: Routledge, 1995), pp. 40–41.

3 Historian John Higham writes that "friendliness turned to fright ... with the so-called 'new immigration,' the flow of peasant and ghetto peoples from Italy, Austria-Hungary, the Balkans, and Russia, which began increasing rapidly in the early 1880s." Italians were considered by some to be as bad as the Chinese, who were themselves the subject of exclusion laws forbidding their entry into the U.S.: John Higham, "Origins of Immigration Restriction, 1882–1897: A Social Analysis," *Mississippi Valley Historical Review* 39, no.1 (June 1952), pp. 77–88.

4 In 1875, Congress required residency permits for Asian immigrants and declared the contracting of "coolies" for labor a felony. The California Land Law of 1913 declared immigrants "ineligible for citizenship" and prohibited them from owning land. The immigrants of the time in California were, of course, Chinese and Japanese. Nativists who thought the law failed to keep pace with the threat encouraged violence. In the 1880s, the novelist Pierton Dooner wrote *The Last Days of the Republic*, condemning white San Franciscans for not murdering more of the Chinese, who had conquered North America and destroyed the American Empire forever.

5 Mae M. Ngai, "The Strange Career of the Illegal Alien: Immigration Restriction and Deportation Policy in the United States, 1921–1965," *Law and History Review* 21, no. 1 (2003), p. 100; see www.historycooperative.org/journals/lhr/21.1/ngai.html.

6 In 1929, Congress passed the Registry Act, allowing "honest, law-abiding alien[s] who may be in the country under some merely technical irregularity" to change their status if they paid a fee of $20, showed they had never left the U.S. since 1921, and were of good moral character. Immigration authorities particularly tempered the prohibition against immigrants "liable to become a public charge (LPC)," benefiting Europeans and Canadians, whose deportation rates for that reason dropped from nearly 2,000 in 1924 to fewer than 500 in 1932. Historian Mai Ngai notes that the "law did not formally favor Europeans over Mexicans. But, of the 115,000 immigrants who registered their prior entries into the country between 1930 and 1940, eighty percent were European or Canadian." According to one economist, many Mexicans qualified but few knew about it, understood it, or could afford the fee. Next, the immigration authorities adopted a policy called pre-examination. In this program, unauthorized immigrants could go to Canada, be examined by an official, and receive permission to re-enter legally. Focusing on the Canadian border also guaranteed that few Mexicans would have the means to use the program. Finally, the INS asked the

attorney general to suspend deportation orders after 1940. Ngai reports that an internal Justice Department study of 389 cases in 1943 revealed that the overwhelming majority of suspensions went to Germans and Italians, while only 8 percent involved Mexicans.

7   More than 500,000 were deported in 1931–34, and over a million were deported each year in 1953–55; see Rodolfo F. Acuña, *Anything But Mexican: Chicanos in Contemporary Los Angeles* (London: Verso, 1996), pp. 112–13.

8   The decade from 1944 to '54 became known in Texas, which was excluded from the Bracero Program, as the "decade of the wetback" (Fred L. Koestler, "Handbook of Texas Online: Operation Wetback," Texas State Historical Association Online, available at www.tshaonline.org/handbook/online/articles/OO/pqo1.html).

9   "Rethinking Mexican Immigration," *New York Times,* July 23, 2001, p. A16.

10   Christine Haughney, "Bush Packs Immigration Initiative for New York Visit," *Washington Post,* July 11, 2001, p. A20.

11   Eric Schmitt, "Bush Says Plan for Immigrants Could Expand," *New York Times,* July 27, 2001.

12   George Kouros and Anne Seymour, "Forging a New U.S.–Mexico Migration Relationship," International Relations Center, September 2001. Accessed at http://americas.irc-online.org/briefs/2001/bl81.html.

13   Mike Allen, "Bush's Mexican Guest Worker Plan to Push English," *Washington Post,* September 1, 2001.

14   Patty Reinert, "Ties That Bind: Bush Won't Focus on Immigration in Visit with Fox," *Houston Chronicle,* September 2, 2001.

15   Juliet P. Stumpf, "The Crimmigration Crisis: Immigrants, Crime, and Sovereign Power," *American University Law Review* 56, no. 367 (2006). Available at SSRN: http://ssrn.com/abstract=935547.

16   Use of undocumented labor is so common that everyone who lived in the society was somehow implicated in it. A number of public officials have been exposed for participating in the practice, usually by hiring undocumented people as domestic workers, or by contracting with companies likely to use them. The list includes Zoe Baird, Bill Clinton's first nominee for attorney general; Massachusetts Governor Mitt Romney; New York City Police Commissioner Bernie Kerik; California Rep. Nancy Pelosi; Vice President Dick Cheney; and Wisconsin Rep. James Sensenbrenner.

17   In 1990, Shine Building Maintenance in California faced an organizing drive by its immigrant janitors. The company told its workers they had to provide new documentation verifying their legal status. When workers couldn't produce it, they were terminated. The immigration check provided a way to eliminate a pro-union workforce without violating legal prohibitions against terminations for union activity. David Bacon, "Organizing Silicon Valley's High-Tech Workers." Available at http://dbacon.igc.org/Unions/04hitec5.htm.

18   By 2001, the General Accounting Office, Congress's nonpartisan research arm, reported that the increase and the fences had not reduced border crossing. They had, however, pushed the crossers into more remote areas, leading to 1,013 deaths over five years, largely by heat exposure or drowning: Robert Collier, "Democrats, GOP in Tug-of-War for Immigration Overhaul," *San Francisco Chronicle,* August 3, 2001, p. A6.

19   In 1994 California voters passed Proposition 187, banning undocumented immigrants from all public services, including subsidized health care, housing, and education. The courts ultimately found the measure unconstitutional, but it set the stage for similarly harsh policies and practices.

20 Almost every immigration statute passed since 1988 has expanded the list of crimes leading to exclusion or deportation. That year, laws vastly expanded the range of crimes leading to deportation by creating a category of "aggravated felonies" that included murder, drug trafficking, and firearms trafficking. In the mid-1990s, Congress added many nonviolent crimes such theft, burglary, and fraud; prostitution; acts related to gambling; alien smuggling; some types of document fraud; obstruction of justice, perjury or bribery, forgery, counterfeiting, vehicle trafficking, and skipping bail.

21 "Because of the lesser substantive and procedural barriers to deportation compared to a criminal conviction, federal officials have been able to undertake initiatives based on citizenship status and ethnicity that are not possible within the criminal justice system." Stumpf, "Crimmigration Crisis," p. 18.

22 This section is drawn from my interviews with Mark Krikorian, September 26 and November 19, 2007.

23 Dena Bunis, "Attack May Alter Debate over Immigration Policies," *Arkansas Democrat-Gazette,* September 17, 2001.

24 Hope Yen, "Customs Agent: Red Flags over 9/11 Hijacker's Visa," Associated Press, January 27, 2004. Available at www.cnn.com/2004/US/01/26/911.commission.ap/index.html.

25 Mark Memmott, Richard Benedetto, and Patrick O'Driscoll, "Poll Finds United Nation: Emotional Survey Shows Support for Long, Costly War, Wariness about Arabs," *USA Today,* September 17, 2001, p. A4.

26 Judy Woodruff, with guests Pat Buchanan and Cecilia Muñoz, *CNN Live Today,* October 23, 2001, Transcript #102311CN.V75.

27 Jane Guskin and David L. Wilson, *The Politics of Immigration: Questions and Answers* (New York: Monthly Review Press, 2007), p. 91.

Chapter 4   Learning to Organize

1 Steven Greenhouse, *New York Times,* June 4, 2002, "Windows on the World Workers Say Their Boss Didn't Do Enough." Available at http://query.nytimes.com/gst/fullpage.html?res=9D07E2DA103AF937A35755C0A9649C8B63.

2 *New York* magazine website, "Best of New York, 2002": http://nymag.com/urban/guides/bestofny/nightlife/02/sportsbar.htm.

3 Anthony DePalma, "15 Years on the Bottom Rung," *New York Times,* May 26, 2005. Available at www.nytimes.com/2005/05/26/national/class/MEXICANS-FINAL.html?_r=1&oref=slogin.

4 Ibid.

5 Restaurant Opportunities Center of New York (ROC-NY) and the New York City Restaurant Industry Coalition, "Behind the Kitchen Door: Pervasive Inequality in New York City's Thriving Restaurant Industry," January 25. 2005. Historical Employment and Wages New York State and Counties, 1975–2000 (SIC-based data) available at www.labor.state.ny.us/workforceindustrydata/employ/historical_qcew.shtm.

Chapter 5   Building a Cooperative Restaurant

1 "The 9-11 Black Hole: LMDC's Secret Ways Keep Little Guys from Getting Rebuilding Bucks," *New York Daily News,* July 6, 2004. Available at www.nydailynews.com/archives/opinions/2004/07/06/2004-07-06_the_9-11_black_hole_lmdc_s_s.html.

Chapter 6   Scaling Up Throughout the Industry

1   Robert Courtney Smith, *Mexican New York: Transnational Lives of New Immigrants* (Berkeley: University of California Press, 2006), p. 19.

2   "NRN Taps Smith & Wollensky Chief Stillman as 2002 Pioneer Award Winner," *Nation's Restaurant News*, April 22, 2002. Available at http://findarticles.com/p/articles/mi_m3190/is_16_36/ai_85017793.

3   Theresa Agovino, "Traveling Epicure Embarks on Bistro," *Crain's New York Business*, April 24, 1989, pp. 3, 49.

4   Seth Wessler interview with Alexis Juárez Cao Romero, sociologist at Benemérita Universidad Autónoma de Puebla, February 15, 2008.

5   Thomas J. Kelly, "Neoliberal Reforms and Rural Poverty," in "Mexico in the 1990s: Economic Crisis, Social Polarization, and Class Struggle, Part 1," special issue, *Latin American Perspectives* 28, no. 3 (May 2001), pp. 84–103.

6   Adriana Sletza Ortega Ramirez, *Migracion Indocumentada Desde Puebla* (Undocumented Migration from Puebla), El Colegio de Michoacán, A.C., 2007. Available at: www.colmich.edu.mx/eventos/2007/diplomadoMigratorios/presentaciones/presenta07.pdf.

7   Michael D. Bordo and Harold James, *The International Monetary Fund: Its Present Role in Historical Perspective* (Cambridge, Mass.: National Bureau of Economic Research, Working Paper No. 7724, November 1999).

8   Santiago Levy and Sweder van Wijnbergen, "Maize and the Free Trade Agreement between Mexico and the United States," *World Bank Economic Review* 6, no. 3 (1992).

9   Thomas Kelly, "Neoliberal Reforms and Rural Poverty," *Latin American Perspectives* 28, no. 3 (May 2001), p. 92.

10   Seth Wessler interview with Professor Jonathan Fox, Dept. of Latin American and Latino Studies, University of California, Santa Cruz, February 15, 2008.

11   Jeff Faux, *Global Class Wars: How America's Bipartisan Elite Lost Our Future—and What It Will Take to Win it Back* (New York: Wiley, 2006), p. 133.

12   Ibid., p. 13.

13   Ibid., p. 139.

14   Ibid., p. 137.

15   *Supreme Court of the State of New York, County of New York. Alan Stillman and La Cite Associates plaintiffs against Saru Jayaraman, Fekkak Mamdouh, Veronica Giminez, Utjok Zaidan, Rosa Fana, Restaurant Opportunities Center of New York, and other unidentified individuals.* Index No. 6000606/04. Filed June 30, 2004.

16   "Special Report 2002: Top 100 Independent Restaurants," *Restaurants and Institutions*, April 1, 2002, p. 4.

17   Restaurant Opportunities Center of New York and the New York City Restaurant Industry Coalition, *Behind the Kitchen Door: Pervasive Inequality in New York City's Thriving Restaurant Industry*, January 25, 2005.

18   Ibid., p. 15.

Chapter 7   Framing the Immigration Debate

1   George W. Bush, "State of the Union Address," January 20, 2004. Accessed at www.whitehouse.gov/news/releases/2004/01/20040120-7.html.

2   Mark Krikorian, "Fool Me Twice, Shame on Me: The McCain/Kennedy Amnesty," *National Review Online*, May 13, 2005; accessed at www.nationalreview.com/comment/krikorian200505130942.asp.

3   Ibid.

4   Eunice Moscoso, "Immigrant Advocates Denounce GOP Bill as Extreme," *Atlanta Journal-Constitution*, December 15, 2005.

5   Josephine Hearn, "CHC 'Livid' at DCCC on Border Bill," *The Hill*, December 20, 2005.

6   Laura Figueroa, Michael Barber, and Richard Dymond, "Rallies Draw Mixed Reaction," *Bradenton* (Florida) *Herald*, May 3, 2006.

7   Knight-Ridder/Tribune News Service, "Editorials on Immigrants' March," May 2, 2006.

8   Charlie Norwood, U.S. Representative, Ninth District, Georgia, "La Raza Mounts Drive to Suppress US Law Enforcement" (press release), September 20, 2006.

9   National Council of La Raza, "The Truth about NCLR: NCLR Answers Critics" (Open Letter to the Public). National Council of La Raza: Viewpoints. Available at www.nclr.org/content/viewpoints/detail/42500/.

10 A cloture vote doesn't guarantee that a bill will pass the Senate floor; it merely cuts off the debate and calls for a floor vote.

11 Janet Murguía. "NCLR President and CEO Janet Murguía's Remarks at the 2007 NCLR Annual Conference." National Council of La Raza: Viewpoints. Available at http://nclr.org/content/viewpoints/detail/47528/.

12 Stephen Dinan, "Hispanic Group Aims to Stop 'Wave of Hate,'" *Washington Times*, July 22, 2007. Available at: www.washingtontimes.com/article/20070722/NATION/107220053/1001.

13 Mark Krikorian, "Legal Good/Illegal Bad? Let's Call the Whole Thing Off," *National Review Online*, June 1, 2007; accessed at www.cis.org/articles/2007/mskoped060107.html.

14 Gary Younge, "Comment and Debate: The US Is Clamping Down on Illegal Migrants, But It Relies on Their Labour," *The Guardian* (London), June 11, 2007.

15 Justin Akers Chacon and Mike Davis, *No One Is Illegal: Fighting Violence and State Repression on the US–Mexico Border* (Chicago: Haymarket Books, 2006).

Chapter 8   Growing a Movement

1   Tom Elliott, "Food Fight: Angry Campaign to End Capitalism in NYC Eateries," *New York Post*, February 4, 2006.

Chapter 9   Dreaming Globally

1   Some details about Mamdouh's friends in Morocco have been changed to protect their identities.

2   World Bank Country Assistance Evaluation, May 14, 2001.

3   Shana Cohen, "Alienation and Globalization in Morocco: Addressing the Social and Political Impact of Market Integration," *Comparative Studies in Society and History* 45, no. 1 (2003), pp. 168–89. Published online by Cambridge University Press. Accessed at http://journals.cambridge.org/action/displayAbstract?fromPage=online&aid=141377.

4   Nicholas Marmie, "Hundreds of Thousands Hold Demonstrations over the Status of Women in Morocco," *Smart Marriages*, March 12, 2000.

5   "Reform, Republics and Monarchies." Bitterlemons-International.org: Middle East Round-table 3, no. 9 (March 10, 2005); available at www.bitterlemons-international.org/previous.php?opt=1&id=75.

6   Kitty Calavita, *Immigrants at the Margins: Law, Race, and Exclusion in Southern Europe* (New York: Cambridge University Press, 2005), p. 36.

7   Ibid., p. 73.

8   Fabrizio Gatti, "Lo, Clandestino a Lampedusa," *L'espresso*. Available at http://espresso. repubblica.it/dettaglio-archivio/1129502.

9   Calavita, *Immigrants at the Margins*, p. 45.

10 Ibid.

11 "Death by Policy: The Fatal Realities of 'Fortress Europe'—More Than 8800 Deaths" (Amsterdam: United for Intercultural Action, n.d.). European network against nationalism, racism, fascism, and in support of migrants and refugees; Website available at www. unitedagainstracism.org/pages/campfatalrealities.htm.

12 Arabs in France had endured dozens of hate crimes and racist murders throughout the 1980s.

13 Emma Charlton, "France Tightens Transport Security on Riot Anniversary," Agence France Presse, October 27, 2006.

14 "A French Perspective on the Riots," *Washington Times*, November 18, 2005.

15 Calavita, *Immigrants at the Margins*, p. 65.

16 John Litchfield, "France Toughens Immigration Controls after Riots, *The Independent* (London), November 30, 2005.

17 Dario Melossi, "Security, Social Control, Democracy and Migration within the 'Constitution' of the EU," *European Law Journal* 11, no. 1 (January 2005), pp. 5–21.

18 "Grenzzaun am Haus," photo account of Moritz_Siebert, May 13, 2006. Available at: www. flickr.com/photos/su_mo/145614781/in/set-72057594134561901/.

Chapter 10   Everybody Means *Everybody*

1   Alex Kotlowitz, "Our Town," *New York Times Magazine*, August 5, 2007. Available at: www. nytimes.com/2007/08/05/magazine/05Immigration-t.html?pagewanted=print.

2   Ibid.

3   Gary Younge, "The U.S. Is Clamping Down on Illegal Immigrants, But It Relies on Their Labour," *The Guardian* (London), June 11, 2007.

4   "LA Cops: Posers Shook Down Immigrants," Associated Press, November 8, 2007.

5   Anthony Faiola, "Looking the Other Way on Immigrants; Some Cities Buck Federal Policies," *Washington Post*, April 10, 2007, p. A01.

6   Randy Capps, Rosa Maria Castañeda, Ajay Chaudry, and Robert Santos, "Paying the Price: The Impact of Immigration Raids on America's Children" (Washington, D.C.: National Council of La Raza, 2007).

7   T. Abu El-Haj, "'I Was Born Here, But My Home, It's Not Here': Educating for Democratic Citizenship in an Era of Transnational Migration and Global Conflict," *Harvard Educational Review* 77, no. 3 (Fall 2007); Research Library, p. 285.

8   James Thomas Tucker, *The ESL Logjam: Waiting Times for Adult ESL Classes and the Impact on English Learners* (Los Angeles: National Association of Latino Elected Officials, September 2006). Available at: http://www.naleo.org/pr100606.html.

9   MacFarquhar, Neil, "To Muslim Girls, Scouts Offer a Chance to Fit In," *New York Times*, November 28, 2007, pp. A1, A22.

10 Annette John-Hall, "Loud and Clear: The Language of Intolerance," *Philadelphia Inquirer*, September 13, 2006, p. E01.

11 National Industry Fact Sheet, National Restaurant Association, Available at: http://www. restaurant.org/research/ind_glance.cfm.

12 Fiscal Policy Institute, "An Economic Update," January 21, 2004 (New York: Fiscal Policy Institute); available at www.fiscalpolicy.org/jan21economicupdate~jobquality.pdf.

13 Faux, *Global Class War*, p. 130.
14 Ibid., p. 129.
15 Ibid., p. 130.
16 Thomas L. Friedman, *The World Is Flat: A Brief History of the Twenty-First Century* (New York: Farrar, Straus, 2005), p. 238.
17 Robin Blackburn, *Age Shock: How Finance Is Failing Us* (London: Verso, 2007).

ACKNOWLEDGMENTS

Many people helped to bring this book into being. Our editor, Johanna Vondeling, tops the list. She is the smartest, the most patient, and the clearest-thinking person in the history of publishing. The entire Berrett-Koehler team was wonderful to work with, and copyeditor Steven Hiatt went far beyond the bounds of duty.

Rinku Sen: The staff and board of the Applied Research Center provided critical financial, moral, and intellectual support; I'm especially grateful for the consistent leadership of our chair, Susan Colson. I was fortunate to have excellent research assistance from Thanu Yakupitiage, Marissa Gutierrez-Vicario, Rhoda Linton, and Seth Wessler. Without my assistant, Megan Izen, I would never get a single thing done. Our associate director, Sonia Peña, took over many of my duties while I worked on the book. The staff and board of the Restaurant Opportunities Center of New York were also wonderful throughout the reporting process.

Many people read and commented on early drafts, including Francis Calpotura, Tram Nguyen, Ellen Bravo, Onnesha Roychoudury, Rob Ellman, Elizabeth Heck, and David Kerns. Gary Delgado, Rhoda Linton, and Kim Fellner helped connect the theory and the story. A number of people introduced us to new ideas and sources, or simply helped us think: David Bacon, Beverly Bell, Jared Bernstein, Deepak Bhargava, D'Vera Cohn, Kim Fellner, Michael Feinberg, Marjorie Fine, Richard Healey, Karla Jackson-Brewer, Kitty Calavita, Vijay Prashad, Mark Randazzo, Aarti Shahani, Larry Solomon, Roger Vann, and Tom Zoellner. More people provided insightful interviews than we could name in the book, including Raoul Altidor, Julio Ansures, Rafael Duran, Caroline Keating, Adil El Maoraki, Daniela Fabbi, Louis Figlia, Jennifer Friedlander, Bill Granfield, Edgar Guttierez, Antonine Lindor, Jeff Mansfield, Chad Parsons, Luigi Perrone, Amanda Ream, Victor Rojas, Andrew Smith, Tom Snyder, Justin Swartz, and Sharda Young.

This is a global book, and I speak only two languages. Donna Hernandez translated for interviews in Spanish. Francesca Maso translated all the Italian written materials. Anna Caputo, Stella Gaetano, Karen Hough, and Najoua Hamed-Allah interpreted for me in Puglia, and Kathryn Webb in Reggio Emilia. I'd like to acknowledge the great work of the Associazione Ricreativa Culturale Italiana and thank them for their hospitality and helpfulness. Finally, Sahid Benali translated for me in Morocco and was also a great source of political history and insight.

The Mesa Refuge in Point Reyes, California, gave me a beautiful quiet space away from the rigors of organizational life. I started working on this book while studying at the Columbia University Graduate School of Journalism. Helen Benedict, David Blum, Stephen Fried, Elizabeth Kadetsky, and Dale Maharidge had a profound effect on my reporting and writing. Christopher Colvin's class "Culture, Trauma, Irony" generated the trauma and national identity ideas. Soyinka Rahim, Yuko Uchikawa, Natalie Kabasakalian, Seema Agnani, Tanya Krupat, and Lori Villarosa provided love, friendship and, quite often, food. Bharati Sen and Chaiti Sen keep me grounded in this world.

I am grateful to Saru Jayaraman and Cecilia Muñoz for the countless hours of interviews they gave me. Finally, if not for Fekkak Mamdouh, this would have been a very different book.

Fekkak Mamdouh: I would like to thank the staff, board, and members of the Restaurant Opportunities Center of New York for their hard work and leadership. Saru Jayaraman is the best political partner and friend anyone can have. It has been an honor to work with Rinku Sen. Many thanks also to Megan Izen for her help. I am also grateful for the love and support of my wife and children, Fatima, Iman, Zackaria, and Mohammed Mamdouh, and that of my mother, Aicha Mamdouh.

Authors' Note

We first met in October 2002, about six months after ROC-NY was founded. Rinku recognized immediately that this multiracial, multilingual community represented the story of immigrants after September 11, and that their work would hold important lessons. We conceived of the book together, and Rinku reported the book from January 2003 to March 2008. In addition to conducting dozens of interviews, she observed meetings and other organizational activities, reviewed media coverage, and analyzed organizational documents and legal filings. She corroborated each of Mamdouh's own recollections with those of at least two additional sources. None of the corporations and restaurant owners targeted in ROC-NY's campaigns responded to requests for interviews. In some cases, people are quoted both from their own writings or press statements as well as from interviews, and we have identified the source of quotes largely in the text itself.

INDEX

ABOUT THE AUTHORS

Rinku Sen is the president and executive director of the Applied Research Center (ARC) and publisher of *ColorLines*, a national newsmagazine on race and politics. She writes and speaks extensively about racial justice, immigration, community organizing, and women's lives for a wide variety of publications. She previously worked as a community organizer and was the co-director of the Center for Third World Organizing. She emigrated to the United States from India when she was a child and studied at Brown and Columbia Universities. Sen is also the author of *Stir It Up: Lessons in Community Organizing and Advocacy*.

Fekkak Mamdouh came to the United States from Morocco in 1988 at the age of twenty-seven. He worked in New York City restaurants, moving to Windows on the World in the World Trade Center after its reopening in 1996. As shop steward for the union at Windows, Mamdouh stood up for the rights of all workers. After September 11, 2001, Mamdouh initially led search parties for the families of the seventy-three victims who lost their lives at Windows, and was later hired by Hotel Employees and Restaurant Employees Local 100 to staff a temporary organization to provide relief services to his fellow displaced workers and to the families of those who had lost their lives at Windows.

Mamdouh helped found the Restaurant Opportunities Center of New York (ROC-NY), which began its work in April 2002. In January 2008, he co-founded the country's first national restaurant worker organization, the Restaurant Opportunities Center United.

About the Organizations

The Applied Research Center (ARC) is a racial justice think tank changing society through research, journalism, and leadership development. Founded in 1981, ARC exposes the racial impact of seemingly neutral policies and practices and provides resources for communities and individuals fighting for racial equity. It uses public policy as a key tool to repair historic injustices by designing and promoting creative solutions to contemporary problems. ARC (www.arc.org) publishes *ColorLines* magazine (www.colorlines.com), the national newsmagazine on race and politics, winner of the Utne Reader General Excellence Award, and hosts "Facing Race," a national conference for people committed to racial justice.

The Restaurant Opportunities Center of New York (ROC-NY, www.rocny.org) was founded after September 11, 2001, to provide support to restaurant workers displaced from the World Trade Center and has grown to organize restaurant workers all over New York City for improved working conditions. Since 2002, they have won more than eight campaigns against powerful restaurant corporations totaling more than $4.5 million in unpaid wages and discrimination payments for immigrant restaurant workers. They also published two ground-breaking reports on the restaurant industry, helped to win a statewide minimum wage increase for tipped workers, organized 40 workers to open a cooperatively owned restaurant, and now include more than 2,000 restaurant workers in their membership.

Based on their successful efforts in New York City, groups in several other cities approached them about initiating ROC branches in their cities. In response, in January 2008 ROC created Restaurant Opportunities Center United (ROC-United), a national intermediary that is developing and providing technical assistance to restaurant worker organizing projects in several large cities across the country, conducting research and policy work on the restaurant industry, and organizing national conferences of restaurant workers.